Culture, Psychotherapy, and Counseling

Culture, Psychotherapy, and Counseling

Critical and Integrative Perspectives

Editor
Lisa Tsoi Hoshmand
Lesley University

SAGE Publications
Thousand Oaks ▪ London ▪ New Delhi

For information:

Sage Publications, Inc.
2455 Teller Road
Thousand Oaks, California 91320
E-mail: order@sagepub.com

Sage Publications Ltd
1 Oliver's Yard
55 City Road
London EC1Y 1SP
United Kingdom

Sage Publications India Pvt. Ltd.
B-42, Panchsheel Enclave
Post Box 4109
New Delhi 110 017 India

Printed in the United States of America

Library of Congress Cataloging-in-Publication Data

Culture, psychotherapy, and counseling : critical and integrative perspectives / edited by Lisa Tsoi Hoshmand.
p. cm.
Includes bibliographical references and indexes.
ISBN 0-7619-3051-5 (hardcover) — ISBN 0-7619-3052-3 (pbk.)
1. Cultural psychiatry. 2. Psychotherapy—Cross-cultural studies.
3. Counseling—Cross-cultural studies. I. Hoshmand, Lisa Tsoi, 1947-
RC455.4.E8C853 2006
616.89—dc22

2005009532

Acquisitions Editor: Arthur T. Pomponio
Editorial Assistant: Veronica Novak
Production Editor: Kristen Gibson
Copy Editor: Taryn Bigelow
Typesetter: C&M Digitals (P) Ltd.
Cover Designer: Janet Foulger

Contents

Preface

Why another book on psychotherapy and counseling? How is culture treated differently here than in the growing literature on counseling the culturally different client? The impetus for this book comes from a desire to focus on what is lacking, and to address schisms in the field of psychotherapy and counseling. At a time when practitioners who are expected to work with time-efficient treatment modalities seem content with their chosen forms of practice so long as they are presumed to be helpful, many of us have continued to feel the need for thoughtful exploration of domains and issues that require attention from the profession.

Due to the fact that much of our theoretical knowledge related to psychological practice is derived from the scientific discipline of psychology, psychotherapy and counseling is viewed as a science-based enterprise. There is a sense, however, that the emphasis on empirically validated treatment approaches and cost-efficiency, driven by reductionistic science and managed care, respectively, have taken away some of the holism and humaneness that we attribute to psychotherapeutic work and the counseling relationship. Furthermore, because of the prevailing scientific ideology, the discussion of moral and spiritual realms of human life has been especially lacking. This state of affairs has created tensions in the field, and posed problems for the practice of psychotherapy and counseling where human understanding, personal worldviews, and existential issues are especially relevant. Our integrity as psychotherapists and counseling professionals also depends on a congruity between our intellectual and moral commitments in the way we practice. Unfortunately, there has been limited allowance in academic discourse and professional education for discussing the integration of the personal and the professional. This has not been helpful to students and new professionals who have to define their orientation in a field with divergent philosophies, theories, and models of practice, and attempt some form of integration.

In spite of increasing acknowledgment of the importance of culture in psychological theory and practice, the implications of culture have continued to be treated as an additional, sometimes only pragmatic, consideration rather than being central to human understanding. This tendency is troubling in view of the current social and political climate and the global escalation of cultural conflicts. When a significant part of the world is sensitive to cultural imperialism, the cultural underpinnings of Western psychology as well as the academic and therapeutic cultures of the profession should be subjected to reflexive, critical evaluation. This is more likely to happen if we would accept the dual nature of psychotherapy and counseling—as an enterprise that is both science-based and fundamentally cultural in nature. Questions of identity, what it means to be human, and how individuals and groups can find sustainable goods in cultural coexistence can then be considered in the broadest sense possible. When issues of psychological and social well-being are raised in contemporary life, with all its multiplicities and challenges, the sources of therapeutic understanding and the nature of this socially embedded enterprise require our in-depth examination. It seems evident that, in addition to the kinds of scientific research and criteria that have defined empirically supported treatments in recent times, a broader approach to accountability is indicated that considers the social and cultural validity of our practice while drawing on the experienced, local knowledge of practice.

I have assembled for this book a group of authors who take the view that psychotherapeutic understanding involves more than theoretical knowledge or the research-tested knowledge associated with technologies of human change. This understanding of the other, while informed by our professional education and training, is conceived as a developmental understanding derived from practice experience and reflection on therapeutic encounters against the backdrop of cultural living. There is as much philosophical intention as there is psychological know-how involved in this process. The mutual expansion of horizons in a therapeutic encounter and counseling relationship also contributes reciprocally to the vision held by both practitioner and client of what constitutes healthy development and well-being. That is why I have asked the authors to share the understanding and vision of human possibilities that have evolved over time in their work. What we hope to offer are personal accounts of diverse pathways to psychotherapeutic understanding in the effort to integrate personal worldviews and existential stances with professional knowledge and practice experience. There is no set formula for the journey, other than achieving some degree of integrity through informed and reflective practice. Such integrity, in many instances, illuminates our existential striving for moral ways of being in our cultural living, and for holism in our work in a fundamentally cultural enterprise.

This book is organized in three sections. In the first section, I introduce the framework for thinking broadly about culture in its multifaceted meanings and implications. I further discuss the centrality of culture to the field of psychotherapy and counseling, reviewing major developments and contributions, and addressing the topics of psychotherapy integration and evidence-based practice. In the second section, the personal accounts of our authors are presented on their reflections on and critique and integration of the field. Each chapter includes for illustration case examples from the authors' clinical practice and experience.

In Chapter 3, John McLeod addresses the cultural resources and processes involved in psychotherapy and counseling from a narrative, meaning-oriented perspective. Chapter 4, by Doralee Grindler Katonah, provides a holistic view of human experience, based on Gendlin's experiential focusing-oriented approach to psychotherapy. These two chapters touch on the generic, cultural processes involved in psychotherapy and counseling. In Chapter 5, William Mikulas discusses the integration of world psychologies, including the Buddhist tradition with Western psychology. Chapter 6, by William Rezentes, presents Hawaiian psychology as an integration of Native Hawaiian concepts and practices of healing and Western psychology. Both chapters illustrate how Western psychology can be integrated with, and learn from, other cultural traditions. Chapter 7, by Dana Becker, provides a feminist, ecological view on psychological practice, including issues of diagnostic practice. Chapter 8, by Susan Gere, offers a woman's view of clinical trauma theory and therapy. These two chapters, in particular, emphasize sensitivity to gender, class, and macro systemic issues, requiring professionals to take a value stance. In Chapter 9, John Christopher further explores the moral dimension of psychotherapy from a hermeneutic perspective. This is followed in Chapter 10 by Del Loewenthal's discussion of issues of values and cultural conflict from a relational, existential perspective.

The final section consists of a summary and discussion of what is learned from the contributed chapters and the perspectives of this group of psychotherapists and counseling educators. Collective themes and recommendations are highlighted. It is my hope that our work will stimulate conversation and reflection in the psychology profession and the related fields, toward a more comprehensive understanding of the cultural nature and implications of psychological theory and practice in the enterprise of psychotherapy and counseling.

In a book that claims to provide critical perspectives on the field, I must also share two qualifications I have about the work presented here. One is that our collective voices would have been further strengthened by the inclusion of additional authors from diverse ethnic, cultural, and national backgrounds. Short of accomplishing this, I hope that colleagues from varied backgrounds and orientations will offer their opinion and critique of our work, and share them in their teaching and publication. The other concern I have is that we may not have addressed sufficiently the organizational and political context of the systems in which our authors have conducted their work as psychotherapists, counseling educators, and researchers. When clinical and relational values so often collide with institutional and political realities, the readers could benefit from knowing more about how professionals manage such tensions. Perhaps some of us will address this in our future work.

Acknowledgments

I wish to express my gratitude to the authors for their willingness to be transparent about their worldviews, therapeutic stances, and personal convictions, and for sharing the insights from their professional work and life experience. It has been a privilege to collaborate with this exceptional group of colleagues. I also want to thank Arthur Pomponio, our editor, and the production and marketing staff at Sage Publications for endorsing and assisting with this project. This work has been partially supported by the sabbatical leave I was granted in the fall semester of 2004 by Lesley University, where my own perspectives on the field have further evolved with teaching and interactions with colleagues. While it is not possible to acknowledge everyone, I would like to mention Susan Gere, Joan Klagsbrun, and Rick Reinkraut, who have provided encouragement or input at different points of this project. I also want to thank my colleague and friend, George Howard, and others who have maintained an interest and enthusiasm for the work that I have chosen to undertake. Finally, I am grateful for my family whose love and hold on my humanity have continued to keep me grounded.

1

Thinking Through Culture

Lisa Tsoi Hoshmand

To explore the relationship between culture and psychotherapy and counseling, I would like to begin by offering some ways of "thinking through culture(s)," a phrase I borrow from Shweder's (1991) book on cultural psychology. I ask students of psychology and practitioners and teachers of psychotherapy and counseling to consider the cultural realm in the broadest terms, and to think deeply about issues that may not be an ordinary part of their professional training and discourse. I invite readers to join me in considering the existential meanings and significance of culture at a time when a great deal is at stake in our understanding and views of culture(s).

To set a framework for understanding culture, I refer to the fields of anthropology and cross-cultural psychology and the more recent development of cultural psychology. From these points of departure I hope to bring attention to the cultural underpinnings of psychological theory and practice, including the cultural appropriation of identity and views of psychological and social well-being. I will consider the contributions of cross-cultural psychology, transcultural psychiatry, and social constructionism to a cultural view of psychotherapy and counseling. My overall goal in this book is to examine, along with the contributing authors, the professional and societal implications of viewing psychological practice from a cultural perspective. With the help of cultural theories and critical perspectives, and a growing awareness of the politics of culture, I argue that for the therapeutic practitioner as well as the public, being able to think through culture(s) is a matter of great urgency. We are in a time of immense cultural change and cultural conflict. This is not to imply that cultural understanding was any less important in history. For as long as there has been human society, culture has provided prescriptions for living, and both symbolic and material means of being and interacting with the other. We can only know culture from our experience of participating in social living. Thus, cultural understanding is simultaneously a reflexive or self-referencing effort and an empathic or other-directed endeavor. In the therapeutic context, this ability to stay on both the personal and the social plane requires the practitioner to integrate the personal with the professional in thought and action. For this reason, I have asked the contributing authors to be transparent about their beliefs and values, and to share how they have integrated their personal worldviews with their professional worldviews in working within the cultural realm.

Following are several ways of thinking about culture that have implications for theory and practice in the psychotherapy and counseling field as well as psychology in general.

Culture and Ethnicity as Sources of Human Diversity

The study of cultures and cultural forms of human diversity historically was undertaken by cultural-social anthropology and cross-cultural psychology. From questioning the conceptual and methodological limitations of these subdisciplines has come cultural psychology (Shweder, 1990; Shweder & Sullivan, 1993). Shweder (1991) defined the field of cultural psychology as "the study of the ways subject and object, self and other, psyche and culture, person and context, figure and ground, practitioner and practice, live together, require each other, and dynamically, dialectically, and jointly make each other up" (p. 73). It is a nonreductionistic approach to understanding the interrelatedness of aspects in the human domain that are of interest to psychotherapists and social scientists. Cultural psychology, which emphasizes the cultural-historical embeddedness of psychological processes (Cole, 1996), is informed by interdisciplinary ideas and the study of culture using cross-paradigm methods. This cross-discipline perspective that I believe is helpful for the purposes of this book acknowledges, but is not identical to, theory and research in cross-cultural psychology.

Cross-cultural psychology as a field has focused on the study of differences between Western and non-Western cultures. Psychologists and other social scientists have brought this science-based knowledge to bear on issues of practice in a multicultural environment. There is a significant body of literature on cross-cultural counseling, mental health, psychiatry, and psychotherapy (e.g., Al-Issa, 1995; Castillo, 1998; Gielen, Fish, & Draguns,

2002; Marsella & White, 1982; Marsella & Yamada, 2000; Pedersen, Draguns, Lonner, & Trimble, 2002; Tseng, 1999). Comparisons of Eastern and Western concepts of self (Marsella, DeVos, & Hsu, 1985) and reports on culture-bound manifestations of psychological disorder (Simons & Hughes, 1985) have informed the mental health field.

Journals such as the *Asian Journal of Counseling, International Journal for the Advancement of Counselling, Transcultural Psychiatry,* and *World Psychology* have reported theoretical and practice developments in different parts of the world. In spite of a relative lack of research on the efficacy of applying Western psychotherapy and counseling to populations in non-Western societies, many countries tend to adopt models of psychotherapy originated from the West. At the same time, most American professionals have not shown a great deal of interest in the theory and research on other groups and cultural traditions that may inform intercultural practice (e.g., Bond, 1996; Paranjpe, Ho, & Rieber, 1988). Where there is an attempt to consider such cultural knowledge, the application of other cultural traditions to therapeutic practice requires critical evaluation. For example, Eastern cultural traditions portrayed by the elite of society may not reflect the cultural realities of the general population under conditions of social change (Hoshmand & Ho, 1995). The internalized culture and identity of a given individual cannot be presumed on the basis of ethnic origin and cultural tradition. While viewing Buddhist psychology and Western psychology in complementary terms, Michalon (2001) further pointed to the limitations and dangers of using an alternative system of belief to replace more culturally congruent concepts of self and psychological practice.

Interest in indigenous psychology (Heelas & Lock, 1981; Kim & Berry, 1993) has led some therapists and counseling practitioners in non-Western societies to reject Western approaches in favor of approaches that are congruent with or derived from the local culture. Indigenous culture provides native ways of knowing what is salient and congruent with the local ethos, and what are credible ways of addressing human problems. Indigenous approaches, however, need to be qualified by judicious adoption and judgment (Yang, 1997). The question remains as to whether it is always more effective to follow indigenous healing practices than to adopt Western psychotherapy and counseling in non-Western contexts (Shek, 1999). We need both psychological analysis of emic or indigenous concepts and practices and indigenous analysis of etic psychological concepts and practices (Kim, Park, & Park, 2000). What complicates the answer to this question about the role of indigenous psychology is the degree of globalization and value-pluralism in contemporary society (Weinrach & Thomas, 1998). Although cultural pluralism promotes diversity and inclusiveness, American models of cultural identity development that have added a cultural dimension to Western models of personality development (Atkinson, Morten, & Sue, 1989; Helms, 1990), have not fully accounted for all world cultures and the effects of globalization. Cultural relativism in Western psychology and the culture at large has not allowed serious attention to the existential meanings and value questions pertaining to human change. This is evident in the challenges experienced, for example, by those who wish to consider issues of spirituality in secular psychotherapy (Helmiak, 2001).

It is therefore important to understand the philosophical underpinnings and cultural values in our paradigms of human change that may exclude certain considerations. One way of evaluating our philosophical and practice assumptions is to learn about psychological theory and practice in other cultures, as in the comparison between Chinese and American perspectives on counseling (Ryback, Wan, Johnson, & Templeton, 2002). An example of philosophical difference concerns the existential meanings of happiness and suffering. Buddhist psychology illuminates the inevitability of human suffering (De Wit, 1996), in contrast to the Western cultural tendency of expecting psychotherapy to be a means of ending suffering and restoring happiness. Perhaps the most salient feature of the Western worldview that differs from non-Western cultures stems from the Cartesian, dualistic assumption of object-subject split that resulted in reductionistic models of psychology and medicine that continue to influence the field. Modernization of society further contributed to mechanistic and materialistic worldviews. These reductionistic and materialistic views are in contrast with more holistic worldviews and models of healing that integrate the spiritual and phenomenological realms with the somatic and behavioral realms. As pointed out by several authors in this volume, part of the criticism of Western psychotherapy comes from the limitations of the reductionistic, materialistic worldviews associated with its theory and practice. These worldviews appear also to be connected with the individualistic bias in Western psychology. American individualism and its religious roots are reflected in concepts of self and society in Western psychology (Sampson, 1988, 2000). Such biases become a concern when cross-cultural theories and research in the West have increased the likelihood of studying the "other" by predominantly Western assumptions and standards. The cultural dimension of individualism versus collectivism is concerned with the relationship between personal autonomy and social obligation. The existential implications of individual autonomy and sociality or heteronomy that emphasizes the relational, as Del Loewenthal discusses in his chapter, point to cultural differences on a moral level.

Given the potential limitations and blind spots in a particular worldview, the hope is that cross-cultural understanding with respect to diverse models of human development and psychological and social well-being can broaden current horizons. Efforts toward integrating different cultural orientations have included exploring how principles of Eastern healing and transpersonal and relational models of self in Eastern cultures can enhance Western models of psychotherapy (Ajaya, 1983; Atwood & Maltin, 1991; Kakar, 1991; Steinberg & Whiteside, 1999). Integration can also be at the personal level, the type of integration that is featured in this book. Murgatroyd (2001) described her spiritual understanding in relation to psychology and counseling from the perspective of one raised in a Buddhist tradition and trained in a Western mental health profession. This literature on the integration of cultural traditions spans a broader scope than what is typically covered by American textbooks on counseling those who are culturally different.

Though serving as a useful resource in understanding human diversity, the value of cross-cultural knowledge is limited by increased cultural assimilation and hybridity resulting from migration and globalization. Hermans and Kempen (1998) suggested that we view culture as moving and dynamic. Cultural differences are no longer bound by geography and ethnic origin. Duan and Wang (2000), for example, reported accommodating both individualistic and collectivist values in a contemporary Chinese context of counseling. Culture-specific approaches run the risk of stereotyping particular cultural groups when global developments have resulted in more rapid cultural change and greater latitude in identity choices than ever before. There is evidence of youth internalizing multiple cultural identities in a globalized world (Jensen, 2003). Cultural studies have been concerned with the role of media and telecommunication in the shaping of identities and societies (Ferguson & Golding, 1997; Lewis, 2002). They suggest that in trying to understand the other and all the differences that represent "otherness," we must learn about not only cultural attitudes, values, and assumptions, but also the diverse cultural sources and processes of appropriating identity. John McLeod, in his chapter, addresses the use of cultural resources and processes in psychotherapy and counseling. In his chapter on Native Hawaiian identity, William Rezentes points to the group history and the experience of acculturation and culture loss. Their work implores us to be cognizant of the moral, social, and political implications of identity in our globalized contemporary world (Hoshmand, 2003b).

Whereas cross-cultural psychology has emphasized cultural variations as scientific phenomena, we need a much broader understanding to comprehend the multilevel implications of cultural issues that can be afforded by multiple disciplines. Cultural psychology, broadly conceived, can be about understanding more than scientifically described differences, including issues related to multiculturalism.

Multiculturalism and the Politics of Identity

Multiculturalism as a social ideology points to the politics of identity and issues of social equity. Taylor, Gutmann, Rockefeller, Walzer, and Wolf (1992) approached multiculturalism in terms of the political recognition of groups with different identities. Social psychology and peace psychology have called attention to identity-based conflict as the most salient feature of intergroup violence (Hoshmand & Kass, 2003). From identity politics and culture wars (Friedman, 1994; Sampson, 1993) to concerns about the normative role of culture in selfhood and society (Adams, 1997), there is much at issue in human existence. Due to the hegemonic nature of the scientific discourse in psychology and the therapeutic professions, however, normative issues often enter into the world of psychological practice in unexamined ways or result in difficult dialogue in the profession. Fowers and Richardson (1996) cautioned against cultural separatism and proposed a hermeneutic perspective for evaluating cultural values. In arguing for more engagement in discussing cultural differences, their attempt to link multiculturalism to the moral traditions and ideals of the West was interpreted by some as elevating the Western traditions. There has not been an easy way for the profession to enter into effective dialogue on culture and identity as politics of difference. As Loewenthal and I comment in subsequent chapters, ideological thoughtfulness and the ability to discuss the politics of identity require related experience and professional socialization that seem lacking in most training programs.

The multidisciplinary field of cultural inquiry, on the other hand, has been so full of controversy and intellectual debate that even anthropologists have questioned the value and meaning of the culture concept (Abu-Lughod, 1991; Brumann, 1999). How culture is supposed to develop in an age of globalization and how cultural forces should define human society in a diverse world are among the questions raised by anthropologists such as Clifford (1988) and political historians such as Huntington (1996). One of the problems is that ethnic and cultural groups that have historical or geographical affinity have been treated as mega-cultures. They include the Western civilization, the Africano, and what has been labeled as Orientalism (Said, 1994). Such mega-culture approaches have made it even more difficult to appreciate within-culture differences and ethnic and national differences.

Cultural historians and political theorists (e.g., Lewis, 1993; Said, 1994) have further discussed the complex issues of culture in a changing world order. Huntington (1996) dramatized the differences between mega-cultures as a clash of civilizations. In a postcolonial age, the study of cultures should assume new meanings. It appears, however, that neoliberalism and neocolonialism have both endorsed capitalism as an organizing principle for the present world order (Schirato & Webb, 2003). Due to patterns of economic and political domination and unequal power, the livelihood and well-being of many groups are at stake. Loewenthal poses critical questions in his chapter about this state of world realities. Practitioners need to be aware that cultural imperialism is a concern for those vulnerable to domination. In interviewing clients from diverse international backgrounds about their experience of psychotherapy in a Western context, Seeley (2000) found cultural resistances that reflect concerns about power imbalance. Clients use a number of ways to protect their indigenous identities from therapeutic tampering. Culture as a descriptive source of human diversity is now entangled with issues of global understanding, identity politics, and social justice.

From understanding culture as a source of human diversity, to recognizing the importance of culture learning in a constantly changing world, some American practitioners have looked to multiculturalism as a community standard and ontological given. The counseling field has responded to changing demographics by emphasizing multicultural competencies for practitioners (Abreu & Atkinson, 2000; Sue, Arredondo, & McDavis, 1992; Sue, Bingham, Porche-Burke, & Vasquez, 1999). The American Psychological Association (2003) has also published guidelines on multicultural education, training, research, practice, and organizational change. Psychotherapists and counseling professionals are expected to engage in culture learning and be responsive to cultural differences in the worldviews and expectations of their clients. Some of these differences are couched in terms of specific attitudinal and behavioral characteristics to be matched with the appropriate interventions. As suggested earlier, however, culture as scientifically depicted difference does not fully account for the possibilities and significance of culture as negotiated identity and social reality.

Psychotherapy and counseling, viewed as a cultural enterprise embedded in social and political context, is about addressing more than descriptive differences across individuals and groups with diverse backgrounds. There is an increasing need to consider ourselves and our clients as world citizens in a particular social and political order. In both local and global contexts, therapists are faced with challenges in culture learning as well as issues of positionality and power. The authority granted professional practitioners embeds us in political structures of social control (Varenne, 2003). Therapeutic practice, like the medical system, is intertwined with the political economy and, in some instances such as communist countries, more obviously defined by political ideology (Tseng, 1999). The fact that political aspects of human interaction are also part of the cultural, multicultural counseling and psychotherapy must address the politics of difference and issues of social justice (Vera & Speight, 2003). Otherwise, it will have a limited role in producing social change. Chasin and Herzig (1994) proposed systemic interventions for the sociopolitical arena of practice, attempting to integrate the personal, professional, and political. Comaz-Diaz (2000) emphasized the ethnopolitical context of therapy and the importance of bearing witness to clients' experience of racism and oppression. Liu and Pope-Davis (2004) further pointed to the interaction between classism, race, and cultural factors in psychotherapy and counseling. Practitioners should be conscious of the social and political history represented by the client as well as the international and local dynamics affecting the client's identity experience. Dana Becker, Susan Gere, and William Rezentes illustrate this consciousness in their chapters. John Christopher and Del Loewenthal urge us to uncover any disguised ideology in psychological theory and practice.

Part of the American literature on multicultural counseling has highlighted issues of race and the dynamics between the dominant Anglo culture and ethnic minority cultures (e.g., Helms, 1990; Helms & Cook, 1999; Sue & Sue, 2002). Yet, the discussion of the personal and the political has been secondary to teaching and learning about descriptive differences between ethnic groups and cultures. The dynamics of culture and identity in therapy are complex (Comas-Diaz & Jacobsen, 1991), and no less complicated in other professional and social settings. As illustrated in Rezentes's chapter, the negotiation of positionality in dealing with culture and identity involves symbolic representation, self-understanding, and interpersonal dialogue. For Susan Gere, the complexities of this process demand deep existential reflection and moral clarity. Therapists engaged in such negotiations with their clients must understand both the symbolic and lived meanings of culture and identity.

Culture as Symbolic Nexus of the Personal and the Social

Cultural psychology has philosophical affinities with the interpretive social sciences and semiotic disciplines that emphasize the symbolic and meaning-driven nature of human existence. Since Berger and Luckmann (1966) wrote about the social construction of reality, there have been examples of cultural study as interpretive social science, such as represented by Geertz (1973) and Rabinow and Sullivan (1987). The emergence of social constructionism in the 1980s further contributed to the view of culture as meaning-making and narrated existence. The postmodern literature on social constructionism and constructivism has influenced the psychology of identity and the theory and practice of psychotherapy (McNamee & Gergen, 1992; Neimeyer & Mahoney, 1995; Shotter & Gergen, 1989). As narrative theory found its way into the human sciences (Polkinghorne, 1988), narrative became a root metaphor for psychology (Sarbin, 1986). Narrative psychology (Hoshmand, 2000) can be considered an extension of cultural psychology that connects culture, identity, and human experience.

Studies of identity development in particular are increasingly focused on the cultural appropriation of stories that we live by. The creation of such stories and the cultural webs of meaning in which they are situated are seen as constitutive of identity and social existence, respectively. Examples of narrative views of identity and cognitive development include the work of Hermans and Kempen (1993), Howard (1991), Markus and Nurius (1986), and McAdams (1985, 1993). Hermans and Hermans-Jansen (1995) and White and Epston (1990) presented a narrative view of psychotherapy, as does John McLeod who writes about psychotherapy and counseling as meaning-oriented cultural work in this volume. In recent years, also as a result of constructivist influence, the cultural view of human dysfunction has gained currency. Neimeyer and Raskin (2000), for example, presented post-modern perspectives on the cultural and social construction of psychological disorder. Further comments on the cultural construction of dysfunction can be found in Dana Becker's chapter.

This reconceptualization of human dysfunction as cultural construction has affinities with meaning-making perspectives of psychotherapy (Rosen & Kuehlwein, 1996) that are fundamentally based in a cultural view. Frankl's (1985) focus on meaning as the key to therapeutic change has been well supported by research on the psychology of meaning. People's sense of purpose and coherence in life, their ability to make meaning of adversity and loss, and their capacity for spiritual or other self-transcendence have been linked to health and wellness (Wong & Fry, 1998). The focusing-oriented approach in psychotherapy described by Doralee Grindler Katonah in her chapter explicates Gendlin's (1962) theory on the integrative and dynamic nature of meaning-making in human experience, and in the process of cultural appropriation and transformation.

The view of cultures as systems of meaning, and life in general as symbolically fashioned, also directs our attention to the understanding of culture as myth and cosmology. From Carl Jung (1998) to the popular contemporary writer Joseph Campbell (1988, 1997), there has been appropriate interest in these aspects of the cultural realm. Whereas cultural-social anthropologists have studied cultural cosmology especially in what may be considered exotic cultures, the psychological meaning of myth (Feinstein & Krippner, 1997; Lukoff, 1997) lends support to a holistic approach to culture and psyche. As William Rezentes and William Mikulas argue in their chapters, respectively, we need to understand the cultural cosmology of clients in psychotherapy, and to consider the wisdom offered by cultural traditions other than our own. To the extent that psychotherapists operate as metaphysicians (O'Donohue, 1989), we also need to examine our role in shaping the cultural cosmology of our society and clients.

For those interested in narrative psychology, one of the most useful concepts is what Bruner (1990) termed narrative knowing as culturally appropriated acts of meaning. He distinguished this mode of knowing, which constitutes much of clinical inquiry, therapeutic dialogue, and practice knowledge, from the hypothetico-deductive forms of scientific knowing that we also use in professional work. In the next chapter, I argue that psychotherapists and counseling practitioners rely on both narrative knowing and the knowledge and methods of psychological science in working with clients. Narrative and experiential therapies (Elliott & Greenberg, 1997; McLeod, 1997; Monk, Winslade, Crocket, & Epston, 1997), in particular, focus on the conversational processes of cultural meaning-making. It is essential to understand such generic processes that connect language and experience, and thought and action. In the narrative conception of psychotherapy cultural scripts are subject to change and re-storying. The possibility for therapists and clients to accept or reject certain dominant cultural stories has many implications. John McLeod explains in his chapter how culture provides resources in the narrativization of experience and the appropriation of identity, and that psychotherapy can be the occasion to sort out cultural polarities and tensions in the search for the good life and what it means to be human.

Narrative psychology may be considered an aspect of cultural psychology, especially if we use cultural psychology as a metatheory (Hoshmand, 1996), a framework that will be developed further. From the standpoint of theoretical integration, the common narrative features of all counseling approaches suggest that a meta-level conceptual framework may be developed with cultural and narrative psychology. The relationship of culture, narratives, and meaning-making to the experience of psychotherapy is of interest to researchers such as those presented in Angus and McLeod (2004). Meaning-oriented approaches to psychotherapy are consistent with the view of culture as symbolic forms of constituting human experience. Understanding such basic processes is essential to a culturally informed psychological practice. The chapters by Grindler Katonah, McLeod, and others address such meaning-making as cultural processes.

Culture as a human creation is a view that has been reinforced by the postmodern philosophy that knowledge and much of human realities are socially constructed (Kvale, 1992). There have been varying degrees of emphasis on the primacy of the personal and the social in constructivist, narrative approaches to psychotherapy and in critical, constructionist approaches, respectively (Freedman & Combs, 1996; Leitner & Epting, 2001). For practitioners, the philosophical difference amounts to one's belief in the extent to which a person can reconstrue and re-story cultural existence, and how much to grant the societal constraints on possibilities of being and living. Some regard these two perspectives as "two sides of the same coin" (McNamee, 2004; Paris & Epting, 2004), consistent with Shweder's earlier definition of cultural psychology as encompassing the dialectical relationship between psyche and culture. Human beings are culture bearing and at the same time capable of self-creating. The notion that we can appropriate from culture what we desire for our identity may seem to suggest endless human potentials. Yet, human agency and control are also part of the makeup of culture, just as physical limitations are part of human constitution. It is more realistic to assert that culture offers both possibilities and constraints (Martin & Sugarman, 1999), a position that is helpful to therapeutic practitioners and their clients when contemplating choices in ways of being. This view acknowledges that the potential for human change is constrained by cultural, social, political, and biological givens.

Culture as Activities, Practices, and Institutionalized Ideology

Although many therapeutic practitioners tend to be most at home with the notion of culture as meaning-making, it is important to remember that culture is more than meanings and how we story human life. Vygotsky (1978) locates the cultural in human activity in social, historical settings whereby learning and cognition are understood as culturally mediated practices. Under the influence of pragmatism, the practice turn in philosophy has helped to promote this view of culture. It conceives of all aspects of human activity and what is institutionalized in human society as cultural in nature. Situating the psychological in the cultural-historical means that we must not allow the psychological to overshadow the ecological. This is important because psychotherapy is limited in its ability to address issues that require social and political solutions (Albee, 1990), a message conveyed in the chapters by Dana Becker, Susan Gere, and others.

In proposing cultural theory as a framework for the history of psychological practice, Voestermans (1992) noted that as a practical science psychology is vulnerable to ideological influences. His formulation of psychological practice as a cultural phenomenon can be applied to psychotherapy as a cultural practice. There are rituals and ideologies characterizing such practices. Two common practices in the mental health field are psychological testing and the application of the diagnostic categories of the *Diagnostic and Statistical Manual.* Their association with reductionistic biases and the medical model, respectively, is seldom questioned, as they have become institutionalized practices. In addition to enabling mental health professionals to describe individual differences, these practices also serve technocratic purposes in determining access to treatment resources, payment for services, and justifying particular interventions and placements of the individuals concerned. As institutionalized practices embedded in the political economy and society, they need to be evaluated as cultural practices that inform psychotherapy. Dawes (1994) questioned the scientific legitimacy of many of the diagnostic and therapeutic practices in common use. The chapter by Dana Becker here also touches on some of the issues arising from diagnostic practices.

Ratner (2000) proposed culture as a comprehensive concept that refers to cultural activities, values, schemas, meanings, and both psychological aspects and physical artifacts that are collectively constructed and distributed with human agency. Cultural understanding includes understanding the practices in which others participate, and knowing about the artifacts, cultural media, and intentions with which people construct their selfhood and identity. This point is illustrated with the Hawaiian culture by Rezentes in his chapter.

The role of human intentions or agency in the creation and appropriation of the cultural has significance not only for therapists and clients, but also for the therapeutic enterprise. We are responsible for the character of our profession and how we do our work. Reflective practice involves a reflexive understanding of the personal and cultural worldviews as well as theoretical assumptions that we bring into the therapeutic encounter. We cannot escape the fact that therapeutic practice, while appropriated from culture, is also a cultural system in itself. Thus, we have the term "therapeutic culture" that refers to the values, assumptions, social ideology, and practices that characterize the community of psychotherapists and counseling practitioners. There are value similarities among counseling practitioners, beyond differences in theoretical orientations (Consoli & Williams, 1999). We need to heed Scarr's (1985) caution that the shared beliefs, theoretical assumptions, and philosophical preferences of the psychology profession are unlikely to be challenged because they are products of our time and supported by the current ideology and culture. This is particularly important because of the role of psychotherapists and counseling practitioners in the cultural transmission of values, as demonstrated by reported shifts in clients toward their therapists' value language and moral stances (Kelly and Strupp, 1992; Rosenthal, 1995).

Therapeutic practice cannot be separated from other social practices and historical contexts that impact the lives of professionals and clients. Ehrenhaus (1993) observed that the therapeutic motif appropriated from cultural narratives can serve social control functions, such as in the political containment of Vietnam veterans. As socially and politically embedded forms of practice that have their own cultural character, psychotherapy and counseling systems mirror their cultures of origin, and can be at times seamless with the popular culture that prevails in the everyday consciousness of people. Lasch (1979) described the cultural trend of the 1960s as one of narcissism supported by a therapeutic culture of individualism that continues to undermine social obligations. Bellah, Madsen, Sullivan, Swidler, and Tipton (1985) found a historic tension between individualism and social commitment in American culture, played out in the search for personal virtues and the good society. Bankart (1997) summarized the feminist critique of Freudian theory and the historical orthodoxy of psychoanalysis, showing that models of psychotherapy and their metaphysics are a function of cultural context and the times.

Cushman (1990, 1995) regarded psychotherapy in the United States to be syntonic with American culture in offering lifestyle solutions to clients who wish to be soothed the same way that they use consumption to fill their existential void. He provided a cultural history of psychotherapy in which he critically examined the role that psychotherapy has played in American society. Applying a hermeneutic perspective in framing psychotherapy as moral discourse, he pointed to the reluctance of therapists to examine the moral and political implications of their theory and practice. Due to the dominance of the scientific model in psychology and its ideology, value issues are seldom part of academic and professional discourse. He attributed this to the Western bias of using the ideology of objectivism to masquerade psychology as a physical science. Such scientistic (as in scientism) biases are contrary to a cultural, humanistic understanding of the psychotherapeutic and counseling enterprise, a schism in the field that will be addressed in the next chapter.

Previously, I had proposed that a reflective profession would critically examine its philosophical foundations and cultural biases (Hoshmand, 1994). The question I want to raise here concerns how members of the therapeutic community can exercise their agency in shaping the therapeutic culture and its relationship to the larger culture. This can include being critical of the effects of cultural trends on psychological health and social well-being. When Mary Pipher (1995) voiced her concerns about the effects of the popular culture on the development of girls she saw in psychotherapy, she was acting as an agent of cultural change. When feminists critique traditional psychotherapy (Brown, 1994; Byrne & McCarthy, 1999), they are serving as cultural critics. Several of our authors refer to aspects of the popular culture that have created issues for the clients they see in their practice. The symbiosis between the therapeutic culture and society becomes more evident when we view culture and psychotherapy in moral and existential terms.

Culture as Moral Ontology and Existential Choices

The philosopher MacIntyre (1981) suggested that each culture offers its stock of characters that represent the embodiment of moral existence. Narrative identities are cultural products that reflect moral ways of being. Understanding human development and psychotherapy in cultural terms requires a moral consciousness, with several implications. One is that we have to acknowledge the moral nature of therapeutic practice in how we interact with clients. Sugarman and Martin (1995) formulated psychotherapy and counseling as a moral conversation, which they were able to support empirically. If psychotherapy or counseling is a venue for moral reflection, such as when discussing clients' intentions and purposes in life, then psychotherapists and counseling practitioners can more consciously engage clients in evaluating the moral consequences of their personal decisions and actions (Doherty, 1995), as well as monitor their own role in this process. Yet, as pointed out previously, the scientistic assumption of neutrality combined with the value relativism that pervades contemporary American society and the therapeutic culture often absolve psychotherapists and counseling practitioners from responsibility as facilitators of moral reflection.

In writing about the psychologist as a moral agent, Peterson (1998) referred to the historic work of London (1964) and Mowrer (1967). London's view of the moral nature of therapeutic practice appeared to be grounded in his religious faith. His work suggests that the professional norm of keeping one's personal beliefs and values out of what is presumed to be scientifically neutral practice (an indication of scientism) does not always serve clients in therapy. Mowrer had argued that psychological "dis-ease" is related to social conscience, and that the modern "sickness of the soul" stems from loss of genuine human communion. Peterson's insight is that in spite of the rejection of the metaphysical in psychological science, psychological practice cannot be without deep moral understanding. Miller (2001) urged clinicians to reclaim moral discourse and acknowledge the moral commitments inherent in clinical work. His concept of moral engagement (Miller, 2004) is consistent with a moral view of psychotherapy and counseling as a cultural enterprise. Whether we consider psychotherapy and counseling to be a response to demoralization (Frank, 1974), human suffering (Miller, 2004), or loss of human communion (Mowrer, 1967), the existential implications are clear. Loewenthal and Christopher in this volume write about the inherently moral nature of a therapeutic relationship. The case example in Susan Gere's chapter further illustrates the moral, existential nature of the therapeutic encounter and client narratives of identity and experience.

Cultural psychology reminds us that what constitutes virtue and moral ways of being are locally defined. Psychotherapists and counseling practitioners need to learn the cultural idioms and moral grammar of their clients' communities. It is likely that discernment of one's moral commitments and failed obligations is related to psychological well-being and distress because they are about a person's relationship with the community. In exploring the cultural roots of concepts of psychological well-being, Christopher (1999) proposed that it is a matter of moral vision and chosen ways of being. Given that there are particular cultural values and assumptions underlying theory and research on psychological well-being, we have to deconstruct the cultural assumptions of our theory and practice. Dueck and Reimer (2003) proposed that rather than impose the liberal tradition of American psychotherapy on clients, we should be sensitive to the moral traditions of our clients. This implies moral pluralism, which is not the same as moral relativism.

Richardson, Fowers, and Guignon (1999) conceptualized the moral dimensions of psychological theory and practice with a hermeneutic perspective that builds on narrative, dialogical views of psychotherapy. This hermeneutic approach to understanding self and others (Gadamer, 1977, 1989) presumes a nonrelativistic ethic while allowing for moral pluralism (Richardson, 2003). Through open dialogue and culture learning, we can broaden the cultural horizons by which we evaluate our own moral stances and other ways of being. Hermeneutic analysis, such as discussed by Eaton (2002), can clarify the moral reasoning and reflections of both therapists and clients. Coming also from a hermeneutic perspective, Christopher (2001) explored the cultural nature of psychotherapy as a moral encounter. Loewenthal and Snell (2001) argued for psychotherapy as the practice of relational ethics in the existential sense of being responsible for the client's responsibility to others. The normative role and existential implications of culture in selfhood, society, and therapeutic practice, which seldom have been part of scientific discourse, are included in a cultural view of psychotherapy and counseling as further developed in subsequent chapters.

Following a narrative, cultural perspective, I have argued previously for a view of psychotherapy as an instrument of culture (Hoshmand, 2001).

Cultural psychology implies that we are not neutral observers of the development of society, but have a role in its development (Poddiakov, 2002). Psychotherapists and counseling practitioners can explore with their clients cultural ways of being, and at the same time critique cultural prescriptions for living. McLeod suggests in his chapter that if psychotherapy and counseling is the arena in which clients reflect on difficulties in their life space or personal niche (that is constructed from cultural resources), then the practitioner can assist in the search for new cultural resources or adaptation of existing ones to resolve such difficulties. The cultural work of psychological practice therefore involves valued possibilities and moral choices. Given Cushman's (1990, 1995) caution about the problem of complicity with a consumerist popular culture, we need to be more critical of the therapeutic enterprise in the types of cultural stories it privileges and the nature of the cultural resources it offers. The work of critical and discursive psychologists (Parker, 1999; Prilleltensky, 1994; Prilleltensky & Walsh-Bowers, 1993) and feminist authors (Brabeck & Ting, 2000; Brown, 1994; Worell & Remer, 1992) has contributed a critical perspective on the interrelationship between the therapeutic enterprise and society at large. A moral perspective that I believe is sorely lacking in professional discourse can strengthen this critical perspective, as expressed by some of our authors.

Rather than making scientistic assumptions of neutrality, we need to bring a critical and moral perspective to the personal and social meanings of psychotherapeutic and counseling practice. Whereas science represents one system of rationality, from the standpoint of cultural psychology, there are multiple rationalities and moral realities (Shweder, 1986). There are as many divergent moral goods and personal virtues as there are multiple communities (Tjeltveit, 2003). The old approach of attempting to maintain neutrality has to be replaced by a conscious attempt to acknowledge the moral spaces in which psychotherapists and clients are located as well as the role we play in enabling, questioning, or diminishing the client's moral possibilities (Benson, 2001).

If psychotherapy is involved in helping clients reflect on their moral understanding of self in relation to others and society, the psychotherapeutic and counseling enterprise should be evaluated by more than scientific criteria (Hoshmand, 2003a). I will summarize in the final chapter some of the ideas suggested by the authors in this regard. In particular, we should consider how issues such as individual freedom and social commitment, as reflected in cultural individualism and collectivism, are addressed in therapeutic practice. As Loewenthal frames it in his chapter, it is a matter of putting the other before oneself. We also need to understand what the realistic limits and moral implications are in attempting to solve social and political problems with psychological means. I explain in the next chapter how a meta-level cultural perspective that includes existential, moral views, and critical perspectives can complement the science-based understanding of therapeutic psychology and counteract problematic scientism.

References

Abreu, J. M., & Atkinson, D. R. (2000). Multicultural counseling training: Past, present, and future directions. *The Counseling Psychologist, 28*(5), 641–656.

Abu-Lughod, L. (1991). Writing against culture. In R. G. Fox (Ed.), *Recapturing anthropology: Working in the present* (pp. 137–162). Santa Fe, NM: School of American Research Press.

Adams, E. M. (1997). *A society fit for human beings.* Albany: State University of New York Press.

Ajaya, S. (1983). *Psychotherapy East and West: A unifying paradigm.* Honesdale, PA: Himalayan Institute Press.

Albee, G. W. (1990). The futility of psychotherapy. *The Journal of Mind and Behavior, 11*(3/4), 369–384.

Al-Issa, I. (Ed.). (1995). *Handbook of culture and mental illness: An international perspective.* Guilford, CT: International Universities Press.

American Psychological Association. (2003). Guidelines on multicultural education, training, research, practice and organizational change for psychologists. *American Psychologist, 58*(5), 377–402.

Angus, L., & McLeod, J. (Eds.). (2004). *The handbook of narrative and psychotherapy: Practice, theory, and research.* Thousand Oaks, CA: Sage.

Atkinson, D. R., Morten, G., & Sue, D. W. (1989). A minority identity development model. In D. R. Atkinson, G. Morten, & D. W. Sue (Eds.), *Counseling American minorities* (pp. 35–52). Dubuque, IA: W. C. Brown.

Atwood, J. D., & Maltin, L. (1991). Putting Eastern philosophies into Western psychotherapies. *American Journal of Psychotherapy, 45*(3), 368–382.

Bankart, P. (1997). *Talking cures: A history of Western and Eastern psychotherapies.* Pacific Grove, CA: Brooks/Cole.

Bellah, R. N., Madsen, R., Sullivan, W. M., Swidler, A., & Tipton, S. M. (1985). *Habits of the heart: Individualism and commitment in American life.* Berkeley: University of California Press.

Benson, C. (2001). *The cultural psychology of self: Place, morality and art in human worlds.* London: Routledge.

Berger, P. L., & Luckmann, T. (1966). *The social construction of reality.* Garden City, NY: Anchor Books.

Bond, M. H. (1996). *The handbook of Chinese psychology.* Hong Kong: Oxford University Press.

Brabeck, M. M., & Ting, K. (2000). Feminist ethics: Lenses for examining ethical psychological practice. In M. M. Brabeck (Ed.), *Practicing feminist ethics in psychology* (pp. 17–35). Washington, DC: American Psychological Association.

Brown, L. S. (1994). *Subversive dialogues: Theory in feminist therapy.* New York: Basic Books.

Brumann, C. (1999). Writing for culture: Why a successful concept should not be discarded. *Current Anthropology, 40,* 19–31.

Bruner, J. (1990). *Acts of meaning.* Cambridge, MA: Harvard University Press.

Byrne, N. O., & McCarthy, I. C. (1999). Feminisms, politics and power in therapeutic discourse: Fragments from the fifth province. In I. Parker (Ed.), *Deconstructing psychotherapy* (pp. 86–102). Thousand Oaks, CA: Sage.

Campbell, J. (1988). *The power of myth.* New York: Doubleday.

Campbell, J. (1997). *The mythic dimension: Selected essays 1959–1987.* San Francisco: Harper.

Castillo, R. J. (1998). *Meanings of madness.* Pacific Grove, CA: Brooks/Cole.

Chasin, R., & Herzig, M. (1994). Creating systemic interventions for the sociopolitical arena. In B. B. Gould & D. H. DeMuth (Eds.), *The global family therapist: Integrating the personal, professional, and political.* New York: Allyn & Bacon.

Christopher, J. C. (1999). Situating psychological well being: Exploring cultural values and assumptions underlying theory and research on psychological well being. *Journal of Counseling and Development, 77,* 141–152.

Christopher, J. C. (2001). Culture and psychotherapy: Toward a hermeneutic approach. *Psychotherapy, 38*(2), 115–128.

Clifford, J. (1988). *The predicament of culture: Twentieth-century ethnography, literature, and art.* Cambridge, MA: Harvard University Press.

Cole, M. (1996). *Cultural psychology: A once and future discipline.* Cambridge, MA: Harvard University Press.

Comas-Diaz, L. (2000). An ethnopolitical approach to working with people of color. *American Psychologist, 55*(11), 1317–1325.

Comas-Diaz, L., & Jacobsen, F. M. (1991). Ethnocultural transference and countertransference in the therapeutic dyad. *American Journal of Orthopsychiatry, 61,* 392–402.

Consoli, A. J., & Williams, L. M. (1999). Commonalities in values among mental health counselors. *Counseling and Values, 43,* 106–115.

Cushman, P. (1990). Why the self is empty: Toward a historically situated psychology. *American Psychologist, 45*(5), 599–611.

Cushman, P. (1995). *Constructing the self, constructing America: A cultural history of psychotherapy.* Cambridge, MA: Perseus.

Dawes, R. (1994). *House of cards.* New York: Free Press.

De Wit, H. (1996). Happiness and suffering in Buddhist psychology. In M. G. T. Kwee & T. C. Holdstock (Eds.), *Western and Buddhist psychology: Clinical perspectives* (pp. 149–174). Delft, The Netherlands: Eburon.

Doherty, W. J. (1995). *Soul searching: Why psychotherapy must promote moral responsibility.* New York: Basic Books.

Duan, C., & Wang, L. (2000). Counseling in the Chinese cultural context: Accommodating both individualistic and collectivist values. *Asian Journal of Counseling, 7*(1), 1–21.

Dueck, A., & Reimer, K. (2003). Retrieving the virtues in psychotherapy: Thick and thin discourse. *American Behavioral Scientist, 47*(4), 427–441.

Eaton, J. (2002). Psychotherapy and moral inquiry. *Theory and Psychology, 12*(3), 367–386.

Ehrenhaus, P. (1993). Cultural narratives and the therapeutic motif: The political containment of Vietnam veterans. In D. Mumby (Ed.), *Narrative and social control: Critical perspectives* (pp. 77–96). Newbury Park, CA: Sage.

Elliott, R., & Greenberg, L. (1997). Multiple voices in process-experiential therapy: Dialogues between aspects of the self. *Journal of Psychotherapy Integration, 7,* 225–240.

Feinstein, D., & Krippner, S. (1997). *The mythic path.* New York: Tarcher.

Ferguson, M., & Golding, P. (1997). *Cultural studies in question.* Thousand Oaks, CA: Sage.

Fowers, B. J., & Richardson, F. C. (1996). Why is multiculturalism good? *American Psychologist, 51*(6), 609–621.

Frank, J. D. (1974). Psychotherapy: The restoration of morale. *American Journal of Psychiatry, 131,* 271–274.

Frankl, V. E. (1985). *Man's search for meaning: An introduction to logotherapy* (L. Lasch, Trans., rev. ed.). New York: Washington University Press.

Freedman, J., & Combs, G. (1996). *Narrative therapy: The social construction of preferred realities.* New York: Norton.

Friedman, J. (1994). *Cultural identity and global process.* Thousand Oaks, CA: Sage.

Gadamer, H. G. (1977). *Philosophical hermeneutics.* Berkeley: University of California Press.

Gadamer, H. G. (1989). *Truth and method* (2nd ed.). New York: Continuum.

Geertz, C. (1973). *The interpretation of cultures.* New York: Basic Books.

Gendlin, E. T. (1962). *Experiencing and the creation of meaning.* Toronto, ON: Free Press of Glencoe.

Gielen, U., Fish, J., & Draguns, J. G. (Eds.). (2002). *Handbook of culture, psychotherapy, and healing.* Boston: Allyn & Bacon.

Heelas, P., & Lock, A. (Eds.). (1981). *Indigenous psychologies: The anthropology of the self.* London: Academic Press.

Helms, J. E. (1990). *Black and White racial identity: Theory, research and practice.* New York: Praeger; Westport, CT: Greenwood.

Helms, J. E., & Cook, D. A. (1999). *Using race in counseling and psychotherapy: Theory and process.* Needham, MA: Allyn & Bacon.

Helmiak, D. A. (2001). Treating spiritual issues in secular psychotherapy. *Counseling and Values, 45*(3), 163–189.

Hermans, H. J. M., & Hermans-Jansen, E. (1995). *Self-narratives: The construction of meaning in psychotherapy.* New York: Guilford.

Hermans, H. J. M., & Kempen, H. J. G. (1993). *The dialogical self: Meaning as movement.* San Diego, CA: Academic Press.

Hermans, H. J. M., & Kempen, H. J. G. (1998). Moving cultures: The perilous problems of cultural dichotomies in a globalizing society. *American Psychologist, 53*(10), 1111–1120.

Hoshmand, L. T. (1994). *Orientation to inquiry in a reflective professional psychology*. Albany: State University of New York Press.

Hoshmand, L. T. (1996). Cultural psychology as metatheory. *Journal of Theoretical and Philosophical Psychology, 16*, 30–48.

Hoshmand, L. T. (2000). Narrative psychology. In A. E. Kazdin (Ed.), *Encyclopedia of psychology* (pp. 382–387). Washington, DC: American Psychological Association; New York: Oxford University Press.

Hoshmand, L. T. (2001). Psychotherapy as an instrument of culture. In B. D. Slife, R. N. Williams, & S. N. Barlow (Eds.), *Critical issues in psychotherapy: Translating new ideas into practice* (pp. 99–113). Thousand Oaks, CA: Sage.

Hoshmand, L. T. (2003a). Applied epistemology in a science-based cultural enterprise. *The Counseling Psychologist, 31*(5), 529–538.

Hoshmand, L. T. (2003b). Moral implications of globalization and identity. *American Psychologist, 58*(10), 814–815.

Hoshmand, L. T., & Ho, D. Y. F. (1995). Moral dimensions of selfhood: Chinese traditions and cultural change. *World Psychology, 1*, 47–69.

Hoshmand, L. T., & Kass, J. (2003). Conceptual and action frameworks for peace. *International Journal for the Advancement of Counselling, 25*(4), 205–213.

Howard, G. S. (1991). Culture tales: A narrative approach to thinking, cross-cultural psychology, and psychotherapy. *American Psychologist, 46*, 187–197.

Huntington, A. P. (1996). *The clash of civilizations and the remaking of world order*. New York: Simon & Schuster.

Jensen, L. A. (2003). Coming of age in a multicultural world: Globalization and adolescent cultural identity formation. *Applied Developmental Science, 7*(3), 189–196.

Jung, C. G. (1998). *Jung on mythology*. Princeton, NJ: Princeton University Press.

Kakar, S. (1991). Western science, Eastern minds. *Wilson Quarterly, 15*(1), 109–115.

Kelly, T. A., & Strupp, H. H. (1992). Patient and therapist values in psychotherapy: Perceived changes, assimilation, similarity, and outcome. *Journal of Consulting and Clinical Psychology, 60*, 34–40.

Kim, U., & Berry, J. (Eds.). (1993). *Indigenous psychologies: Research and experience in cultural context*. Cambridge, UK: Cambridge University Press.

Kim, U., Park, Y., & Park, D. (2000). The challenge of cross-cultural psychology: The role of indigenous psychologies. *Journal of Cross-Cultural Psychology, 31*(1), 63–79.

Kvale, S. (1992). *Psychology and postmodernism*. Newbury Park, CA: Sage.

Lasch, C. (1979). *The culture of narcissism*. New York: Norton.

Leitner, L. M., & Epting, F. R. (2001). Constructivist approaches to therapy. In K. J. Schneider, J. F. T. Bugental, & J. F. Pierson (Eds.), *The handbook of humanistic psychology* (pp. 421–431). Thousand Oaks, CA: Sage.

Lewis, B. (1993). *Islam and the West*. New York: Oxford University Press.

Lewis, J. (2002). *Cultural studies*. Thousand Oaks, CA: Sage.

Liu, W. M., & Pope-Davis, D. B. (2004). Understanding classism to effect personal change. In T. B. Smith (Ed.), *Practicing multiculturalism: Affirming diversity in counseling and psychology* (pp. 294–310). Boston: Pearson.

Loewenthal, D., & Snell, R. (2001). Psychotherapy as the practice of ethics. In F. P. Barnes & L. Murdin (Eds.), *Values and ethics in the practice of psychotherapy and counseling* (pp. 23–31). Philadelphia: Open University Press.

London, P. (1964). *The modes and morals of psychotherapy*. New York: Holt, Rinehart & Winston.

Lukoff, D. (1997). The psychologist as mythologist. *Journal of Humanistic Psychology, 37*(3), 34–58.

MacIntyre, A. (1981). *After virtue: A study in moral theory*. Notre Dame, IN: University of Notre Dame Press.

Markus, H., & Nurius, P. S. (1986). Possible selves. *American Psychologist, 41*, 954–969.

Marsella, A. J., DeVos, G. A., & Hsu, F. L. K. (Eds.). (1985). *Culture and self: Asian and Western perspectives*. New York: Tavistock.

Marsella, A. J., & White, G. M. (Eds.). (1982). *Cultural conceptions of mental health and therapy*. Dordrecht, The Netherlands: D. Reidel.

Marsella, A. J., & Yamada, A. M. (2000). Culture and mental health: An introduction and overview of foundations, concepts and issues. In I. Cuella & F. A. Paniagua (Eds.), *Handbook of multicultural mental health: Assessment and treatment of culturally diverse populations* (pp. 3–24). New York: Academic Press.

Martin, J., & Sugarman, J. (1999). *The psychology of human possibility and constraint*. Albany: State University of New York Press.

McAdams, D. P. (1985). *Power, intimacy, and the life story: Personological inquiry into identity*. Chicago: Dorsey.

McAdams, D. P. (1993). *The stories we live by: Personal myths and the making of the self*. New York: William Morrow.

McLeod, J. (1997). *Narrative in psychotherapy*. Thousand Oaks, CA: Sage.

McNamee, S. (2004). Relational bridges between constructionism and constructivism. In J. D. Raskin & S. K. Bridges (Eds.), *Studies in meaning 2: Bridging the personal and social in constructivist psychology* (pp. 37–50). New York: Pace University Press.

McNamee, A., & Gergen, K. J. (1992). *Therapy as social construction*. Newbury Park, CA: Sage.

Michalon, M. (2001). "Selflessness" in the service of the ego: Contributions, limitations and dangers of Buddhist psychology for Western psychology. *American Journal of Psychotherapy, 55*(2), 202–218.

Miller, R. B. (2001). Scientific vs. clinical-based knowledge in psychology: A concealed moral conflict. *American Journal of Psychotherapy, 55*(3), 344–356.

Miller, R. B. (2004). *Facing human suffering: Psychology and psychotherapy*. Washington, DC: American Psychological Association.

Monk, G., Winslade, J., Crocket, K., & Epston, D. (Eds.). (1997). *Narrative therapy in practice*. San Francisco: Jossey-Bass.

Mowrer, O. H. (1967). *Morality and mental health*. Chicago: Rand McNally.

Murgatroyd, W. (2001). The Buddhist spiritual path. *Counseling and Values, 45*(2), 94–102.

Neimeyer, R. A., & Mahoney, M. J. (1995). *Constructivism in psychotherapy.* Washington, DC: American Psychological Association.

Neimeyer, R. A., & Raskin, J. D. (Eds.). (2000). *Constructions of disorder: Meaning-making frameworks for psychotherapy.* Washington, DC: American Psychological Association.

O'Donohue, W. (1989). The (even) bolder model: The clinical psychologist as metaphysician-scientist-practitioner. *American Psychologist, 44,* 1460–1468.

Paranjpe, A. C., Ho, D. Y. F., & Rieber, R. W. (Eds.). (1988). *Asian contributions to psychology.* New York: Praeger.

Paris, M. E., & Epting, F. (2004). Social and personal construction: Two sides of the same coin. In J. D. Raskin & S. K. Bridges (Eds.), *Studies in meaning 2: Bridging the personal and social in constructivist psychology* (pp. 3–35). New York: Pace University Press.

Parker, I. (Ed.). (1999). *Deconstructing psychotherapy.* Thousand Oaks, CA: Sage.

Pedersen, P. B., Draguns, J. G., Lonner, W. J., & Trimble, J. E. (2002). *Counseling across cultures.* Thousand Oaks, CA: Sage.

Peterson, D. R. (1998). The professional psychologist as a moral agent. In L. T. Hoshmand (Ed.), *Creativity and moral vision in psychology: Narratives on identity and commitment in a postmodern age* (pp. 29–49). Thousand Oaks, CA: Sage.

Pipher, M. (1995). *Reviving Ophelia: Saving the selves of adolescent girls.* New York: Ballantine.

Poddiakov, A. (2002). The space of responsibility of cultural psychology. *Culture and Psychology, 8*(3), 327–336.

Polkinghorne, D. E. (1988). *Narrative knowing and the human sciences.* Albany: State University of New York Press.

Prilleltensky, I. (1994). *The morals and politics of psychology: Psychological discourse and the status quo.* Albany: State University of New York Press.

Prilleltensky, I., & Walsh-Bowers, R. (1993). Psychology and the moral imperative. *Journal of Theoretical and Philosophical Psychology, 13,* 310–319.

Rabinow, P., & Sullivan, W. M. (Eds.). (1987). *Interpretive social science.* Berkeley: University of California Press.

Ratner, C. (2000). *Cultural psychology and qualitative methodology.* New York: Plenum.

Richardson, F. C. (2003). Virtue ethics, dialogue, and "reverence." *American Behavioral Scientist, 47*(4), 442–458.

Richardson, F. C., Fowers, B. J., & Guignon, C. B. (1999). *Re-envisioning psychology: Moral dimensions of theory and practice.* San Francisco: Jossey-Bass.

Rosen, H., & Kuehlwein, H. T. (1996). *Constructing realities: Meaning-making perspectives for psychotherapists.* San Francisco: Jossey-Bass.

Rosenthal, D. (1995). Changes in some moral values following psychotherapy. *Journal of Consulting and Clinical Psychology, 19,* 431–436.

Ryback, C. J., Wan, G., Johnson, C., & Templeton, R. A. (2002). Bridging Eastern and Western philosophies and models. *International Journal for the Advancement of Counselling, 24,* 43–56.

Said, E. W. (1994). *Culture and imperialism.* New York: Vintage.

Sampson, E. E. (1988). The debate on individualism: Indigenous psychologies of the individual and their role in personal and societal functioning. *American Psychologist, 43*(1), 15–22.

Sampson, E. E. (1993). Identity politics: Challenges to psychology's understanding. *American Psychologist, 48,* 1219–1230.

Sampson, E. E. (2000). Reinterpreting individualism and collectivism: Their religious roots and monologic versus dialogic person-other relationship. *American Psychologist, 55*(12), 1425–1432.

Sarbin, T. (Ed.). (1986). *Narrative psychology: The storied nature of human conduct.* New York: Praeger.

Scarr, S. W. (1985). Constructing psychology: Making facts and fables for our times. *American Psychologist, 40,* 499–512.

Schirato, T., & Webb, J. (2003). *Understanding globalization.* Thousand Oaks, CA: Sage.

Seeley, K. M. (2000). *Cultural psychotherapy.* Northvale, NJ: Jason Aronson.

Shek, D. T. L. (1999). The development of counseling in four Asian communities: A critical review of the review papers. *Asian Journal of Counseling, 6*(2), 97–114.

Shotter, J., & Gergen, K. (1989). *Texts of identity.* Newbury Park, CA: Sage.

Shweder, R. A. (1986). Divergent rationalities. In D. W. Fiske & R. A. Shweder (Eds.), *Metatheory in social science: Pluralisms and subjectivities* (pp. 163–196). Chicago: University of Chicago Press.

Shweder, R. A. (1990). Cultural psychology—What is it? In J. W. Stigler, R. A. Shweder, & G. Herdt (Eds.), *Cultural psychology: Essays on comparative human development* (pp. 1–43). Cambridge, UK: Cambridge University Press.

Shweder, R. A. (1991). *Thinking through cultures: Expeditions in cultural psychology.* Cambridge, MA: Harvard University Press.

Shweder, R. A., & Sullivan, M. A. (1993). Cultural psychology: Who needs it? *Annual Review of Psychology, 44,* 497–523.

Simons, R. C., & Hughes, C. C. (Eds.). (1985). *Culture-bound syndromes.* Boston: D. Reidel.

Steinberg, F. E., & Whiteside, R. G. (1999). *Whispers from the East: Applying the perspective of Eastern healing to psychotherapy.* Phoenix, AZ: Zeig, Tucker & Co.

Sue, D. W., Arredondo, P., & McDavis, R. J. (1992). Multicultural counseling competences and standards: A call to the profession. *Journal of Counseling and Development, 70,* 477–486.

Sue, D. W., Bingham, R. P., Porche-Burke, L., & Vasquez, M. (1999). The diversification of psychology: A multicultural revolution. *American Psychologist, 54,* 1061–1069.

Sue, D. W., & Sue, D. (2002). *Counseling the culturally different* (4th ed.). New York: John Wiley.

Sugarman, J., & Martin, J. (1995). The moral dimension: A conceptualization and empirical demonstration of the moral nature of psychotherapeutic conversations. *The Counseling Psychologist, 23*(2), 324–347.

Taylor, C., Gutmann, A., Rockefeller, S. C., Walzer, M., & Wolf, S. (1992). *Multiculturalism and the politics of recognition.* Princeton, NJ: Princeton University Press.

Tjeltveit, A. C. (2003). Implicit virtues, divergent goods, multiple communities. *American Behavioral Scientist, 47*(4), 395–414.

Tseng, W. S. (1999). Culture and psychotherapy: Review and practical guidelines. *Transcultural Psychiatry, 36*(2), 131–179.

Varenne, H. (2003). On internationalizing counseling psychology: A view from cultural anthropology. *The Counseling Psychologist, 31*(4), 404–411.

Vera, E. M., & Speight, S. L. (2003). Multicultural competence, social justice, and counseling psychology: Expanding our roles. *The Counseling Psychologist, 31*(3), 253–272.

Voestermans, P. (1992). Psychological practice as a cultural phenomenon. *New Ideas in Psychology, 10*(3), 331–346.

Vygotsky, L. (1978). *Mind in society* (M. Cole, Ed.). Cambridge, MA: Harvard University Press.

Weinrach, S. G., & Thomas, K. R. (1998). Diversity-sensitive counseling today—A postmodern clash of values. *Journal of Counseling and Development, 76,* 115–122.

White, M., & Epston, D. (1990). *Narrative means to therapeutic ends.* New York: Norton.

Wong, P., & Fry, P. S. (Eds.). (1998). *The human request for meaning.* London: Lawrence Erlbaum.

Worell, J., & Remer, P. (1992). *Feminist perspectives in therapy: An empowerment model for women.* New York: John Wiley.

Yang, K. S. (1997). Indigenizing Westernized Chinese psychology. In M. H. Bond (Ed.), *Working at the interface of cultures: Eighteen lies in social science* (pp. 62–76). New York: Routledge.

2

Culture and the Field of Psychotherapy and Counseling

Lisa Tsoi Hoshmand

In this chapter, I review culture-centered views of psychotherapy and counseling, exploring the implications of a cultural view of psychological practice. I discuss issues in the field, in particular the two topics of psychotherapy integration and evidence-based practice. In addition to considering a broadly conceived cultural perspective as a meta-level understanding about psychological practice, developmental integration at the personal level is emphasized, to be illustrated by the chapters that follow. I suggest how students and practitioners in training can reflect on their own integrative understanding of psychotherapy and counseling. Further thoughts are given to the dual nature of psychotherapy as a science-based cultural enterprise. I propose that a metalevel cultural perspective can provide what is lacking in a purely scientific, and sometimes scientistic, view of psychological practice. In considering the implications of culture for psychotherapy and counseling, I suggest that we return to the fundamental questions of how human experience is understood in the therapeutic encounter, and how human potentials can be realized in the therapeutic relationship.

Cultural Views of Psychological Practice

A cultural point of view is not new to psychological practice. It has taken time, however, for the theoretical and philosophical implications of culture to be fully recognized. The work of Watts (1961) is an example of early interest in the role of psychotherapy and Eastern philosophies and religions in respectively offering human liberation and critique of culture. This was followed by three decades of excursion into new frontiers in search of alternative models of healing (Moyers, 1993). The study of holistic traditions has given rise to practice that integrates mind, body, and spirituality (e.g., Bakal, 1999; Cortright, 1997; Mikulas, 2002; Miller, 1999; Richards & Bergin, 2000), and the development of transpersonal and consciousness studies in humanistic psychology (Goleman, 1993; Walsh, 1993) and integral psychology (Marquis, Holden, & Warren, 2001; Wilber, 1999). Nonetheless, there has been no commonly endorsed, unifying cultural framework of therapeutic practice. This lack of total integration is to be expected because the broadening and negotiation of theoretical and practice horizons can only be a continuous, incomplete process. The issue lies more with hegemonic tendencies that exclude a broader cultural grounding, as pointed out by Mikulas, Rezentes and Christopher in this volume. Meanwhile, psychological practice has been evaluated over time for its effectiveness, and is expected increasingly to be evidence-based. As I will explain subsequently, the scientific and cultural-moral validity of our theory and practice are both in question. More attention to questions of value issues and social validity is needed in the field.

Rieff (1966) discussed the role of the therapeutic and its fit with the culture(s) in which it is institutionalized. He observed that in contrast to the preference for self-centered approaches in individualistic Western societies, commitment therapies that offer individual transformation and symbolic return to the community are found in more traditional and collectivist societies. While the goals and rituals involved may differ as a function of culture, therapeutic systems (whether administered by therapist, shaman, or priest) serve similar functions in society. In this sense, there is commonality in the social roles and functions of therapeutic enterprises.

Frank (Frank, 1973; Frank & Frank, 1991) anticipated the current research on common factors in psychotherapy outcome by emphasizing the importance of cultural expectations and relational aspects of healing across cultures. Similarly, Torrey (1996) described the common features of healing across cultures. Simek-Downing (1989) examined cross-cultural factors in the study of psychotherapy process, lending support for the concept of common factors in helping relationships. Beyond the scientific question of what brings symptomatic relief, Frank (1974, 1978) recognized the need for the helping professions to address demoralization and the human predicament. Inherent in his arguments is the connection between therapeutic practice, societal malaise, and the human condition. It is a point of view that recognizes the moral and ontological significance of psychotherapy as a cultural practice.

Unfortunately, few have developed Frank's thesis as a therapeutic philosophy. Graduate students and practitioners in clinical and counseling psychology who have not read this seminal work are encouraged to do so.

In the counseling field, Patterson (1978) had proposed intercultural psychotherapy, based on commonalities in human experience and the assumption that society is moving toward a world culture. Though largely subscribing to a client-centered perspective that eschewed offering simplified, structured psychotherapy and counseling to the poor or the mentally disabled, it was an early attempt to strike a balance against parochial, culture-bound views of helping. More recently, Pedersen (2001) proposed a generic culture-centered perspective in counseling that encompasses global concerns for health, social justice, and moral and spiritual development with the goal of adaptive coexistence. This perspective can be considered as complementing the emphasis on culture-specific approaches that tend to be techniques-oriented. Vontress and Epp (2001) proposed cross-cultural counseling that gives equal attention to the physical and spiritual, and the public and private as existential spheres. The value of such holistic frameworks is in complementing reductionistic, culture-specific interventions with a broader understanding of cultural ways of being and the ecological context of cultural living.

Coming from cross-cultural psychology, Draguns (1975) conceptualized psychotherapy as resocialization into culture. Having conducted global research on culture, psychotherapy, and healing (Draguns, 2001, 2002; Gielen, Fish, & Draguns, 2002), he acknowledged the complexities of taking a worldwide view of psychotherapy.

The prospect of internationalizing American counseling psychology, for example, is questionable because of cultural encapsulation, political resistance to American or Western dominance, and the ethics of crossing boundaries in a divided global village with incommensurable values (Lemert, 2004; Pedersen, 2003; Varenne, 2003). Transcultural inquiry, with appropriate political sensitivity, is preferred to the multiculturalism associated with American ideology that also tends to reify discrete cultures when there is constant cultural change.

In psychiatry, Kleinman (1988) advocated for legitimating a more substantial form of symbolic healing in biomedicine, after learning that most symbolic healing around the world occurs in the family, community, and folk culture. The work of both Frank and Kleinman has advanced transcultural psychiatry. Writing in this tradition on cultural psychotherapy, Seeley (2000) described cultural differences in the presentation of problems, transferences and countertransferences among clients from diverse backgrounds. Kleinman (1988) suggested additionally that we evaluate different healing systems and sectors of care in different societies and cultures. In this chapter, I will pose the questions of criteria for such evaluation and what may constitute evidence of therapeutic and societal benefit in a cultural view of psychotherapy, questions that we will revisit in the final chapter of this book.

Vontress (2001) urged practitioners to integrate traditional healing with modern approaches. Such attempts would involve developing certain meta-perspectives for understanding the field. In view of tensions between proponents of culture-specific emic approaches and proponents of universal etic approaches in multicultural counseling, the common-factors perspective can go a significant distance in providing conceptual integration. This possibility and the role of culture will be further considered in relation to the topics of psychotherapy integration, evidence-based practice, and the related issues in the field.

Culture and Psychotherapy Integration

The field of psychotherapy is characterized by multiple theories and diverse systems of practice, resulting in concerns about proliferation and fragmentation. When each therapeutic approach proffers idealized answers to psychological health while minimizing competing theories (Fancher, 1995), it becomes a problem as to how practitioners can choose wisely and adopt a coherent approach to practice. In response to these concerns, there have been several decades of interest and effort in psychotherapy integration, supported by the Society for the Exploration of Psychotherapy Integration (SEPI), the *International Journal of Eclectic Psychotherapy,* and, more recently, the *Journal of Psychotherapy Integration.* It is not within the scope of this chapter to review the extensive literature on psychotherapy integration, including its history such as found in Hollanders (2000). Rather, I will identify the main developments and issues, and attempt to explore the implications of a broad cultural view of psychotherapy in relation to the work on psychotherapy integration.

The movement toward psychotherapy integration favored eclecticism before and during the 1980s (Norcross, 1986), with a number of advocates taking positions that have been described variously as theoretical eclecticism, strategic eclecticism, and technical eclecticism. Due to the fact that different theoretical schools of therapy subscribe to different philosophical views of human nature and human change, theoretical integration cannot be the same as theoretical eclecticism. Norcross (1986) based the possibility of psychotherapy integration on the profession's ability to generate a unified body of empirical work that informs practice, a point that is relevant to the more recent topic of evidence-based practice. In view of the problems with theoretical eclecticism, other forms of eclecticism were followed (Norcross & Goldfried, 1992; Stricker & Gold, 1993). Technical eclecticism involves deriving procedures from different sources without necessarily subscribing to the theories that spawned them (Lazarus, Beutler, & Norcross, 1992). Prior surveys estimated that one-third to one-half of practitioners were eclectic (e.g., Norcross, Prochaska, & Gallagher, 1989; Watkins & Watts, 1995). This seems to have continued, with many therapists and counseling professionals practicing some form of eclecticism. What is noteworthy is that this kind of eclectic approach has been broadened beyond theories and techniques to a focus on therapist variables and relationship stances. This is appropriate because research findings have indicated that these common factors account for more of the variance in treatment outcome than techniques per se (Bergin & Garfield, 1994; Lambert, Shapiro, & Bergin, 1986; Wampold, 2001).

It should be pointed out, however, that the literature on psychotherapy integration primarily has involved the integration of Western models, with little attention to the body of knowledge on theory and practice from cross-cultural sources. This is in spite of the fact that a growing percentage of the membership of the SEPI is international in background, and that SEPI has held international conferences. As Mikulas indicates in his chapter, exploring the integration of cultural traditions has not been a main focus of psychotherapy integration in the United States. Even in terms of local diversity, the issue of culture has not been an emphasis in discussions about psychotherapy integration. Commenting on multicultural issues in eclectic and integrative psychotherapy and counseling, Lago and Moodley (2000) expressed the view that a broad repertoire of approaches probably can serve culturally diverse clients better than single approaches, so long as the practitioner is culturally sensitive and competent. This still leaves the role of culture as an added factor, rather than at center stage.

Before addressing the question of how culture fits into psychotherapy integration, one should consider the possibility of conceptual bridging and integration. Obviously, it is not possible or desirable to try to integrate incompatible theories and systems of practice. The apparent futility of theoretical rapprochement, however, should not discourage us from seeking a meta-level perspective that provides some commonality and continuity between theoretical models. Short of a complete metatheoretical integration, compatibility of certain basic concepts also permits a kind of syncretism rather than unreflective eclecticism. The language of cultural psychology seems to be sufficiently inclusive of diverse theories of psychological practice to serve as a meta-level perspective. Psychotherapy and counseling have common narrative features, processes, and goals that are culturally appropriated. As some of the proponents of a culture-centered view of psychotherapy have pointed out, there are common processes of healing and problem solving across cultural systems, even if the content and form may vary. The respective roles of practitioner and client are also culturally defined. Thinking in cultural terms allows us to see more continuity within the current enterprise, beyond the shared values in the therapeutic culture and its distinct local (in this case, American) character. All of these commonalities should be in clear view as much as the apparent differences between approaches. Common cultural assumptions can then be critiqued, such as when an individualistic worldview is applied to populations with more collectivist worldviews.

Fischer, Jome, and Atkinson (1998) conceptualized multicultural counseling in terms of universal healing conditions in a culturally specific context. They used the common-factors framework as a transtheoretical perspective, reviewing the extant literature and related empirical research. They also evaluated a number of integrative models in multicultural counseling in terms of how they may fit into the organizing framework of a common-factors perspective. In discussing the implications for culturally competent practice, these authors emphasized again the therapeutic relationship, client expectancies, shared worldviews, and the importance of practitioners being aware of the limits of their cultural understanding.

Hansen (2002) challenged the modern science context of prior theoretical integration and compared it with the postmodern view of knowledge as a context for integration. He argued that the narratives in counseling, being meaning structures appropriated from the culture and society in which they are used, are not likely to be refuted in the manner of scientific truths even if the theoretical narratives used by practitioners are initially associated with science. In other words, he viewed the postmodern epistemic context as more honest in giving up on the notion of theoretical truths. This radical view, which is consistent with critical and social constructionist perspectives, may not be readily accepted by the profession. This is because of scientific ideology and the socioeconomic reasons for legitimating psychological practice with science. Hansen also drew attention to the common narrative features of counseling and psychotherapy in the co-constructing of truths and healing narratives by practitioners and clients. Although he did not frame this in terms of cultural validity, his proposal moves us from focusing only on the scientific validity of therapeutic models to their social validity and cultural pragmatics in the search for evidence of therapeutic benefit. Hence, the possibility of developing a more integrative meta-perspective is not unrelated to the topic of evidence-based practice.

Evidence-Based Practice and Research on Psychotherapy

By evidence-based practice, I refer to one kind of terminology currently proposed for use by those interested in the empirical evaluation of psychotherapy and counseling outcome (Chwalisz, 2003). The more common usage is that of empirically supported interventions, previously referred to as empirically validated treatment (EVT) and empirically supported treatment (EST) that were mostly manualized treatments for specific diagnostic groups. I prefer the concept of evidence-based practice, not necessarily because I agree with all of the arguments presented by Chwalisz, but because a cultural perspective requires a more inclusive term, separate from the connotations of EVT and EST. There are epistemic and sociological reasons for the lack of consensus in the field as far as the empirical evaluation of therapeutic and counseling practice (see Hoshmand [2003] for my comments on Chwalisz [2003]). The existing differences also reflect a cultural divide within the profession (Peterson, 1991; Rice, 1997), to which I will return later.

It is important to understand how the historical context and current realities of practice have interacted with our academic and professional cultures. Psychologists' concerns about being included as health care providers under managed care, and a desire to compete with biological psychiatry, have been part of the reasons for advocating empirically supported interventions. Wampold, Lichtenberg, and Waehler (2002) provided a historical analysis of the socioeconomic and professional context of the movement toward empirically supported treatments in the psychotherapy and counseling field. We need to complement this contextual understanding with a more critically reflexive understanding of the therapeutic enterprise and the academic and practice cultures that have shaped it. This involves questioning biases in the therapeutic culture such as those mentioned in the previous chapter.

Wampold et al. (2002) also presented seven principles of empirically supported interventions that clarify, in a thorough and well-reasoned manner, how scientific standards can be upheld in the effort toward identifying empirically supported interventions. Although client factors, cultural characteristics, and population specificity are included in the principles they proposed, culture does not appear to be the major consideration. As pointed out by Quintana and Atkinson (2002), treatment efficacy for subpopulations must be evaluated in the local, cultural context, taking into account its cultural acceptability and conformity with professional standards of service delivery to ethnic and linguistic minorities. The accumulation of evidence, a goal of empirically supported interventions, should apply differently to indigenous practices and etic practices that require cultural adaptation. Furthermore, we should be aware of the fact that an intrapsychic, symptom-relief emphasis in outcome evaluation is likely to ignore the ecological and political realities that affect minority clients whose difficulties may be the result of discrimination and other experiences due to their minority status.

Additionally, there is ample research showing that the common factors emphasized in cultural views of psychotherapy and counseling described earlier account for the majority of the variance in treatment outcome (Fischer, Jome, & Atkinson, 1998; Wampold, 2001). As our authors illustrate in this book, cultural factors affect the therapeutic relationship, client expectations, treatment acceptability, and what are valued outcomes. Hence, they have to be accommodated in the conception of evidence and the criteria for the evaluation of therapeutic benefit. Empirical research on psychotherapy should aim to understand also the processes of cultural meaning-making and the narrative construction of identity and moral choices, such as discussed in the chapters by McLeod, Grindler Katonah, and others. This kind of research can illuminate and broaden our understanding of both evidence and criteria in a culturally informed way.

The tensions in the field between those who support the movement toward empirically supported interventions and those who resist a science-based conception of therapeutic practice are in part due to differences in preferred ways of knowing. (For a discussion of the practice implications of philosophical differences underlying different paradigms of knowing, the reader is referred to Cheston [2000], Hoshmand [1994], and Downing [2000].) In the commonly endorsed scientist-practitioner model, research is privileged as the primary way of informing theory and practice. Although Wampold et al. (2002) indicated that the relationship between science and practice should be dialectical rather than unidirectional, there is no equal acknowledgment in the field of the role of practice knowledge and the judgments of practitioners in the implementation and evaluation of psychological interventions. Whether in the sense of the experiential knowledge of reflective practice (Hoshmand & Polkinghorne, 1992), or practitioners acting as local scientists (Stricker & Trierweiler, 1995), the processes involved are relevant to therapeutic practice in diverse cultural settings. In the case of indigenous practices, the reliance on the oral tradition and native, narrative knowing would be especially pertinent. The judgments and standards of local practice communities, often based on native knowledge of the culture, are an essential part of practice knowledge that should not be dismissed.

The role of clinical judgment in case formulation and treatment decisions was acknowledged by both the proponents and those skeptical of empirically supported interventions (Persons & Silverschatz, 1998; Shoham & Rohrbaugh, 1996; Task Force on Promotion and Dissemination of Psychological Procedures, 1995). This case-by-case type of judgment that is associated with the knowledge of practice, developed in context, is emphasized in a pragmatist view of psychological practice (Fishman, 1999). It has been supported by cognitive psychology and a number of philosophical traditions (Polkinghorne, 2004). Clinical judgment is a function of the "internal database" of the practitioner, interpreted through reflective, personal integration of cultural understanding and professional knowledge, which we hope to illustrate in the remainder of this book. Such ways of knowing should have a complementary role with conventional research-based knowledge. In the chapters by Mikulas and Rezentes, the integration of cultural traditions involves using both principles of human change derived from research-based psychological theories and knowledge and the time-tested native knowledge of practice informed by culture.

There have been legitimate concerns about the limitations of quantitative hypothesis-testing research associated with the traditional philosophy of science, leading to the call for methodological pluralism (Hoshmand, 1989, 1994). Wampold's (2003) reaction to Chwalisz's (2003) call for broadening our research methods and the definition of evidence is an example of the opposite concern that methodological pluralism and broadened sources of evidence might undermine scientific values. While it is not my purpose here to provide the philosophical arguments for dispelling such fears, the following practical points are worth noting. One is that ethnographic research and qualitative methods are particularly suited for the study of cultures and cultural phenomena. Applying judgment on a case-by-case basis, as in case study research, also allows for the maximal consideration of local ecology and client factors. Thus, methodological pluralism, which includes case study methodology as one possible inquiry approach, is friendly to a cultural view of psychotherapy evaluation. Pluralism is inclusive of the standard research paradigm, even if additional or different epistemic standards may be involved with the use of qualitative methods of inquiry. Cultural diversity necessarily means differences in what constitutes evidence of therapeutic benefit and the criteria for judging such benefits, as well as who will exercise judgment about therapeutic efficacy. It is consistent with a cultural perspective to broaden the sources and kinds of evidence to be used.

In a cultural, ecological view, the criteria and evidence for therapeutic benefit would come from stakeholders in local communities, and not just professional practitioners and researchers. The social validity of psychotherapy and counseling ought to be evaluated not only at the individual level, but also systemically. Prilleltensky and Prilleltensky (2003) suggested that a critical health psychology practice should be informed by three kinds of values—values pertaining to personal wellness for individuals, values on relational wellness for groups and organizations, and values of collective wellness for the community and society. The practice of psychotherapy and counseling can be similarly evaluated at these different levels. This is where case study methodology, with its allowance for contextual and conceptual complexity, can be especially helpful.

The issue of values, however, shows that the tensions in the field go deeper. In the previous chapter, I commented on the reluctance of psychologists to engage in moral discourse, and the reluctance of psychological practitioners to acknowledge their role in facilitating moral reflection in psychotherapy and counseling. This is because the separation of fact and value is part of scientific ideology and the academic culture. Some members of the profession seem to feel that even if we are to grant the moral nature of our undertaking, psychology does not have to wear a moral face under its self-definition as a science. A cultural view of psychotherapy, on the other hand, requires us to engage in moral discourse and to acknowledge our role in a fundamentally moral enterprise. To bridge the divide in the field between a purely science-based definition of the enterprise and a moral, critical view, changes in the ideology and sociology of the profession are needed (Hoshmand, 2003). For practitioners, including those trained on a scientist-practitioner model, the ability to deal with existing tensions and schisms in the field is a developmental process.

Developmental Integration as Reflective Practice

Although a cultural view of psychotherapy can be helpful in addressing related issues in the field, the integration for individual practitioners remains at the personal level. There are few books on psychotherapy that address such integration. Shay and Wheelis (2000) included therapists' reflections on changes in their beliefs about psychotherapy, subscribing to the notion that the professional is the personal. The therapists were asked to include all factors that have influenced their convictions, including theory, research, practice, personal experience as well as the social ethos. Kahn and Fromm (2000) focused on how experiences with clients can have reverberations in practitioners' lives. In particular, they showed that efforts in working through therapeutic relationships could change the therapist's beliefs, feelings, and actions. The adage that therapists grow with their clients is consistent not only with a developmental view, but also an existential and moral view of the therapeutic encounter. Loewenthal in his chapter conceptualizes this as relational learning.

The developmental approach to integration is described by those who emphasize professional identity development that integrates personal and professional selves (Fear & Woolfe, 2000; Skovholt & Ronnestad, 1992).

Part of this development is epistemic, including the development of reflective judgment (Kitchener & King, 1981) and one's theory-in-action that is not the same as espoused theory or formal theoretical orientation from one's training (Poznanski & McLennon, 1995). In focusing on the individual practitioner, I do not mean that the therapist is the only locus of integration. Much occurs in the therapeutic relationship and also with the acquiring of metatheoretical understanding from other sources. Horan (2000) provided an excellent description of the elements and process of developmental integration, with a checklist for self-inquiry that can be used by students and practitioners in training. He distinguished between personal belief system, formal theory, clinical theory, and therapist operations. Included in the personal belief system are values and views of cultural identity and differences, in addition to views of the counseling process. Most of these aspects that are not frequently discussed in professional training need to be articulated. He also summarized several principles of change in clinical theory, and offered additional principles for developing a personal integration.

Developmental integration is progressive and evolving, inseparable from the development of professional identity. A function of reflective practice, it is the process by which practitioners achieve integrity in their professional worldviews and practice. To understand the developmental nature of how practitioners integrate diverse theories and practice models as well as their personal beliefs and values, I have asked our authors here to provide information on formative influences and the context of their development. I also asked them to be as transparent as possible about their professional and personal worldviews. My hope is that such reflection, along with case examples from their practice, will illustrate different paths to integration. In view of the judgment-based and case-based nature of psychotherapy and counseling work, the chapters with case examples should be looked at in terms of what has informed the practice orientation and judgments in each case. Due to the requirements of conciseness, however, some allowance should be given for any simplification and omission of information on the overall contexts involved.

The path to integration is personal, but to the extent that it is informed by what one learns from practice and other professional knowledge and experience, not arbitrary. While such integration often occurs gradually with professional growth, and is more pronounced in seasoned practitioners, it needs to begin at an early stage of professional development. Instructors can encourage students to start the process with writing a reflective essay on their personal theories of human nature and human change. Such reflection, repeated periodically after significant learning and supervised practice, can help to facilitate integration that will have an increasing degree of philosophical and personal congruence. This type of exercise serves several purposes. Students and practitioners in training are asked to make explicit their beliefs and assumptions. With encouragement and modeling, they may also uncover personal values and biases, becoming more aware of their own cultural encapsulation. Facilitated discussions of issues of culture and identity, as noted in the previous chapter, that pertain to oneself and one's personal experience should be part of the learning environment. This is more likely when there is an emphasis on the personal development of the practitioner, in balance with the academic preparation and technical training emphasized in graduate clinical psychology programs and counseling programs with a strong scientist-practitioner orientation.

The implications of this type of developmental integration for the issues in the field will be summarized and discussed in the final chapter of this book. Collectively, it may be illuminating to look at the criteria for psychological and social well-being shared by these different therapists. Along with these criteria, one may identify the kinds of evidence that would be appropriate to include for the evaluation of psychological practice within certain cultural and personal parameters.

To summarize the approach to the field of psychotherapy and counseling that I am suggesting, a few more thoughts about the dual nature of the enterprise are offered next. I will further discuss issues that are brought forth by a critical, existential cultural view, returning to how we could understand human experience and potentials in the therapeutic encounter.

Psychotherapy and Counseling as a Science-Based Cultural Enterprise

In framing psychotherapy and counseling as a science-based cultural enterprise, I am taking the middle ground between a purely scientific (and sometimes scientistic) view of psychological practice on the one hand, and a cultural, humanistic view of psychological practice on the other. There are many reasons for this position. The psychological knowledge that informs practice, though incomplete and partial or even biased in certain ways, is valuable to practitioners especially if moderated by cultural and contextual understanding. Inasmuch as the definition of the discipline is open to question (Hoshmand, 2003), its scientific epistemology combined with a healthy skepticism can keep us from being irresponsible to the public that we serve. We certainly need continuing research on the efficacy of psychological interventions with culturally diverse populations (Sue, 1988; Sue, Zane, & Young, 1994). A professional enterprise without self-evaluation and public accountability will only result in hazardous practice (Sussman, 1995).

I mentioned in the last chapter Bruner's (1990) distinction between the scientific paradigmatic mode of knowing and culturally appropriated narrative knowing. The former tends to be emphasized in scientist-practitioner training, whereas narrative knowing is native to our cultural being and ability to construct knowledge in story form. The fact that both modes of knowing are involved in practice is consistent with the dual nature of psychotherapy as a science-based cultural enterprise. In my clinical teaching and supervision, I have observed that novice practitioners tend to rely mainly on the scientific, paradigmatic knowing emphasized in their training, whereas mature practitioners seem more free to use the native, narrative knowing from their practice and life experience, in addition to scientific ways of knowing. I found in my own development as a practitioner that the two modes of knowing came together in a complementary way only with more professional and life experience. It is when practitioners make a conscious effort to fully acknowledge their own cultural ways of being and knowing that our narrative mode of knowing is affirmed. Through reflective practice, both kinds of knowing can be developed and integrated.

Woolfolk (1998) argued that the scientific (and I would consider scientistic) assumption that psychotherapy involves the application of value-free knowledge ignores the social function of psychotherapy and its inherent humanistic purpose. Acknowledging the reciprocal relationship between psychotherapy and modern culture, he suggested that psychotherapy has a cultural role beyond helping clients. He considered the therapeutic enterprise a historical response to the decline of traditional institutions that had served as resources for cultural and moral existence. His point is similar to what others have observed about how people in contemporary Western societies try to fill their existential void and empty selves with the secular equivalent of religion (Cushman, 1990, 1995; Johnson & Sandage, 1999). Recognizing also the antagonism toward managed care and the technologizing of services, Woolfolk proposed a complementary relationship between the scientific and humanistic traditions. I would propose that the schism in the field between scientific and humanistic views can be avoided if we view psychotherapy as a science-based cultural enterprise. The cultural perspective (as described in the previous chapter and proposed here) has broader implications than those emphasized in humanistic psychology and philosophy.

Yet another way to appreciate these tensions in the field is in terms of the simultaneous presence of skepticism or uncertainty and a necessary degree of conviction and certitude with which practitioners (including scientist-practitioners) have to function. Downing (2000) reasoned that we need to have both of these attitudes so that the various ways of professional knowing can serve as checks and balances. The scientific attitude of questioning is perhaps more readily understood than what informs the practitioner's conviction and certitude when working with clients in psychotherapy. A combination of factors are likely involved in the latter, including the goals and values of the practitioner, the experienced knowledge of practice, and the practitioner's cultural sense of the client and the therapeutic contract. This is illustrated by the case examples in the chapters that follow.

To return to culture as moral ontology and the issue of values in psychotherapy and counseling, it is imperative that we acknowledge the cultural nature of the enterprise and the biases of the therapeutic culture. Only when we grant the dual nature of the therapeutic enterprise and avoid scientistic assumptions would we be able to engage in critical discourse about the moral, existential implications of our theory and practice. I agree with Miller (2001) that there should be truth in moral packaging. The issue is no longer whether psychological practice is a moral undertaking, but rather, how we shape the way that it is (already) moral. As Miller (2004) further argued, there is a critical difference between having implicit, assumptive moral values, and having explicit, examined moral values in our theory and practice. Denying the moral nature of psychotherapeutic endeavors will be at our own and our clients' peril. Miller sees the morally engaged practitioner as the bulwark against the demoralizing forces of contemporary life. In working with clients' experiences, life purpose, and choices, we need not just the theories and tools of scientific psychology, but a deep understanding of the cultural realm and its existential implications. It is not the professional norm, however, to confront the moral in our theory and practice. This leads me to conclude that we have to infuse the cultural into all parts of graduate curriculum in the education of psychotherapists and counseling professionals, and to address culture as moral ontology as a topic in the discussion of professional ethics. Additional readings such as suggested by Miller (2004), and cocurricular enrichment in the form of multidisciplinary conversations with moral philosophers and social theorists, may be helpful.

Perhaps part of the reluctance in psychologists when it comes to fully engaging with the moral realm stems from the general ambivalence in contemporary society toward discussions of the moral. It is a highly charged area in which there have been few experiences of successful dialogue. If one thinks of the psychotherapeutic encounter as a microcosm of social discourse and as a moral conversation, it behooves practitioners to approach such interactions with a clear framework. While it is beyond the scope of this chapter to explain possible frameworks, I want to point to four sources of ideas—communitarian theories of dialogue (Etzioni, 1996, 1998), hermeneutic perspectives (Gadamer, 1989; Taylor, 1989), practical virtue ethics (MacIntyre, 1981), and phenomenological-existential perspectives (see

Davis [1996] on Levinas and May [1953]). Within the psychology profession a number of authors have integrated these sources of ideas into moral frameworks for psychological theory and practice (Christopher, 2001; Cushman, 1995; Loewenthal & Snell, 2001; Miller, 2004; Richardson, Fowers, & Guignon, 1999; Woolfolk, 1998). They offer an understanding of how cultural conflict can be addressed with dialogical processes, how the self is culturally appropriated and defined in relation to society and the other, and how psychotherapy and counseling may facilitate moral reflection and the development of practical knowledge constitutive of personal virtues in living. These dialogical, hermeneutic, and communitarian frameworks grant that finding moral and political consensus about the goals and valued outcomes of psychological practice, framed as personal virtues or social goods, requires the respectful negotiation of cultural horizons.

How might these frameworks and thinking culturally about the moral realm translate into action? Tyler, Susswell, and Williams-McCoy (1995) proposed in their model of ethnic validity that the therapeutic task is to optimize both the convergence and divergence in the cultural interaction between the practitioner and the client while containing conflicting factors that may emerge. Given that there are potential risks and benefits in the encounter and negotiation of identities, especially in relationships that are asymmetrical in power, communication that preserves each party's integrity is essential. Practitioners need to engage in culture learning with their clients in a sensitive negotiation of therapeutic identities. The therapeutic conversation can validate the client's goals and values and encourage moral reflection on their life choices and ways of being. The results are expected to be applied to the client's practical living. There needs to be both formal and informal research and supervision that examine the therapeutic process in terms of such cultural negotiation, beyond what has been conceptualized as transference and countertransference.

Ibrahim (1996) suggested that a multicultural perspective requires a paradigm shift in understanding moral outlook. Rejecting relativism and absolutism, he proposed a more dynamic view that takes into account diverse moral systems while acknowledging universal processes. Instead of imposing Western models of morality, practitioners should consider their role in their clients' character development in a multicultural society, encouraging perspective taking and the learning of communication skills and behavioral flexibility. These qualities and skills would enable clients to participate in dialogues about differences, and to understand the moral horizons of others while reflecting on their own. In other words, clients will engage in culture learning that is the key factor in the hermeneutic, dialogical perspective. Using new learning, one may then critically evaluate the limitations of one's worldview and moral outlook as a result of cultural encapsulation. With this dynamic manner of transforming cultural horizons, psychotherapy and counseling would not simply perpetuate the cultural status quo.

Hanna, Bemak, and Chung (1999) proposed using the transcultural concept of wisdom to conceptualize the orientation of counselors and psychotherapists needed in multicultural work. It includes both affective and cognitive dimensions. Affective areas include empathy, compassion, emotional awareness, resistance to automatic thought and action, sagacity as reflected in self-knowledge, an ability to learn from mistakes, and deep insight into humankind. The cognitive areas include dialectical reasoning, recognition of context and interdependency, tolerance of ambiguity, metacognitive and problem-solving skills, and the capacity to accurately interpret situations. Many of the qualities and skills associated with wisdom are similar to those recommended for clients as ways of being in a multicultural environment with diverse worldviews and moral beliefs. A combination of affective and cognitive capacities is needed for the development of moral and existential awareness.

Our acknowledgment of the inescapable moralities of human existence helps to affirm the social ties and moral obligations with which people have to live. Many clients come into psychotherapy and counseling because of demoralization and value conflicts. Framing identity issues and interpersonal issues in moral terms allows clients to deal with the root of their problems that would not be possible with a symptom-relief approach. In this sense, clients develop moral knowledge about what it means to be a virtuous person as a practical form of knowledge for cultural living. Therapists and counseling professionals would be able to discharge their moral responsibility by attending to their clients' existential responsibility to others. Such motivation also stems from an appreciation of the existential and moral obligations to the other of being virtuous persons.

On a communal level, the type of processes involved in the negotiation of cultural and moral horizons is emphasized in the communitarian perspective of how we may improve the social order by allowing autonomous identities and seeking cohesion at the same time. Finding political and moral consensus on the goals and valued outcomes or the personal and social goods of psychological practice requires the kind of dialogue emphasized in both hermeneutic and communitarian perspectives. As members of our profession and the community of practitioners, we need to do more in engaging one another in negotiating our cultural and identity differences against the current social horizon.

Returning to Human Experience and Potentials

What does it all mean for the practitioner and psychotherapeutic and counseling work? As psychological practitioners, we bring to the understanding of human experience and human change not only the knowledge of our profession, but also our cultural ways of being and moral vision of the world. To the extent that our ways of knowing are conducive to a holistic and inclusive approach to human experience, we may be able to discover the full range of ways by which others from diverse backgrounds and different societies fashion their cultural existence. The therapeutic encounter becomes an opportunity for culture learning, narrative exploration, and world making (Hoshmand, 2001). We should be familiar with how such processes work in psychotherapy and counseling, keeping in mind the issues involved in the construction of identities and the negotiation of cultural horizons. In the next chapter, John McLeod addresses the cultural resources and processes of appropriation in psychotherapy and counseling. In the chapter that follows, Doralee Grindler Katonah provides a view of how human experience and human potentials can be understood and nurtured, respectively, in the therapeutic context.

References

Bakal, D. (1999). *Minding the body: Clinical uses of somatic awareness.* New York: Guilford.

Bergin, A. E., & Garfield, S. L. (Eds.). (1994). *Handbook of psychotherapy and behavior change* (4th ed.). New York: John Wiley.

Bruner, J. (1990). *Acts of meaning.* Cambridge, MA: Harvard University Press.

Cheston, S. E. (2000). A new paradigm for teaching counseling theory and practice. *Counselor Education and Supervision, 39*(4), 254–269.

Christopher, J. C. (2001). Culture and psychotherapy: Toward a hermeneutic approach. *Psychotherapy, 38*(2), 115–128.

Chwalisz, K. (2003). Evidence-based practice: A framework for twenty-first-century scientist-practitioner training. *The Counseling Psychologist, 31*(5), 497–528.

Cortright, B. (1997). *Psychotherapy and spirit: Theory and practice in transpersonal psychotherapy.* Albany: State University of New York Press.

Cushman, P. (1990). Why the self is empty: Toward a historically situated psychology. *American Psychologist, 45*(5), 599–611.

Cushman, P. (1995). *Constructing the self, constructing America: A cultural history of psychotherapy.* Cambridge, MA: Perseus.

Davis, C. (1996). *Levinas: An introduction.* Notre Dame, IN: University of Notre Dame Press.

Downing, J. (2000). *Between conviction and uncertainty: Philosophical guidelines for the practicing psychotherapist.* Albany: State University of New York Press.

Draguns, J. G. (1975). Resocialization into culture: The complexities of taking a worldwide view of psychotherapy. In R. W. Brislin, S. Bochner, & W. J. Lonner (Eds.), *Cross-cultural perspectives on learning* (pp. 273–289). New York: Wiley Halsted Press.

Draguns, J. G. (2001). Toward a truly international psychology: Beyond English only. *American Psychologist, 56*(11), 1019–1030.

Draguns, J. G. (2002). Universal and cultural aspects of counseling and psychotherapy. In P. B. Pedersen, J. G. Draguns, W. J. Lonner, & J. E. Trimble (Eds.), *Counseling across cultures* (5th ed., pp. 29–50). Thousand Oaks, CA: Sage.

Etzioni, A. (1996). *The new golden rule: Community and morality in a democratic society.* New York: Basic Books.

Etzioni, A. (Ed.). (1998). *The essential communitarian reader.* Lanham, MD: Rowman & Littlefield.

Fancher, R. (1995). *Cultures of healing: Correcting the image of American mental health care.* New York: Freeman.

Fear, R., & Woolfe, R. (2000). The personal, the professional and the basis of integrative practice. In S. Palmer & R. Woolfe (Eds.), *Integrative and eclectic counselling and psychotherapy* (pp. 329–340). Thousand Oaks, CA: Sage.

Fischer, A. R., Jome, L. M., & Atkinson, D. R. (1998). Reconceptualizing multicultural counseling: Universal healing conditions in a culturally specific context. *The Counseling Psychologist, 26*(4), 525–588.

Fishman, D. B. (1999). *The case for pragmatic psychology.* New York: New York University Press.

Frank, J. D. (1973). *Persuasion and healing: A comparative study of psychotherapy* (Rev. ed.). Baltimore: Johns Hopkins University Press.

Frank, J. D. (1974). Psychotherapy: The restoration of morale. *American Journal of Psychiatry, 131,* 271–274.

Frank, J. D. (1978). *Psychotherapy and the human predicament.* New York: Schocken.

Frank, J. D., & Frank, J. B. (1991). *Persuasion and healing: A comparative study of psychotherapy* (Rev. ed.). Baltimore: Johns Hopkins University Press.

Gadamer, H. G. (1989). *Truth and method* (2nd ed.). New York: Continuum.

Gielen, U., Fish, J., & Draguns, J. G. (Eds.). (2002). *Handbook of culture, psychotherapy, and healing.* Boston: Allyn & Bacon.

Goleman, D. (1993). Psychology, reality, and consciousness. In R. Walsh & F. Vaughan (Eds.), *Paths beyond ego: The transpersonal vision* (pp. 13–17). Los Angeles: Tarcher.

Hanna, F. J., Bemak, F., & Chung, R. C. (1999). Toward a new paradigm for multicultural counseling. *Journal of Counseling and Development, 77,* 125–134.

Hansen, J. (2002). Postmodern implications for theoretical integration of counseling approaches. *Journal of Counseling and Development, 80,* 315–321.

Hollanders, H. (2000). Eclecticism/integration: Historical developments. In S. Palmer & R. Woolfe (Eds.), *Integrative and eclectic counselling and psychotherapy* (pp. 1–30). Thousand Oaks, CA: Sage.

Horan, I. (2000). Principles and practice of a personal integration. In S. Palmer & R. Woolfe (Eds.), *Integrative and eclectic counselling and psychotherapy* (pp. 315–328 and 341–344). Thousand Oaks, CA: Sage.

Hoshmand, L. T. (1989). Alternate research paradigms: A review and teaching proposal. *The Counseling Psychologist, 17,* 3–79.

Hoshmand, L. T. (1994). *Orientation to inquiry in a reflective professional psychology.* Albany: State University of New York Press.

Hoshmand, L. T. (2001). Psychotherapy as an instrument of culture. In B. D. Slife, R. N. Williams, & S. N. Barlow (Eds.), *Critical issues in psychotherapy: Translating new ideas into practice* (pp. 99–113). Thousand Oaks, CA: Sage.

Hoshmand, L. T. (2003). Applied epistemology and professional training in a science-based cultural enterprise. *The Counseling Psychologist, 31*(5), 529–538.

Hoshmand, L. T., & Polkinghorne, D. E. (1992). Redefining the science-practice relationship and professional training. *American Psychologist, 47,* 55–66.

Ibrahim, F. A. (1996). A multicultural perspective on principle and virtue ethics. *The Counseling Psychologist, 26*(1), 22–32.

Johnson, E., & Sandage, S. (1999). A postmodern reconstruction of psychotherapy: Orienteering, religion, and the healing of the soul. *Psychotherapy, 36,* 1–15.

Kahn, S., & Fromm, E. (Eds.). (2000). *Changes in the therapist.* Wokingham, UK: Lea Publishing.

Kitchener, K. S., & King, P. (1981). Reflective judgment: Concepts of justification and their relationship to age and education. *Journal of Applied Developmental Psychology, 2,* 89–116.

Kleinman, A. (1988). *Rethinking psychiatry: From cultural category to personal experience.* New York: Free Press.

Lago, C., & Moodley, R. (2000). Multicultural issues in eclectic and integrative counseling and psychotherapy. In S. Palmer & R. Woolfe (Eds.), *Integrative and eclectic counselling and psychotherapy* (pp. 233–251). Thousand Oaks, CA: Sage.

Lambert, M. J., Shapiro, D. A., & Bergin, A. E. (1986). The effectiveness of psychotherapy. In S. L. Garfield & A. E. Bergin (Eds.), *Handbook of psychotherapy and behavior change* (3rd ed., pp. 157–211). New York: John Wiley.

Lazarus, A. A., Beutler, L. E., & Norcross, J. C. (1992). The future of technical eclecticism. *Psychotherapy, 29,* 11–20.

Lemert, C. (2004). Can the worlds be changed? On ethics and the multicultural dream. *Thesis Eleven, 78,* 46–60.

Loewenthal, D., & Snell, R. (2001). Psychotherapy as the practice of ethics. In F. P. Barnes & L. Murdin (Eds.), *Values and ethics in the practice of psychotherapy and counseling* (pp. 23–31). Philadelphia: Open University Press.

MacIntyre, A. (1981). *After virtue: A study in moral theory.* Notre Dame, IN: University of Notre Dame Press.

Marquis, A., Holden, J. M., & Warren, E. S. (2001). An integral psychology response to Helmiak's "Treating spiritual issues in secular psychotherapy." *Counseling and Values, 45*(3), 218–236.

May, R. (1953). *Man's search for himself.* New York: Dell.

Mikulas, W. L. (2002). *The integrative helper.* Pacific Grove, CA: Wadsworth.

Miller, R. B. (2001). Scientific vs. clinical-based knowledge in psychology: A concealed moral conflict. *American Journal of Psychotherapy, 55*(3), 344–356.

Miller, R. B. (2004). *Facing human suffering: Psychology and psychotherapy.* Washington, DC: American Psychological Association.

Miller, W. R. (Ed.). (1999). *Integrating spirituality in treatment: Resources for practitioners.* Washington, DC: American Psychological Association.

Moyers, S. B. (1993). *Healing and the mind.* New York: Doubleday.

Norcross, J. C. (Ed.). (1986). *Handbook of eclectic psychotherapy.* New York: Brunner/Mazel.

Norcross, J. C., & Goldfried, M. R. (Eds.). (1992). *Handbook of psychotherapy integration.* New York: Basic Books.

Norcross, J. C., Prochaska, J. O., & Gallagher, K. M. (1989). Clinical psychologists in the 1980's: II. Theory, research and practice. *The Clinical Psychologist, 42,* 45–53.

Patterson, C. H. (1978). Cross-cultural or intercultural psychotherapy. *International Journal for the Advancement of Counselling, 1*(3), 231–247.

Pedersen, P. B. (2001). Mobilizing the generic potential of culture-centered counseling. *International Journal for the Advancement of Counselling, 23,* 165–177.

Pedersen, P. B. (2003). Culturally biased assumptions in counseling psychology. *The Counseling Psychologist, 31*(4), 396–403.

Persons, J. B., & Silverschatz, G. (1998). Are results of randomized controlled trials useful to psychotherapists? *Journal of Consulting and Clinical Psychology, 66,* 126–135.

Peterson, D. R. (1991). Connection and disconnection of research and practice in the education of professional psychologists. *American Psychologist, 40,* 441–451.

Polkinghorne, D. E. (2004). *Practice and the human sciences: The case for a judgment-based practice of care.* Albany: State University of New York Press.

Poznanski, J. J., & McLennon, J. (1995). Conceptualizing and measuring counselors' theoretical orientations. *Journal of Counselling Psychology, 42*(4), 411–422.

Prilleltensky, I., & Prilleltensky, O. (2003). Toward a critical health psychology practice. *Journal of Health Psychology, 8*(2), 197–210.

Quintana, S. M., & Atkinson, D. R. (2002). A multicultural perspective on principles of empirically supported interventions. *The Counseling Psychologist, 30*(2), 281–291.

Rice, C. E. (1997). Scenarios: The scientist-practitioner split and the future of psychology. *American Psychologist, 52*(11), 1173–1181.

Richards, P. S., & Bergin, A. E. (2000). *Handbook of psychotherapy and religious diversity.* Washington, DC: American Psychological Association.

Richardson, F. C., Fowers, B. J., & Guignon, C. (1999). *Re-envisioning psychology: Moral dimensions of theory and practice*. San Francisco: Jossey-Bass.

Rieff, P. (1966). *The triumph of the therapeutic: Uses of faith after Freud*. Chicago: University of Chicago Press.

Seeley, K. M. (2000). *Cultural psychotherapy*. Northvale, NJ: Jason Aronson.

Shay, J., & Wheelis, J. (2000). *Odysseys in psychotherapy*. New York: Ardent Media.

Shoham, V., & Rohrbaugh, M. (1996). Promises and perils of empirically supported psychotherapy integration. *Journal of Psychotherapy Integration, 6*, 191–206.

Simek-Downing, L. (Ed.). (1989). *International psychotherapy: Theories, research, and cross-cultural implications*. New York: Praeger.

Skovholt, T. M., & Ronnestad, M. H. (1992). *The evolving professional self: Stages and themes in therapist and counselor development*. Chichester, UK: John Wiley.

Stricker, G., & Gold, J. R. (Eds.). (1993). *Comprehensive handbook of psychotherapy integration*. New York: Plenum.

Stricker, G., & Trierweiler, S. T. (1995). The local clinical scientist: A bridge between science and practice. *American Psychologist, 50*, 995–1002.

Sue, S. (1988). Psychotherapeutic services for ethnic minorities: Two decades of research findings. *American Psychologist, 43*, 301–308.

Sue, S., Zane, N., & Young, K. (1994). Research on psychotherapy with culturally diverse populations. In A. E. Bergin & S. L. Garfield (Eds.), *Handbook of psychotherapy and behavior change* (4th ed., pp. 783–817). New York: John Wiley.

Sussman, M. B. (Ed.). (1995). *A perilous calling: The hazards of psychotherapy practice*. New York: John Wiley.

Task Force on Promotion and Dissemination of Psychological Procedures. (1995). Training in and dissemination of empirically-validated psychological treatments. *The Clinical Psychologist, 48*, 3–23.

Taylor, C. (1989). *Sources of the self*. Cambridge, MA: Harvard University Press.

Torrey, E. F. (1996). *Witchdoctors and psychiatrists: The common roots of psychotherapy and its future*. New York: Harper & Row.

Tyler, F. B., Susswell, D. R., & Williams-McCoy, J. (1995). Ethnic validity in psychotherapy. In N. R. Goldberger & J. B. Veroff (Eds.), *The culture and psychology reader* (pp. 789–807). New York: New York University Press.

Varenne, H. (2003). On internationalizing counseling psychology: A view from cultural anthropology. *The Counseling Psychologist, 31*(4), 404–411.

Vontress, C. E. (2001). Cross-cultural counseling in the 21st century. *International Journal for the Advancement of Counselling, 23*, 83–97.

Vontress, C. E., & Epp, L. R. (2001). Existential cross-cultural counseling. In K. J. Schneider, J. F. T. Bugental, & J. F. Pierson (Eds.), *The handbook of humanistic psychology* (pp. 371–387). Thousand Oaks, CA: Sage.

Walsh, R. (1993). The transpersonal movement: A history and state of the art. *Journal of Transpersonal Psychology, 25*, 123–140.

Wampold, B. E. (2001). *The great psychotherapy debate: Models, methods, and findings*. Mahwah, NJ: Lawrence Erlbaum.

Wampold, B. E. (2003). Bashing positivism and revering a medical model under the guise of evidence. *The Counseling Psychologist, 31*(5), 539–545.

Wampold, B. E., Lichtenberg, J. W., & Waehler, C. A. (2002). Principles of empirically supported interventions in counseling psychology. *The Counseling Psychologist, 30*(2), 197–217.

Watkins, C. E., Jr., & Watts, R. E. (1995). Psychotherapy survey research studies: Some consistent findings and integrative conclusions. *Psychotherapy in Private Practice, 13,* 49–68.

Watts, A. W. (1961). *Psychotherapy East and West.* New York: Ballantine.

Wilber, K. (1999). *Integral psychology: Consciousness, spirit, psychology.* Boston, MA: Shambhala.

Woolfolk, R. L. (1998). *The cure of souls: Science, values, and psychotherapy.* San Francisco: Jossey-Bass.

3

Counselling and Psychotherapy as Cultural Work

John McLeod

For many years in her childhood, Debbie had experienced physical, emotional, and sexual abuse from members of her immediate family. Her strategies for surviving this, then and later, were based on the development of a denial of the possibility of physical pleasure and avoidance of touch or bodily contact. She could not see how she could ever belong, how she could ever become a valued member of a group, how she could ever be physically intimate. In psychotherapy, she began to see that other ways of being with people were possible, but could not see how she could ever achieve these for herself. One week, in therapy, she announced that she had started to attend a martial arts class, and talked with great energy about the bodily excitement of the Aikido exercises she was learning, and the spirit of acceptance in the group.

Alec had been retired for four years from a successful career as a factory manager. He and his wife enjoyed the freedom given by retirement, particularly the chance to meet with friends and to travel. The diagnosis of multiple sclerosis threw Alec into a crisis. He could see his horizons closing in. He began to withdraw from relationships. A conversation with his health counsellor centred on the idea of telling. He told his church minister of the diagnosis. In a moment of great closeness and meaning, they prayed together. Alec then went on to tell other people in his social circle, and to talk with them about the implications of his illness.

The stories of Debbie and Alec illustrate some of the basic processes involved in an understanding of counselling and psychotherapy as forms of cultural work. These two people found themselves at a moment when they were excluded in some aspect of their life, unable to participate in an aspect of everyday social interaction that had meaning for them. They each found a counsellor, a person external to their situation, who was able to help them to gain some perspective on what was happening, in terms of their historic patterns within their life as a whole, and in terms of current patterns of relationship, action, and emotion (McLeod, 1999). At this point, both Debbie and Alec were able to identify cultural resources that could be drawn into service to enable them to make a move back in the direction of personal agency—being in control of their life—and connection with others. These cultural resources were already there. Debbie knew people who were involved in martial arts; Alec was a church member. What was therapeutic was the realisation that, out of all the possible cultural resources that were available to Debbie and Alec at that point, these particular cultural arenas provided the most creative possibilities for moving forward in their lives.

In this chapter I explore the role of counselling or psychotherapy as a means of gaining access to cultural resources that can be used to solve or resolve problems in living, and to construct a life that has meaning and purpose. The concept of cultural resources is briefly examined in relation to therapy, followed by an example of the kind of "cultural work" that can take place in therapy. I then consider some of the implications of these ideas for training, practice and research in counselling, and psychotherapy.

Understanding Culture: Implications for Counselling and Psychotherapy

The idea of culture can be understood from several different perspectives (Williams, 1981), but is used here in a broad sense, to refer to the way that a group of people live their lives. Culture includes tangible physical objects such as buildings, books, and works of art, and observable forms of human organisation such as institutions (the BBC, the Church of Scotland), family and kinship networks, and patterns of behaviour (e.g., greeting rituals). It also encompasses the less tangible ideas, values, and narratives that knit together these objects and activities and give them some degree of coherent meaning. A useful way of making sense of a culture is to regard it as a *tradition* (Gadamer,

1975) within which previous ways of living provide sedimented layers of meaning that provide the depth to current activity. A tradition or a culture that is alive and developing always incorporates polarities and tensions, or competing voices, within it (MacIntyre, 1981). Thus, we can view culture then at some level as a conversation about what it means to be human, and how the good life should be defined and lived (Taylor, 1989).

A human being is born into a culture, and is assigned an identity (for example, a name, a birth story, a family role) that is drawn from the identity repertoire available within that cultural system. From the beginning, the way that the child is touched, held, and fed constructs a pattern of relationship and emotional life that replicates the fundamental way of being that is characteristic of the cultural world into which the person has been born. As Williams (1961) puts it, a culture is organised around a "structure of feeling."

I believe that it is mistaken to regard a cultural perspective on personality as implying any kind of total social determinism. Culture is built upon individual human agency and reflexivity. Cultural values and practices are never static, but shift to reflect the ways that individual members develop strategies for responding to environmental, political, and technological events and processes. From the point of view of the individual, the culture within which he or she lives represents the material with which identity and a life can be constructed in terms of future possibilities, as well as the material from which he or she *has been* constructed, in terms of who he or she is now. A culture is like a traditional marketplace, in which a huge array of identities, virtues, and practices is on offer, but also within which individuals can seek to sell their own cultural products. What is bought and sold within this market is the result of negotiation—culture is always co-constructed. The use of the marketplace as an image of cultural life can also be used to highlight some of the major shifts that have taken place in the cultures of industrial societies in recent years. In a traditional, weekly rural market, the majority of participants are primary producers, of such commodities as vegetables, seeds, and cloth, who meet face-to-face to buy and sell. In contemporary society, markets are increasingly mediated by information technology, with the majority of participants being passive *consumers* rather than producers.

The necessary existence of tensions and polarities within any viable cultural system, as argued by Macintyre (1981) and others, has important implications for individuals, and for the practice of psychotherapy because it introduces into life the inevitability of *multiplicity*. It would appear that cultural belief systems and mythologies have always incorporated good and bad polarities (angels and devils) that represent a simple way of condensing the different kinds of moral choices that were open to people. It seems likely then, in earlier times, at least in Christian cultures, there was a high degree of consensus around what was good, right or Godly, and what was a bad or wicked course of action. At some point in history, associated with the so-called "Enlightenment," this began to change, and multiplicity became more problematic. The spread of written language provided a powerful means for distancing personal reflection from action and experience (Abram, 1997), and introduced people to a wider range of ideas. Global travel, migration, and trade meant that people were sharply confronted with a whole spectrum of expressions of "other-ness." As Van den Berg (1974) has pointed out, at some stage during the 1800s, the experience of being human began to be one in which a sense of being divided within oneself was increasingly commonplace. In 1886, Robert Louis Stevenson wrote *The Strange Case of Dr. Jekyll and Mr. Hyde,* the first representation within popular literature of multiple personality. At the same time, Sigmund Freud was developing the psychological theory of the "unconscious," a hidden part of the self present in every person. By the 1990s, Kenneth Gergen (1991) was describing a "saturated" self, a form of postmodern selfhood organised around a multiplicity of compartmentalised relationships and settings.

In cultural terms, divided experience can be understood as a process of standing within different cultures. Very few of us can claim to be unequivocally a member of a single culture. Our parents, or grandparents, may represent contrasting religious or ethnic communities. The trajectory of our lives may have brought us into contact with different cultural ideas and practices. The psychologist Ingrid Josephs (2002) has described a series of events within her own life that led to her, a German woman, visiting San Francisco and buying a Hopi silver ring. The ring, and story that she was told about it by the American Indian man who sold it to her, took on great personal significance. She read about Hopi culture and became aware of what she and her friends recognised as "the Hopi in me," a voice within her that represented strength, security, and harmony in her relationships and in her sense of her personal autobiography. The story told by Josephs is not remarkable in itself—at a time of global communications, travel, and trade, we are all exposed to ideas from other cultures. It offers, however, an example of a positive and life-affirming instance of divided experience, in which the "Hopi voice" gave expression to a set of values and practices that were presumably not readily available in the European culture within which Ingrid Josephs had grown up.

The French postmodern philosophers Deleuze and Guattari (1988) approach the question of cultural life through the metaphor of the rhizome. A rhizome is a plant whose root system extends under the earth, hidden from sight. Separate plants may appear in different places, but underneath they are all joined up, part of a whole. It seems to me that one of the (many) things they are saying is that individuality is more apparent than real. We may consider ourselves to be autonomous bounded selves (Cushman, 1990), but in fact we are part of a greater whole. They are also saying, I believe, that the elements of thought and feeling that define this system are the same, no matter where we look. The same values, practices, and discourses of modern culture are expressed in furniture design, TV schedules, music, political campaigns, as well as in psychotherapy theories and practices. The study carried out by the anthropologist Victor Turner (1964) into psychotherapeutic healing practices within the Ndembu, an African tribal community, can be used to exemplify this principle.

Turner (1964) vividly describes the climax of a therapeutic ritual that involves all of the members of a village community, during which they engage in music and dance, visit the surrounding forest to collect sacred plants, and express their feelings about the behaviour of the "patient." The therapeutic process is highly collectivist. Everyone takes part, and all facets of the physical world possess meaning in relation to the problem that is being ritually addressed. In a modern setting, by contrast, the "patient" would in all likelihood meet individually with a psychotherapist, and might use his leisure time to consume music and visit the outdoors. The contrast with Ndembu healing ritual highlights the individualised, compartmentalised, and commodified nature of contemporary cultural life, apparent across all three of these seemingly separate elements of modern cultural life (therapy, music, and outdoor pursuits).

This brief outline of some ideas about how culture might be understood has a number of implications for the theory and practice of counselling and psychotherapy. First, a cultural perspective opens up possibilities for new ways of making sense of people who seek therapy, or service users. Most approaches to therapy are based in psychological theories of the person—psychodynamic, humanistic, cognitive-behavioural. A cultural perspective brings with it an image of the person as an actor within social and cultural networks, and draws attention to the ways in which identity is constructed and maintained in relation to these networks. The focus of attention becomes the space *between* the person and the cultural world within which he or she lives, rather than the intrapsychic space *within* the person's "self." The theoretical implications of this shift have been articulated most fully by White and Epston (1990) in their description of a narrative therapy that draws on the post-structuralist philosophy of writers such as Michel Foucault.

A second implication of a cultural perspective is to invite a therapeutic focus on the use of *language* within therapeutic conversations. Language is a primary means through which a culture is represented, and brought into being. The different historical traditions within a culture can be regarded as existing as discourses (ways of talking). The concept of subject *positioning*

(Harre & Van Langenhove, 1991) presents a powerful tool for exploring the relationship of the individual within the dominant discourses of his or her culture, and additionally for making sense of the ways that client and therapist position themselves, each in relation to the other (McLeod, 2004a). For example, in a case analysed by McLeod and Lynch (2000), the key issues presented by a client could be seen to be grounded in a conflict between competing cultural discourses within which her life was lived out, and her relationship to her therapist was largely organised around her engagement with, and resistance to, the discursive practices of the therapist.

Finally, a cultural perspective invites counsellors and psychotherapists to be curious about the actual cultural worlds of the people who consult them. The narratives of clients can be viewed as "openings" into the cultural world of the client (McLeod, 2002; McLeod & Balamoutsou, 2000), and an approach that encourages and respects storytelling is likely to provide a therapist with rich material about that world. Culturally-sensitive therapists also initiate conversations around the meaning for the person of critical aspects of his or her life space. If cultural life is organised around a principle of interconnectedness, such as Deleuze and Guattari's (1988) rhizome, then both the tensions and impasses within a person's life and the potential resources for change and development may be found in many different domains within that life. The notion that the way forward for a person may emerge from any aspect of the life space of the person was illustrated in the stories of Debbie and Alec, at the beginning of this chapter, and is explored more fully in the following section.

The Personal Niche: Assembling Cultural Resources

Culture, as the way of life of a group of people, is about survival. We are able to live because of the other people who live with us, and those who have gone before. Modern society, probably more than any other previous form of human social organisation, relies on a massive amount of interdependence. There are very few of us who could deal with the everyday necessities of food, shelter, and health in the absence of the complex cultural structures that exist within contemporary society. Within these structures, each of us makes our own individual life space within which a life can be lived out. The psychotherapist Juerg Willi (1999) describes this process as that of constructing a personal niche:

> The personal niche is the space in which a person develops his or her interactive effectiveness. By this we mean the actual part of the environment with which they truly relate. In this personal niche, individuals relate to the material environment and to other people. The material environment includes

> specific objects, homes and furnishings, the place of work, cherished objects, work objects, achievements and products. The people in the niche include partners, significant others, and the representatives of the cultural environment with which the person is currently relating. (p. x)

The materials from which a personal niche can be constructed can be understood as *cultural resources*. Anything that has meaning to a person can be a cultural resource. Within Western culture, the Bible is a pervasive cultural resource, available in almost every home and public building. It provides a way of thinking, a set of narratives, a range of personalities and identities, and a way of talking. A person can draw on this cultural resource in many different ways, in the construction of his or her personal niche. Passages or phrases and concepts from the Bible may be memorised, and brought into conversation. Images from the Bible may be displayed on the walls of the person's home. His or her niche may incorporate visiting a church, reading a newspaper, or watching a television programme—all places within which Biblical ideas may be overtly or covertly enacted.

The Bible is a highly visible, pervasive cultural resource. There are other forms of cultural resource that are more idiosyncratic. In my own study, I have a square glass vase that contains a collection of white pebbles. These pebbles have been collected while walking on the nearby beach with my dog. There is a story that I can tell about why and when I started to collect these pebbles. Visitors to my study have engaged in conversations about these pebbles, and have attributed their own meanings to them. My study is an important space within my personal niche, and this jar of pebbles represents a valued cultural resource within that space. It signifies meanings connected to my relationship with nature, the importance of hope in my life, and my relationships with other people who are close to me. This jar of pebbles is an asset, a source of support, something that helps me to live the kind of life I want to live. Its loss would diminish my life.

There are many types of cultural resources that can be used in the construction of a personal niche: stories, places, objects, art, music, work, sport. People—present, absent, or imagined—are always central to a niche. The cultural world within which a person lives can shape the kinds of personal relationships that are possible. For example, cultures differ a great deal in terms of how they encourage relationships across gender, age, ethnic and social class boundaries. The majority of cities can be viewed as cultural landscapes in which subgroups of people (rich/poor, old/young, Black/White, able-bodied/disabled) inhabit different territories, participate in their own cultural activities, and rarely meet. In many patriarchal, traditional communities, relationships between men and women are similarly codified and controlled.

It can be useful to think about counselling or psychotherapy as an arena within which a person can reflect on difficulties within a personal niche, and find new cultural resources, or adapt existing ones that can be used to resolve these difficulties. An example of this process can be seen in the following case, drawn from an ongoing research study of cultural factors in therapeutic change that I am conducting. The study comprises an "enhanced" outcome study, in which routine questionnaire measures of outcome have been supplemented with intensive interviews with clients, and analysis of session transcripts. The client has given permission for this material to be used; information that might allow the client to be identified has been changed or omitted.

Case Example

Ian, a teacher, came to therapy because he "felt stressed and tired all the time." As in any life, what was happening for Ian was not simple. There were many threads to his story. The brief account presented here specifically highlights ways in which his use of therapy illustrates the culturally-embedded nature of some fairly typical problems in living, and also some of the ways in which the reconstruction of his personal niche, involving the discovery and use of cultural resources, made a difference to him.

Ian described himself as being under pressure at work, "trudging back and forward, like a soldier in the trenches," just "responding to demands from other people," with no power to change this pattern. In reflecting on these issues in cultural terms, Ian quickly realised that he was not alone in experiencing the workplace as oppressive. He knew that many other colleagues had similar feelings. He knew that the teaching profession reported one of the highest stress and early retirement levels of any profession. He came across a book by a sociologist, Bunting (2004), that helped him to accept that his exhaustion was not a personal failing, but was in reality characteristic of working life in modern organisations. His therapist drew attention to the harshly critical manner in which he sometimes talked about himself, and introduced the idea of "soothing." Over time, this theme developed into a discussion of a "masculine" way of being, reflecting images of warfare, in conflict with a silenced "feminine" way of being, which reflected images of creativity and caring.

The key event, the "why now?" of Ian's life that had brought him to therapy, was his new fear of enclosed spaces: plane journeys, being in lifts, travelling in the underground, attending formal meetings in packed rooms. Encouraged by his therapist to talk about what happened during these panic attacks, when they took place, and his strategies for coping with them, Ian began to conceptualise fear as an external force, something that he could invite into his life, or not (White & Epston, 1990). In his battle against panic, he used everyday cultural resources that were available to him. He defined it as a project. He made lists and maps, and carried out research. In an internet search, he found CBT-based self-help materials for panic attacks, which he began to practice.

His therapist, who was not a CBT practitioner, continued to invite Ian to report on what it was like to be on a plane and be having a panic attack, to re-experience the panic in the therapy room. "It is like being in a closed box. Outside the box are these monsters. They want to take me with them. They are telling me I need to feel pain, rather than being cut off and locked away." Later, Ian realised that he had seen these monsters before in the Tate Gallery in London, a series of paintings by Francis Bacon, the *Triphtych 1944*. He went to view them again, and came back to tell his therapist that he had realised: "there is someone else who has known this."

The outcome of this therapy can be viewed from different perspectives. Assessed in terms of conventional diagnostic categories, Ian represented a "good outcome" case. In his responses to a symptom questionnaire administered by his therapist at the end of treatment, he reported being less anxious, less depressed, more hopeful, and with better social support. From a cultural perspective, other factors were more salient. In his personal niche were a notebook with a list of strategies for preventing panic, a postcard of Bacon's *Triptych,* a blanket, some different stories he told about himself and his work, and some new projects.

While this account of Ian's therapy is undoubtedly subject to "narrative smoothing" (Spence, 1989), and omits important detail, it nevertheless makes it possible to identify some of the key ways in which psychotherapy and counselling can be understood as a form of cultural work. First, the weekly therapy session provided a space outside of his everyday life, from which he could reflect on what had been happening for him. The fixed, ritualised structure of the therapy session made it possible to be active in the use of the weekly space, for example by planning and anticipating issues that he wanted to talk about, and thinking about them in advance, or carrying out "homework" and reporting back at the next session. Second, the therapy operated as an arena in which cultural resources could be considered, or tried out. In the case of Ian, many of the cultural resources that he found helpful, such as breathing exercises to forestall panic, were identified first of all between sessions and then discussed in a therapy session. Other resources, however, were initiated by the therapist, including, for example, the exploration of the "harsh critic/soothing" narrative. This kind of intervention can be regarded as an example of the application of what Fairclough (1992) has described as "discourse technology"—the therapist consistently uses a particular way of talking, or discourse, and re-frames the client's narrative in terms of this set of discursive practices. For example, when Ian talked about his panic attacks, he positioned himself as an external narrator, and reported (in a highly critical style) as if "objectively" observing the scene, who was accounting for his actions to an implicitly judgmental interlocutor. His therapist invited a re-telling of the same event from the position of the experiencing subject, as if sharing the moment with a caring companion. This had the effect of allowing Ian to develop competence in initiating such conversations in other situations, for example telling other people in his life—his wife, friends—directly about his distress, and enlisting their support. This enabled him, after a while, to view strangers in scary places, such as aeroplanes, as potential participants in such soothing conversations, rather than as potential critics. Ian also began to reflect on the occasions when the voice of the harsh critic appeared in his conversations, and to begin to make sense of the broader significance of this voice in his life, including its positive value.

Another important cultural dimension of the case of Ian was the role of art within the change process. In a post-therapy interview, Ian reported that the image of sharp-toothed, open-mouthed monsters crowding into his life space, and the representation of this image in the paintings of Francis Bacon, was a crucial turning point for him. The image captured multiple threads of meaning in his life (fear, threat, constriction, pain, and isolation) while at the same time opening up possibilities for new action (Who or what are these monsters? What do I say to them? What are they saying to me?). This image, and the events that surrounded its creation, were highly memorable, and continued to function as a *source of meaning* many months later. For other clients in therapy, the art work that they create in therapy may be a metaphor, or a speech, a piece of gardening, or an object stolen or borrowed from the therapist's room (Arthern & Madill, 1999). One of the intriguing hypotheses that a cultural perspective opens up for psychotherapy is that, in each case in which therapy is in some sense successful, the still-point for the person (Jevne, 1988) is crystallised in a personal construction that functions, for that individual, as a personal piece of art. It is clear that this kind of process is built into the arts therapies that make specific use of drama, painting, music, sculpture, and dance (Anderson, 1977). But there is evidence that it also occurs in more conventional talking therapies. Art can be understood as an object or event that discloses something significant of *what it means to be human.* It makes sense, therefore, that the moments in our lives when we are seeking to renew or rediscover our sense of what it means to be human (for example, in therapy) can result in the production of personal art. Artists, moreover, can be regarded as specialists, experts, or pioneers within a culture in relation to the task of capturing and creating (in images, words, sounds, and objects) still-points in which human-ness is disclosed. While it is undoubtedly the case that art serves many functions, such as that of reinforcing power, class, and gender relationships within a culture (Berger, 1972), it cannot be denied that art is also a fundamental cultural resource that, somehow, traps meaning in a form that can be revisited and remain generative over long periods of time. A cultural perspective on therapy invites consideration and reflection on the role of art-works, and the personal production of art objects, within the life space or niche of the person.

Personal Reflection on the Challenge of a Culturally-Informed Therapy

In my own life and work, I have become increasingly aware of the importance of culture, rather than individual psychology, as the starting point for making sense of my own, and other people's, behaviour and actions. I was born into a working-class family in Dundee, an industrial town on the East coast of Scotland, in which working hard and doing well were core values. I then suffered two major cultural dislocations. After the war, my father got a job with a jute company in Calcutta, and I lived until the age of 6 in India. Returning to Scotland to attend school, I might as well have arrived from another planet. I spoke a different language and operated according to different rules. Then, at the age of 18, I was the first member of my extended family to go to university. Here, I was introduced to another language and set of rules. Each of these biographical events had a major impact on my identity. Much later, reading about research into the family experiences of people who went on to become psychotherapists (Henry, 1977), I experienced a shock of recognition that other people, many other people, had taken a childhood pattern of self-reliance and being a cultural outsider, and found in the role of counsellor or psychotherapist an arena in which survival strategies assembled in early life could be put to good use. I have therefore been able reflexively to make a link between my own cultural positioning and my career choice.

Within the British academic system, the doctoral thesis is a major, self-initiated, self-defining *rite de passage* into the academy. Understandably, in the light of my life experiences, I chose to study the topic of what gives meaning to life. At the time, I thought I was investigating personality change in adulthood. I carried out a qualitative, participant observation study of two sets of people, who were involved either in Transcendental Meditation or in week-long personal development intensive encounter groups. What I learned, and wrote about (McLeod, 1981, 1984), was that each of these activities could be viewed as providing participants with entry into a distinctive cultural world, or moral arena, with its own values, bodily practices, and discourse.

My subsequent career involved training in person-centred counselling and psychotherapy (Mearns & Thorne, 1999), and employment as a counsellor and counselling/psychotherapy educator and researcher, within the context of an emerging counselling profession in Britain. My textbook, *An Introduction to Counselling* (McLeod, 2003), can be read as both a map of the culture of counselling in Britain and as an attempt to shape that culture in the direction of a more socially critical and politically oriented worldview. In that book, I discussed theories of counselling within their historical and social contexts, included chapters on culture and power, and made reference to sociological and anthropological research. In the 1990s, I became very interested in the idea that therapy is fundamentally a process of storytelling and "re-authoring" (McLeod, 1997), and studied the work of narrative therapists such as Michael White and David Epston (White & Epston, 1990).

I now believe that these theorists are using the term "narrative" in a particular way, which intersects only partially with the wider interest and body of theory and research around narrative and storytelling that has emerged in psychology, counselling, and psychotherapy in recent years (Angus & McLeod, 2004). It seems to me that White and Epston (1990) have developed a form of therapy that is primarily oriented toward social action. It is a therapy that makes heavy use of cultural objects and resources such as letters, certificates, and teddy bears. The ultimate goal, however, appears to be to create new forms of social organisation that sustain alternative, anti-oppressive, ways of being. A good example of this kind of social action is the "anti-anorexia league," a network of people who come together to challenge and resist the narratives and practices of perfectionism and thinness that control many people, particularly women, in our culture (Epston, Morris, & Maisel, 1995). This is, to me, an attractive and powerful concept. The notion of the personal niche, as articulated by Willi (1999), provides an immensely valuable means of beginning to make sense of the relationship between the person and his or her cultural environment. Although Willi writes vividly about the importance of close, intimate love partnerships in niche-building, he is largely silent on forms of social organisation that extend beyond the couple relationship. The case examples that permeate the narrative therapy literature, by contrast, are full of examples of therapists facilitating the construction of support networks that can involve schoolmates, neighbours, family members, therapy centre users, and other forms of collectivity.

Despite the potential of culturally-oriented approaches to therapy, such as ecological psychotherapy (Willi, 1999) and narrative therapy (White & Epston, 1990), there seems little immediate likelihood that psychotherapy and counselling practice as a whole might be moving in the direction of becoming explicitly a form of "cultural work." Returning to my own life story, I observed earlier that my biography, which is probably typical of many people who become psychologists, counsellors, and psychotherapists, involved two stages of turning away from my root culture—once as a result of migration in childhood, and once as a result of professional socialisation at university. My experience has been that these turns have distanced me from everyday culture, while at the same time inducting me into a globalised, international discipline-based "club." This process has been described by Michael White (1997) in the following terms:

> In the culture of the professional disciplines . . . there is an overriding expectation that the membership of a person's life will be constituted of others who have met the eligibility requirements of the formal organs of these disciplines. . . . In this formalisation of the membership of a person's life, the 'common' memberships of life—the 'ordinary,' everyday and historical associations—are dishonoured. . . . For example, upon entering the culture of psychotherapy . . . it is not at all uncommon for a person to be subject to systems of understanding that are pathologising of the significant relationships in their lives, and especially of their familial relationships (and, more often than not, of their relationship with their mother). This can be understood as part of an induction or initiation process, one in which the significant memberships that feature in the history of a person's life are downgraded and frequently disqualified. . . . In this process the associations of the monoculture of psychotherapy are substituted for the diverse, historical and local associations of persons' lives. (pp. 12–13)

What White calls the "monoculture of psychotherapy" can be overwhelming and total. Training, supervision, continuing professional development, personal therapy, service on committees, keeping up to date with theory and research—all this and more in addition to the day-to-day work of seeing clients. It is hardly surprising that participants in a recent study that explored the perceptions of members of a minority community viewed psychologists and psychotherapists as remote, cold, and not interested in their culture (Thompson, Bazile, & Akbar, 2004).

In my experience, the discourses and practices of psychology have not been consistent with cultural curiosity and the cultivation of cultural resources. The perspective on the world that is inculcated by mainstream psychology education and training, results in what Bruner (1986) characterised as a "paradigmatic" way of knowing, based around the application of abstract, timeless, decontextualised categories and if-then formulas, leading to what McAdams (1996) has described as a "psychology of the stranger." Cultural phenomena are, ultimately, grounded in what Bruner calls "narrative knowing"—the telling and performance of stories that refer to historically situated, concrete events, and invoke a moral order. Within counselling and psychotherapy, the growth in interest in cultural dimensions, as exhibited within the last 20 years in the emergence of multicultural approaches to counselling (e.g., Pedersen, 1991), primarily has been driven, I would argue, by a paradigmatic worldview. It has largely focused on an analysis of the culture of the "other," most of the time from a rather detached stance.

It seems to me that the possibilities of cultural and social understandings in counselling and psychotherapy will only be realised through the pursuit of critical reflexivity by which we, as therapy practitioners and educators, examine the ways in which our own cultural identity shapes our practice. The collection of essays by McGoldrick (1998) represents a powerful move in this direction. I also believe that wider use of cultural products—novels, movies, music, art, architecture—as allowable data in psychological inquiry, and as educational materials in therapy training, will be necessary if a truly culturally-informed therapy is to be constructed. Within many training programmes in medicine, for example, students are required to read and discuss works of fiction as a means of enhancing their appreciation of the experience of patients (see, for example, Murray, 1998). The work of Knights (1995) has demonstrated the value of this approach within counselling and psychotherapy training. Further initiatives along these lines would contribute to the development of a deeper appreciation within the counselling and psychotherapy community of what Mair (1989) has described as the *poetics* of human experience. In relation to the important issue of the effectiveness of therapy, it would be valuable to supplement research that was essentially based on data gathered through form-filling, with an analysis of the impact that therapy can have on the engagement and participation in cultural and social life of those who make use of this type of personal learning, such as through life history studies. An acceptance that counselling and psychotherapy are forms of cultural work, rather than quasi-medical interventions, would do much to clear a space for the development of new avenues of inquiry that made use of insights from cultural studies, the humanities, and sociology to construct a knowledge base for post-psychological therapeutic practice (Couture & Strong, 2004; McLeod, 2004b).

Concluding Thoughts

The idea of a culturally-based approach to counselling and psychotherapy is, for me, part of a much larger contemporary movement that seeks to promote a particular vision of psychological and social well-being, and the creation of a better world, along the lines of Illich (1973). Some of the key elements of this movement are: active preservation of nature and the physical environment;

rejection of military solutions to conflict and huge expenditures on armaments; and combating economic systems that are organised around passive consumerism. I suspect that many people would support these principles, even if they have little opportunity to vote for political representatives who might put such ideas into practice. It seems obvious, given the sustained assault that has been made on social capital and community throughout the 20th century, and the increasing disparity between images of wealth that are readily available in magazines and television, set against the reality of most people's lives, that dealing with depression should have become one of the main health priorities in recent years. My own sense is that we live in a culture in which the powerful, decision-making majority—members of the educated professional classes in industrialised societies—live their lives mainly encapsulated within spheres of personal control and pleasure: comfortable cars and homes, nice restaurants, good schools and hospitals, unthreatening television, art, and literature, well-stocked supermarkets, and pensions. Behind this economy of pleasure and personal fulfilment, most of the time hidden from view, are the poverty-ridden populations of producer countries, the erosion of the biosphere, and the loss of myth and tradition.

The argument for an approach to counselling and psychotherapy that views it as a form of cultural work is relatively straightforward. The conditions of modern life are destructive of social capital, historical consciousness, caring, and the ecology of human community. Many thousands of people are treated, in effect, as *waste* (Bauman, 2004). All of this causes emotional pain for the individual and many groups. The solutions that are most readily to hand—medication, consumerism, and psychotherapy—perpetuate an individualism that further erodes community and any sense of a shared culture or structure of feeling. There is, however, the possibility to use counselling and psychotherapy to contribute to a process of culture-building. This is the choice that we face. The work of the Dulwich Centre in Australia (Epston & White, 1992), and the Just Therapy collective in New Zealand (Waldegrave, Tamasese, Tuhaka, & Campbell, 2003) provide models of approaches to therapy that make a positive contribution to the construction of community and cultural life, and demonstrate practical ways in which counselling and psychotherapy can be conducted from a perspective that seeks to support social change.

References

Abram, D. (1997). *The spell of the sensuous. Perception and language in a more-than-human world.* New York: Vintage.

Anderson, W. (Ed.). (1977). *Therapy and the arts: Tools of consciousness.* New York: Harper & Row.

Angus, L., & McLeod, J. (Eds.). (2004). *The handbook of narrative and psychotherapy: Practice, theory and research.* Thousand Oaks, CA: SAGE.

Arthern, J., & Madill, A. (1999). How do transition objects work? The therapist's view. *British Journal of Medical Psychology, 72,* 1–21.

Bauman, Z. (2004). *Wasted lives. Modernity and its outcasts.* Cambridge, UK: Polity Press.

Berger, J. (1972). *Ways of seeing.* Harmondsworth, UK: Penguin.

Bruner, J. (1986). *Actual minds, possible worlds.* Cambridge, MA: Harvard University Press.

Bunting, M. (2004). *Willing slaves: How the overwork culture is ruling our lives.* London: HarperCollins.

Couture, S. J., & Strong, T. (2004). Turning differences into possibilities: Using discourse analysis to investigate change in therapy with adolescents and their families. *Counselling and Psychotherapy Research, 4,* 90–101.

Cushman, P. (1990). Why the self is empty: Toward a historically-situated psychology. *American Psychologist, 45,* 599–611.

Deleuze, G., & Guattari, F. (1988). *A thousand plateaus: Capitalism and schizophrenia.* London: Continuum.

Epston, D., Morris, F., & Maisel, R. (1995). A narrative approach to so-called anorexia/bulimia. In K. Weingarten (Ed.), *Cultural resistance: Challenging beliefs about men, women and therapy* (pp. 69–96). New York: Haworth.

Epston, D., & White, M. (Eds.). (1992). *Experience, contradiction, narrative and imagination: Selected papers.* Adelaide, South Australia: Dulwich Centre Publications.

Fairclough, N. (1992). *Discourse and social change.* Cambridge, UK: Polity Press.

Gadamer, H. (1975). *Truth and method* (2nd ed.). New York: Continuum.

Gergen, K. J. (1991). *The saturated self: Dilemmas of identity in modern life.* New York: Basic Books.

Harre, R., & Van Langenhove, L. (1991). Varieties of positioning. *Journal for the Theory of Social Behaviour, 21,* 393–407.

Henry, W. E. (1977). Personal and social identities of psychotherapists. In A. S. Gurman & A. M. Razin (Eds.), *Effective psychotherapy: A handbook of research* (pp. 211–247). Oxford, UK: Pergamon.

Illich, I. (1973). *Tools for conviviality.* London: Calder and Boyars.

Jevne, R. F. (1988). Creating stillpoints: beyond a rational approach to counselling cancer patients. *Journal of Psychosocial Oncology, 5,* 1–15.

Josephs, I. E. (2002). "The Hopi in me." The construction of a voice in the dialogical self from a cultural psychological perspective. *Theory and Psychology, 12,* 161–173.

Knights, B. (1995). *The listening reader: Fiction and poetry for counsellors and psychotherapists.* London: Jessica Kingsley.

MacIntyre, A. (1981). *After virtue: A study in moral theory.* London: Duckworth.

Mair, M. (1989). *Between psychology and psychotherapy: A poetics of experience.* London: Routledge.

McAdams, D. P. (1996). Personality, modernity, and the storied self: A contemporary framework for studying persons. *Psychological Inquiry, 7,* 295–321.

McGoldrick, M. (Ed.). (1998). *Re-visioning family therapy*. New York: Guilford.

McLeod, J. (1981). The social context of TM. *Journal of Humanistic Psychology, 21,* 17–31.

McLeod, J. (1984). Group process as drama. *Small Group Behavior, 15,* 319–332.

McLeod. J. (1997). *Narrative and psychotherapy*. London: Sage.

McLeod, J. (1999). Counselling as a social process. *Counselling, 10,* 217–226.

McLeod, J. (2002). Lists, stories and dreams: Strategic invitation to relationship in psychotherapy narrative. In W. Patterson (Ed.), *Strategic narrative: New perspectives on the power of personal and cultural stories* (pp. 89–106). Lanham, MA: Lexington.

McLeod, J. (2003). An introduction to counselling (3rd ed.). Buckingham, UK: Open University Press.

McLeod, J. (2004a). Social construction, narrative and psychotherapy. In L. Angus & J. McLeod (Eds.). *The handbook of narrative and psychotherapy: practice, theory and research* (pp. 355–366). Thousand Oaks, CA: Sage.

McLeod, J. (2004b). The significance of narrative and storytelling in postpsychological counselling and psychotherapy. In A. Lieblich, D. P. McAdams, & R. Josselson (Eds.), *Healing plots: The narrative basis of psychotherapy* (pp. 11–27). Washington, DC: American Psychological Association.

McLeod, J., & Balamoutsou, S. (2000). Narrative process in the assimilation of a problemtic experience: Qualitative analysis of a single case. *Zeitschrift fur Qualitative Bildungs—Beratungs—und Sozialforschung, 2,* 283–302.

McLeod, J., & Lynch, G. (2000). "This is our life": Strong evaluation in psychotherapy narrative. *European Journal of Psychotherapy, Counselling and Health, 3,* 389–406.

Mearns, D., & Thorne, B. (1999). *Person-centred counselling in action* (2nd ed.). London: Sage.

Murray, R. (1998). Communicating about ethical dilemmas: a medical humanities approach. In R. Bayne, P. Nicholson, & I. Horton (Eds.), *Counselling and communication skills for medical and health professionals* (pp. 189–203). Leicester, UK: British Psychological Society.

Pedersen, P. B. (1991). Multiculturalism as a generic approach to counseling. *Journal of Counseling and Development, 70,* 6–12.

Spence, D. P. (1989). Rhetoric vs. evidence as a source of persuasion: A critique of the case study genre. In M. J. Packer & R. B. Addison (Eds.), *Entering the circle: Hermeneutic investigation in psychology* (pp. 124–175). New York: New York University Press.

Taylor, C. (1989). Sources of the self: The making of modern identity. Cambridge, UK: Cambridge University Press.

Thompson, V. L. S., Bazile, A., & Akbar, M. (2004). African Americans' perceptions of psychotherapy and psychotherapists. *Professional Psychology: Research and Practice, 35,* 19–26.

Turner, V. W. (1964). An Ndembu doctor in practice. In A. Kiev (Ed.), *Magic, faith and healing: Studies in primitive psychiatry today* (pp. 230–263). London: Free Press of Glencoe.

Van den Berg, J. H. (1974). *Divided existence and complex society.* Pittsburgh, PA: Duquesne University Press.

Waldegrave, C., Tamasese, K., Tuhaka, F., & Campbell, W. (2003). Just therapy—a journey. Adelaide, South Australia: Dulwich Centre Publications.

White, M. (1997). Narratives of therapists' lives. Adelaide, South Australia: Dulwich Centre Publications.

White, M., & Epston, D. (1990). *Narrative means to therapeutic ends.* New York: Norton.

Willi, J. (1999). Ecological psychotherapy: Developing by shaping the personal niche. Seattle, WA: Hogrefe and Huber.

Williams, R. (1961). *The long revolution.* London: Chatto and Windus.

Williams, R. (1981). *Culture.* London: Fontana.

4

The *Felt Sense* as Avenue of Human Experiencing for Integrative Growth

Doralee Grindler Katonah

I have been living as a Focusing-Oriented Psychotherapist for 25 years. I have been fortunate to work at a center for complementary medicine located on a hospital campus. We are one of the few centers that offers an integrated approach in which each patient is staffed by the whole team, which includes professionals practicing Western medicine, acupuncture, homeopathic medicine, chiropractic treatment, massage therapies, and clinical psychology. I am a health psychologist and a transpersonal psychologist who has found the focusing-oriented experiential theory (Gendlin, 1962, 1981, 1996) the most conceptually clear and experientially powerful way to integrate mind, body, and spirit in my work.

How should we think about the *relationship* between the person and culture? What therapeutic processes will enable personal development beyond known patterns? How can people develop freely and diversely to full potential? In this chapter, I discuss and demonstrate an understanding of the person in interaction with culture as a psychological process that can be facilitated within the psychotherapeutic relationship through working with the *felt sense,* a bodily sense of the whole, felt but not known. In addressing the limitations of the Cartesian model of science, I provide the theoretical underpinnings and ways of knowing of a new paradigm that integrates mind, body, and spirit for the sake of health and healing. I try to show the client-therapist interactions that illuminate the ways in which the *felt sense* is the place within our bodies where mind, body, and spirit are already an integrated whole. I explain how, by directly attending to the *felt sense,* physical healing and personal and spiritual growth are possible. This way of working challenges the current medical culture of healing and the secular culture of psychology.

My integration of this way of working has many roots in pivotal experiences in my life, which later resonated with the experiential focusing orientation. This interplay between my way of living and my developing skill as a clinical psychologist was central to my ability to work in this way. By sharing my story and my practice experience, I hope that the reader will begin to see how the theory of experiential focusing is a phenomenology of an inherently natural process.

Culture and Ways of Being: Making Meaning of Human Experience

We cannot begin with only the person; nor can we begin with only culture. We must begin with both as an interaction. It is important to understand that human beings live in relation to their own creations. Living is not just instinctual—humans generate symbolic meanings that become our environment (Gendlin, 1997b). Cultures are creative expressions of meaning shared by groups of people. Yet every culture in this world is evolving in response to interaction with the rest of the world. If we only view cultural change in this general way, however, we do not address the nature of the psychological processes that occur as a person lives life in interaction with his or her environment.

I believe that human beings are not entirely bound by culture. In Eugene Gendlin's Philosophy of the Implicit, culture is defined as "the structure of situations, the patternings of human interactions" (Gendlin, 1997b, p. 17). He goes on to say, however, that living processes are fundamentally unfinished and carry "potential patterns for further interactions with our environment" (Gendlin, 1962, p. 25). Current considerations of culture tend to err on the end of looking for the construction of meanings through culture. This postmodern view, carried to its extreme, concludes that meaning-making is essentially arbitrary and human beings are more products of culture rather than creators; "meaning is created for me by vast networks of background contexts about which I consciously know very little. I do not fashion this meaning; this meaning fashions me" (Wilber, 2000, p. 166). The logical extreme of postmodernism leaves us without a sophisticated understanding of change. Although we are shaped by our context, there is always "the more," lived in the body, about to be formed out of the person's actual experiencing now. No experience is a repeat of an already known patterning. In actuality, human living is an interaction in which the organism can bring its own responsive order to cultural meanings such that a known meaning is transformed into a furthering of newly patterned living. Although cultural meanings are included within the responsive order, the newly differentiated meaning becomes a freshly lived experience beyond known patterns or form.

Gendlin has devoted his life to understanding the interaction between experiencing and symbolization. He differentiates the felt level of implicit meaning that is involved when a person participates in living. He terms this the *felt sense.* This level of meaning is felt in the body as a whole and carries multiple, intricate, and unfinished meanings. The *felt sense* is experienced first as concretely felt body sensations without words. Gendlin's contribution to this discussion of cultural psychology is his clarification of the way in which symbols function in relation to felt experience. Symbolization does not merely define, describe, or prescribe. Rather, symbolization functions to further differentiate felt meaning beyond known concepts, cultural response patterns, and language definitions. An unfinished, yet exact new symbolization emerges from this interaction in such a way that newly created meaning changes the whole again. Thus the emphasis shifts from content to the manner of process and cuts across the existing cultural distinctions.

The field of linguistics has helped us understand this dynamic. The model arising from scientific materialism broke meaning down into units and definitions. In contrast, the philosopher Ludwig Wittgenstein (Stern, 1996) showed us that words continuously develop new meanings as they function differently in situations or contexts of usage. We speak *from* something felt inside that is "the more" and words emerge from the *felt sense* in novel ways. "The word would not be *that word,* if it did not actually *bring* its old uses and schemes *into* the new situation, so that old meaning and new situation 'cross,' and just this new meaning results" (Levin, 1997, p. 48).

The discovery of the *felt sense* also brings a new understanding of emotion and its function in human experience. Emotion is understood to be about the main tendency of the person's problem or situation, whereas the *felt sense* is broader than the emotion and carries the wider context that lends intricate and often different meanings to the situation. It is through this wider sense that new information emerges that moves the person beyond the known version of the situation. "Emotions arise out of the wider context, which their coming then narrows. This has not been well understood. One cannot recover the origin of an emotion by sensing only the emotion itself" (Gendlin, 1991, p. 261). Current theories of psychology identify emotion itself as the psychological process to work with to facilitate change. Working with only the emotion itself keeps the person within the cultural pattern. In contrast, the *felt sense* enables an articulation of experience that interacts with cultural meanings. It is only through pausing the whole behavioral sequence and accessing the *felt sense* that a new pattern emerges from within the person, which could not emerge only through the cultural pattern. This new understanding provides a framework to facilitate a psychological change process that helps people find their own pattern of expression, shaped but not determined entirely by culture.

For example, Focusing-oriented psychotherapy is the most frequently reported therapy in the Japanese *Journal of Humanistic Psychology* (Ikemi, 2003), and is said to be the second-most frequently reported therapy among Japanese clinical psychologists as a whole (Ikemi, personal communication, November 24, 2004). Many Japanese found that through engaging in a *focusing* process, they valued aspects of their own tradition that have been rejected by modernity. By checking with the *felt sense,* cultural meanings are also selectively valued according to this bodily resonance and so a new form of cultural expression becomes possible. Akira Ikemi (2001), a professor of counseling psychology at Kobe College, Japan, transforms his understanding of Buddhism through an interaction with Gendlin's concept of *felt sense*:

> As Focusing-Oriented Therapists, we are very Buddhist, in a way. We are letting go of the forms and then from the empty space, we are letting form some new forms. . . . We trust "the more" arising in the client, rather than the client's same old cognitions. (p. 4)

Alannah Earl Young is a counselor at the First Nations House of Learning in British Columbia, Canada. She is a First Nation Musikeginiwak Cree from the central plains area in Canada. She finds that focusing works with the concepts of the Medicine Circle and brings the bodily awareness that enables a coming of a fresh, personal meaning. In her article (Young, 1998, p. 10), she describes a *focusing* process in which the traditional reference to ancestors becomes a symbolization that carries forward a more personally felt meaning:

Dialogue:

You have pressure on your right chest.

I feel like it is dragging me down.

What do you need to feel more comfortable there?

I need to make some space between the flat stone and me.

How is this related to your life right now?

In my relationship I need to take some space and slow down.

Really take that message in.

Is there anything you need to help you with that right now?

Yes, my grandmother. . . . She is behind me and protecting me.

This understanding of the responsive order also illuminates the kind of process that can bridge communication between cultures in conflict. For example, Atsmaout Perlstein (Kirschner, 2004), an Israeli, is now teaching focusing to Palestinians on the Gaza Strip. She helps people to step back from the cultural stereotypes and pause to find the felt meaning in the body. "This allows a person to live from their felt experience, even when it contradicts outside expectations" (p. 8).

This articulation of human potential to make felt meaning a direct referent reveals a new evolutionary development that comes after culture, language and emotion, which enables us to further differentiate experience. As Hendricks (2003) states:

> All individuals have many strands of experience which could be differentiated and which do not fit the cultural patterns. But to allow the whole of this ongoing experience to form as a bodily *felt sense* one has to pause the cultural story. . . . The *felt sense* is the inner datum of "how this whole situation is for me." This is wider than what a typical acculturated person feels. (p. 5)

We live in a world with extraordinarily complex problems. The domination of scientific materialism has led to the devaluing of subjective experience, the belief that the mind and the body are separate, the ultimate valuing of material goods and technology, and the rejection of spirituality as a psychological dimension impacting health and healing. As Lisa Hoshmand states in Chapter 1, it is important to understand the philosophical underpinnings and cultural values in our paradigms of human change that may exclude certain considerations. We cannot address the whole person while working within a dualistic and reductionistic framework. The cultures of modern science and clinical psychology perpetuate a circumscribed understanding of the person. Under the assumption of mind/body dualism we seldom consider meaning as also processed from the body, not only the mind.

Within the paradigm of scientific materialism we cannot consider the realm of spirit as a reality and investigate how spirituality is related to health, healing, and the development of the person. We desperately need access to human processes that restore our capacity to address the whole person.

Following is my own story about how I came to adopt and integrate a holistic perspective in my life.

Personal Journey

One day, when I was in high school, my French teacher decided to take us on a field trip to the St. Louis Art Museum. She took us to the room where the French Impressionist paintings were displayed. As I looked at a Monet painting for the first time, I shook within as suddenly my own inner world became vividly and consciously alive for me. It was not just the rapture of discovering the beauty of these paintings. A vibration of recognition shot through my body and I was filled with excitement as I realized that this "vivid, impressionistic view" is how I had been seeing the world my whole life. Prior to this moment, I did not know this. This self-recognition brought relief—now that I recognized myself—I came alive to myself. There was a distinct bodily release in this recognition and with it, a freeing of energy and self-confidence. From here, I became interested in the world of art. Both inner and outer worlds began to develop.

I did not know at the time that this experience was an instance of experiential focusing. What I experienced was what Gendlin theorizes to be the primary human process that carries life forward into further development—the interaction between experiencing and symbolization that creates new meaning and in turn implies a further meaning. Our experiencing is not fully lived and cannot develop further until there is a symbolization that carries forward what is implied by the body. The Monet painting was such a symbol.

There was something else I did not know about myself for a long time, yet it was functioning within me. When I was in college, I often became caught up in the theology papers I was assigned to write. One time we were asked to critically analyze a scriptural passage from the New Testament. I found somewhere on campus where I could be totally alone and just sat. (I did not want anyone to see me doing this. It seemed too weird at the time.) I sat quietly with the assignment for a long time, finding there was nothing to write. All that I was aware of were certain uncomfortable sensations in my body. I knew on some level that my thoughts were in there if I just waited. Then it felt like words or thoughts surged up into my awareness and over time, if I just let these thoughts come, there was a cogency to what I was writing, and my body released as I got each sentence to say what was there *exactly*. Then I was filled with such excitement as my whole body seemed to be involved in the creation and explication of a knowing I was now saying. It was even further reassuring that what I formulated actually communicated well to my professors. But then if someone tried to talk to me about what I had written, I was tongue-tied. I would feel inadequate and empty. I could not speak or think in a kind of fast, analytical way.

Only later did I come to understand that we are already implicitly guided by a knowing that is first felt in the body as a vague body sensation. This *felt sense* carries already integrated complex meanings beyond what we could think about analytically. What matters is this ability to pay attention to this level and not let our conscious thought process interfere with what is capable of emerging from the body. This attending, waiting, and checking with the body are new ego functions. When I consciously took the stance of "not knowing," I was enabling a different kind of knowing to emerge.

When I began my studies at The Divinity School at University of Chicago, I was already open on a spiritual level. I became deeply immersed in the study of world religions and was introduced through the eyes of many religions to the mystical thread of spirituality. As I entered the world of the Catholic Mystics of early Christianity, I was adamant: They are not talking about ideas. They are describing personal experiences of a spiritual reality that are part of the spectrum of human potential, universally available to all who seek. This stirred a longing within me to find this inner potential. This is an example of moving from the cultural religious expressions to the personalized *felt sense* and back again.

It was during this time that I met Eugene Gendlin and began to learn about the experiential focusing process and its philosophical underpinnings. I was fortunate to have been part of the initial developments of this process. Originally, when we began teaching people focusing and helping people find this *felt sense* level within their bodies, the emphasis had been on problems. As we became more skilled, we began to wonder what would happen if we could find a place in our bodies where we are free from our problems, a kind of open space of well-being *directly felt*. We began to wonder whether we have the potential of attending to a bodily sense of well-being that is not contingent upon whether or not our problems are solved. Well, I could not quite imagine this at the time, but every night as I was walking home from work I would try to find this state in my body. I tried and I tried. "What would it feel like in my body if I was all fine now?" I would direct my attention to the center of my body and when a problem arose I would notice it and place it spatially at a distance.

One night it happened! It kind of popped in. This vast, inner space opened up from inside my body and I felt a sense of calm and well-being that was "just there." In the same instant, I realized that on a fundamental level I am not my problems; whatever problems I have are there and part of my life but that "I" am really this vast space of well-being opening up. I also realized that the meaning of the problems began to change as well, just in this shift of my inner relationship to these problems. I cried with joy over the realization that this was the kind of experience I had been reading about in the mystical literature. This was it! This was a doorway I had discovered within ME. The crucial connection that I began to make here, which has since informed my work, is that this connection to spirit comes through the body. Mind/body/spirit now were all related and my life took on a whole new level of meaning. Gendlin (1981) later called this process "clearing a space" and now it is part of all Focusing training.

My meditation practice evolved and I would sit in this silent open space. I became able to open into my existential situation and let go of many self-definitions I had carried in a rigid fashion. I began to learn that in this open space is a seamless connection to a larger consciousness from which a kind of universal wisdom arises that shifts my perspective. During this time, I also discovered how this kind of experience and understanding of the mind is greatly developed within the Buddhist tradition and became curious about the convergences between the Philosophy of the Implicit and Eastern thought.

About 15 years ago, my 14-year-old nephew died of an asthma attack. This was devastating—a young life ended. I was so agitated I could not sleep; I had to keep moving but in a frantic, directionless way. I could not imagine how I could live through the many weeks ahead. Then I remembered to meditate. I went into my little room, which had become my sacred space. I usually do some form of breathing and stretching to help me find that meditative place. I had to force myself to begin my ritual. My breathing was shallow and I stretched, feeling my pain open out to spirit. I stretched more and my breathing deepened and I cried out, "Why?" I rested in meditation. Suddenly strong, loud words came up and flowed through me: "You can't control life!" My whole body shook and then relaxed as if a burden was lifted. These words of healing came through my body and my body released. I felt comforted and I "knew" this was a deeper truth that gave me the courage to be present for both my family and myself during a very difficult time. This was when I became confident that a spiritual force engages each person's existential reality for the sake of healing.

But my crucial personal development did not stop here. A former student of mine called me one day. She was devastated to learn that the cancer of the uterus in her had returned and metastasized to the colon. She had tried the Simonton Method of Guided Imagery, but it did not feel right to her. She wondered whether Focusing would help. We worked together to learn how to engage *focusing* with her healing process. What we learned was that the body gave her the next steps of living that reduced side effects to her medical treatments, and opened up depth of meaning and direction for her life. Here is where I learned with her that the *felt sense* also has a contribution toward the healing of physical disease and quality of life.

Now, we have case studies (Gendlin, Grindler, & McGuire, 1984; Grindler Katonah, 1999a, 1999b; Kanter 1999; Krycka, 1999) and research evidence (Grindler Katonah, 1991; Lutgendorf, Antoni, Kumar, & Schneiderman, 1994) that indicate that bodily explicated meaning is processed on a physiological level with the potential to restore the healing capacities of the body. Mind/body constitutes one whole. Unlived potential meanings are held by the body if not accurately symbolized. Thus, physical symptoms become an expression of a need for further symbolization to carry life forward. A new symbolization becomes recognized as "true" as it is filtered through the body's knowing/resonating. Often a physical symptom is expressed through a cultural pattern. These expressions evoke a *felt sense* that interacts with the cultural meaning. Physical healing then becomes related to furthering of lived meaning.

I continue to strive to live in relation to the *felt sense* level in my personal and professional life. The underpinnings of focusing-oriented psychotherapy are further explained next.

Philosophical and Conceptual Framework of Focusing-Oriented Psychotherapy

Focusing-oriented psychotherapy is an emerging family of psychotherapies inspired by Gendlin's (1996, 1997a, 1997b) discovery of Focusing and its roots in the Philosophy of the Implicit. It has some support from Rogerian psychotherapy (Rogers, 1951), and psychotherapy outcome research (Gendlin, Beebe, Cassens, Klein, & Oberlander, 1968; Hendricks, 2001). Gendlin's Philosophy of the Implicit and his Theory of Experiencing offer a new paradigm that posits *"interaction first"* as the fundamental process sustaining and creating all life. Central to Gendlin's (1987) critique of narcissism, it opens up new consideration of human possibility and the role of culture in human development. Living beings are not separate entities. Every aspect of the living organism, from cellular process to cultural contexts, to personal meaning-making, to spiritual engagement is inherently interactive. Our lungs imply the air. Our leg structure implies the earth. Babies cry for their parents to hear. Cultural forms do not just shape the individual; rather human beings respond back to culture in unique ways. It is assumed that our experience is about our interaction with the world in an open way, neither mechanical nor determined. This open way activates a responsive order of creative magnitude, fresh in the moment, both nondetermined and exact. This interactional structure is noniconic (it does not look like earth and legs imply each other); it is one organization that is already in interaction in their creation and ongoing functioning. Therefore, a change in any part already affects all the other parts. Thus, what changes is the whole (Gendlin, 1997b, p. 3). This holistic paradigm offers a way of understanding the role of felt meaning in the cultural symbolization of human growth and experience.

A basic question for psychology is: What kinds of processes generate and sustain aliveness? Aliveness does not neatly fit into the modern scientific model. Descartes's separation of mind and body, along with an ultimate valuing of mathematical reasoning led to the belief that the person is more like a machine. Science is currently understood as an inquiry into parts with logical relationships. The mind is not considered to be of the body, so there cannot be an organismic intelligence known through the whole. In addition, the physical view of the mind, as a product of brain functioning only, abdicates the possibility that consciousness is more than what is internal to brain physiology (Tart, 2000). Transpersonal understanding proposes that human experience extends beyond the individual to "encompass wider aspects of humankind, life, psyche, and cosmos" (Walsh & Vaughan, 1996, p. 17). Considering human nature beyond the mechanistic view opens us to think about the human capacity to live from an interactive whole, which includes the mind and body, the environment, cultures, and the transpersonal whole as already integrated (Gendlin, 1997b).

Fundamental to the Philosophy of the Implicit is the explicit attending to a bodily *felt sense* of an issue. The *felt sense* is a concretely felt body sensation connected to an issue but conceptually vague. What is implicit is felt only, not yet symbolized. When a meaning is implicit, it is not experienced. This *felt sense* level of experiencing is just below normal consciousness and carries the whole meaning of a situation and a directionality of change. Only when interaction with fitting symbols actually occurs, is something lived further. This is called "carrying forward." Further steps of change are possible from this *new opening*.

What differentiates human process from other living processes is the capacity to make this *felt sense* a direct referent. By bringing a nonjudgmental attention to the quality of the *felt sense* and waiting, symbolization emerges that resonates with the body. This new explicit meaning has a complexity to it that cannot be conceived through existing categories alone (Gendlin, 1962, pp. 138–173). The symbolization is not a logical explanation, but rather a resonating produced by an exact fit, which then opens up further meaning that is lived. This *felt sense* level of change is going on within many human processes; thus, focusing-oriented psychotherapy brings depth to any other psychotherapeutic approach. When focusing and the function of the implicit in psychotherapeutic change are not known, psychotherapy (no matter what the orientation is) may lose its potential to initiate deep and lasting change. This loss occurs when insights, meanings, and behavioral change are not checked with or modified by the bodily sense. Only if there is a resonance in the body does a person "feel differently" and "live differently."

A mature Focusing-oriented psychotherapist may integrate *focusing* with other psychotherapeutic interventions and ways of working (Gendlin, 1996). Content does not define the methodology; therefore, the unique aspects of the person become more central to the psychotherapeutic process and cross-cultural work moves between symbol and this bodily checking. For example, recently I was working with a Buddhist priest from Japan. He was attending to a *felt sense* (in his body) and asking himself what he needs to continue living his spirituality. The word that emerged was: *nothing.* At first he was perplexed because he could only think of the Zen connotation of this word as a kind of emptiness. I explained to him that what this word means to him right now as it interacts with his body sense is a new meaning of this word. So I invited him to check inside with his bodily *felt sense* to see what more emerged. When the image of a snake and the words "stillness and action" came, he felt a release in his body and a more personal sense of how his spirituality, while grounded in the shared cultural meaning, moves a step further from this interaction between felt meaning and known symbol.

Focusing-oriented psychotherapy demands of the clinician a way of living that honors the *felt sense* level. It operates from the following assumptions: (a) The interactive whole is implicit and felt in the body, (b) The interaction between felt meaning and symbol generates new meaning, (c) Human beings are part of a larger responsive order, and (d) The interactive whole of mind/body/spirit is a dynamic unity. The first two assumptions have been alluded to previously. What many call a larger consciousness, or the transpersonal, can also be described as the life-force that is within and between, permeating and transcending all forms of life and interacting with the openness (or unfinished furthering of living) within the person. This life-force carries the furthering of life as a dynamic—that is, it is actively creating through engagement with living beings. As Thomas Merton (1968) said: "The metaphysical intuition of Being is an intuition of a ground of openness, indeed a kind of ontological openness and an infinite generosity which communicates itself to everything that is" (pp. 24–25). I will term this intangible, universal openness to life, *spirit.* Spirit interacts with personal life through the body. In the bodily opening there is an opening to a larger patterning that opens something more within the person. Our spiritual nature moves us beyond ourselves to engage with the life-force of the world. This interactive whole of mind/body/spirit, accessed through the *felt sense,* can further the development of the person.

The Clinical Integration of Mind, Body, and Spirit

Focusing-oriented psychotherapy is about a way of being in the interaction that supports and elicits the client's capacity to relate to his or her own felt meaning and to allow the symbolization process to arise and resonate back with the body. The therapist is attending not only to the implicit felt experiencing within the client, but is also attending within herself at the same time to how she is resonating with the client's process as well as noticing what emerges. In this view, diagnostic or personality categorizations of the person are not of inherent truth-value. These understandings can be valuable only as they function to further the explication of meaning, which by their explication will then change.

The "self" from this orientation is understood to be the person's capacity to be present to whatever is emerging into new form in the moment. Current conceptualizations of experience are relinquished for the sake of continued openness into potential. There is a wide range of ways in which it is difficult for people to relate in this way to themselves (Hendricks, 1986). Thus, the therapy also includes working with these difficulties for the sake of nurturing the development of this capacity. It is important that the therapist not fall into the trap of being wedded to either his or her own or the client's conceptualizations of self. What matters is the quality of presence lived by the therapist that allows him or her to discern and newly constellate the *felt sense* level of processing in the interaction.

Such understanding of the interaction between experiencing and symbolization gives us a new method for working cross-culturally. As a clinician of a different culture, we can learn to engage the cultural patternings in this new manner by facilitating the formation of a *felt sense* in response to cultural patterns. For example, a Focusing teacher taught focusing to Afghan volunteers for the Coordination of Humanitarian Assistance (Lawrence, 2004). She introduced Focusing through excerpts from Sufi poetry and then guided people to attend to their *felt sense* response to the poem. Not only did the poems symbolize their own cultural/religious meanings, but the inner checking with the *felt sense* brought a personal meaning as well, that was empowering and releasing of inner stress and despair. As practitioners, we may not fully understand the culture itself (especially if we have not lived in the culture extensively); but rather, we understand this psychological process of further symbolization as it resonates with the body. There is an inherent respect for the person communicated through this process as meanings and categories are not imposed. Instead, there is a reverence toward whatever emerges from the *felt sense.* A volunteer in the workshop commented: "Focusing is in the history here. It is in the literature, the poems. Mohammad even sat in the cave before becoming the messenger of God doing something like Focusing. So what have we been doing these 1,000 and more years? Why doesn't everybody know this?" (Lawrence, 2004, p. 2). A deep sense of personal connection and empowerment is the result.

The clinical presentations below illuminate this holism. The emphasis is on the moment-to-moment interactions. I will demonstrate the healing within this triadic dynamism of mind/body/spirit activated by the *felt sense.* Specifically, I will illustrate (a) how the *felt sense* shifts the mind/body relationship, (b) how the *felt sense* of a physical symptom heals the symptom, and (c) how spiritual symbolization interacts with the *felt sense* to further spiritual development. At the same time, I will highlight the ways of engaging with this *felt sense* dynamic in the therapeutic interaction, thus showing both the macro and micro level of experiential processing.

Case Examples: The *Felt Sense* Shifts the Mind/Body Relationship

The benefits of guided imagery, relaxation, biofeedback, and many forms of meditation have been shown to have an impact on health, stress-reduction, and recovery from a serious illness. The benefits of these familiar processes have been shown through research to activate the parasympathetic nervous system. Experiential focusing is another mind/body process that includes the physiological benefits of relaxation and meditation but also engages the *felt sense.* If this layer of bodily sensed experience is identified and given attention, specific steps of change emerge from within the person, which guide the person in the direction of further health.

A client I will call Michelle was the first person with cancer with whom I worked. In preparation for the *focusing,* I guided her in a progressive relaxation exercise. I asked her to relax the part of the body that had the cancer. As she tried to do that she exclaimed: "I can't believe it! I cut that part off!" There was shock in her voice as it hit her that she was so frightened that she mentally cut off that part of her body. She had been blaming her body for the illness and saw her body as the enemy. I now know this is a common coping strategy.

Focusing begins with this kind of body awareness, moving out of our heads and normal ways of talking to a noticing of body sensations. We notice these sensations in a nonjudgmental way and clear a space by allowing what is there to move to a space further out.

I asked her to find a place in her body where she felt some good energy. She was quiet for a very long time and then she said: "I can't do that. I'm sick! Like I'm bad in some way because of being sick!" I responded to her by saying: "It feels like that's all of you, being sick. And so there is no good energy."

Notice the effect of identifying with the problem. Often, when someone is trying to cope with a life-threatening illness, this sense of a larger self collapses into the illness (I am my illness) and thus the person is cut off from the energy and resources that are available to them. In this case, the client does not know how to use her attention in such a way to create a space between "I" and her illness. There is not a "more" to the "I" yet. This collapsing is a shutting down of the *focusing* process. The *felt sense* needs to be related to as a direct referent—there needs to be an "I" that is relating to the "It." This inner activity of noticing and placing each concern at a metaphorical distance brings the conscious self (the part of us that attends) into direct contact with the largest sense of one's life and the steps to move forward. A Focusing-oriented therapeutic response will strengthen this "I" that is a "more" and is with whatever is there.

I invited Michelle to look around for where in her body she might experience good energy. "Maybe there is some place in your body where you still carry some good energy, even if it is at the tip of your toe." She was quiet again for a while and then she said: "Oh, it's amazing, I was able to move past that idea that somehow I'm bad because I'm sick, and I got to a place in my head where I feel some creative energy. It feels really good!" She then expressed a desire to begin to care about that part of her body that had been carrying the disease. She described how she began to channel her breathing into the part of her body that had the cancer. A seed was planted for developing a new relationship with her body as an implying of further living.

Notice how just clearing a space, finding that open potential space inside the body, automatically begins to generate steps of change. These steps are not exactly "ideas" but rather the combination of a particular action and felt desire that comes from this deep wanting of further living. This desire to begin to care about the part of her body that had the cancer was a dramatic change (as she had cut that part out), which occurred within about 20 minutes of *focusing*.

The changes that come through Focusing have a lasting impact. There is a strengthening of the Self that is sustained at the structural level. In contrast to such practices as relaxation or guided imagery, which bring relief felt in the moment, the effects of practicing Focusing continue over time. In my pilot study, I was able to measure the effects of Focusing over time. This study evaluated the usefulness of Focusing for cancer patients with regard to depression, hardy coping mechanisms, body cathexis, body attitudes, and physical activity level for 12 cancer patients between the ages of 30 and 55. A 6-month follow-up evaluated the change over time. Results showed a significant decrease in depression and a significant improvement in body image for the treatment group when compared to the waiting-list group. A trend toward significance appeared in the hardiness scores and the body cathexis scores. At the 6-month follow-up, no significant differences in the scores emerged for the treatment group, suggesting that subjects had sustained the changes achieved with this intervention over time (Grindler Katonah, 1991).

I will show in another case how symbolization interacts with felt experience. This client I will call Sally was devastated when she was told that her ovarian cancer had returned. She felt she had done everything right to heal herself after the first diagnosis and now she felt betrayed by God and angry at this injustice. She also was frightened and worried because "my attitude just isn't very good." Not only was she facing more chemotherapy but also she was frightened that she might die. This uncertainty about her future left her with overwhelming grief as she contemplated that she may not experience her daughter graduating from high school or see her children marry. In our previous session, she had begun to talk about her wish that her children would know "the artist in her," as she had been a painter before she had children. In the following session, she was experiencing much emotion yet she was not consciously connected to a *felt sense*. I asked her to take a moment and notice this sense of uncertainty in her body:

Client: (Silence) . . . I feel it in my head. . . . Now it has moved down into my chest area.

Often when we bring our attention to our body, we first begin to sense in our head, where we think about everything. If we stay with the body then the sensation often moves to a lower location where a *felt sense* forms.

Therapist: You talked about this as uncertainty. When you say that back to your body—"uncertainty"—does that resonate?

Client: (Silence . . . checking the word with the body sense) No. . . . It's more like a dark hole with no end to it. . . . (Tears)

Here I am working directly with this process of checking a symbol to see if it fits what the body knows. The word "uncertainty" did not resonate.

If we had stayed with this inaccurate symbolization an experiential process would not occur. Fortunately, because she did check back with her body, she was able to sense further into the felt meaning and a more accurate symbol emerged ("a dark hole with no end to it"). Often tears come in response to this deep resonating as natural bodily release.

Therapist: Just stay with this sense of the dark hole with no end to it with gentleness and warmth. . . . If it feels right, take that sense of the dark hole and place it at a little distance from yourself.

Here I invite her to *clear a space* with the understanding that shifting the relationship one has with the problem begins to open bodily-informed meaning. This is one way to bring the client to the "I" that notices.

Client: I can't today. Usually it works to put it in God's hands . . . today that feels hard to do.

Therapist: So as you checked inside, it doesn't feel right to make too big a space there with all of that. It needs your attention now. Let's trust that and see what emerges if you just stay with that.

In this instance, her body let her know that this issue needs close attention. Even with this checking, however, there is a strengthening of the "I" that is more than this problem. She is not just inside this issue now. There is now a larger self, who is bringing an inner presence to this hard feeling place.

Client: (Tears) . . . I can't talk to my family about how all of this upsets me. So I guess I do want to stay with it. (She talks about how letting go and living in the present is easier for older people because they have accomplished all they set out to accomplish; whereas for her, letting go is more difficult as she is raising young children and living for their futures.)

Therapist: You're sensing your own deep longing to fulfill your purpose in life, which includes raising your children.

Client: Yes. (Eyes open wide, head nods . . . silence)

Therapist: Let that live . . . that deep desire.

It is important to not forget that the words are connected to a *felt sense* that is present at this moment. Not only is she talking about this stage of life issue, but she also is *feeling* a deep sense of *wanting* to fulfill her purpose. So it is important to invite the person to stay with the bodily feel of this desire, rather than just go on talking about it. This way she stays engaged with the *felt sense,* which has the next steps of living in it.

Client: (Silence . . . sitting with the feel of it all). (Noticeable shift in affective presence . . . as she comments on feeling lighter and less burdened.) You know, my husband picked up the paintings of mine I had framed and they turned out to be wonderful—I feel pleased. . . . Now I will frame more of them.

Therapist: So you are following through on this purpose you had identified last week. . . . You are living this now . . . the purpose of enabling your children to know the artist in you.

Client: Yes . . . and I feel clear about the summer—that I am doing what I most want to do. . . . (Silence) . . . My children seem happier now. They are more independent. . . . That's what I've been helping them with.

What mattered to Sally is to continue to live out her sense of purpose and not let the illness and her fears about the future stop her. Sally continued working with the *focusing* process in subsequent sessions. At one point, she was worried because her tumor count was not going down after many chemo treatments. Through *focusing* on this concern, she got the message: "Cut the tumor out." Although her physician felt that surgery would not work, she sought a second opinion and eventually she had the surgery. It was amazing that the tumor was actually quite small and self-contained (no lymph glands affected). It is now 2 years later and she remains in remission.

Often people with physical illness or physical symptoms interpret them to mean: "I cannot live my life fully." These examples lead me to wonder whether the opposite could be true—that it is in activating the forward direction and continuing to live life fully that the physical illness/symptom may heal.

Case Example: The *Felt Sense* Can Release Physical Symptoms

There is so much we do not know about physical disease. If we begin with the assumption that we are one whole organism that is in interaction with environment, culture, and spirit, then physical disease is an interaction as well. I want to highlight in this case example what can happen when we treat a physical symptom as a *felt sense;* that is, the physical symptom carries bodily felt meanings that imply further living.

A 45-year-old man I will call John has been learning Focusing. He has recently returned from Arizona where his father died and was buried. He is married with two children. He begins the session:

Client Response 1: I didn't feel like coming today. My chronic bronchitis is acting up again. I am so stuffy I can hardly breathe. I've been living with this all day at work. I'm tired. I just want to go to bed.

Therapist Response 1: So it's important to allow that tiredness and stuffiness to be . . . to acknowledge in a gentle way that your body has been carrying this all day. And you are wondering whether you should have even come today.

Client Response 2: Yes. . . . (Silence) . . . (Deeper breaths, deep sighs) . . . It feels a little better just being with it.

In client response 1, he is describing uncomfortable physical symptoms but he has not yet brought his awareness into his body. In order to create an inner sense of being with his body as it is, I invited him to notice and acknowledge how it is in his body. Just this inner act brings a gentle movement, or a shift from being stuck or static, to an easing and more of an opening. In client response 2, the deep sighs and the deeper breathing express this easing. I notice this bodily communication, which tells me he is ready for a *felt sense* to begin to form.

Therapist Response 2: Could you describe what *that whole thing* is like; living with this stuffiness—the chronic bronchitis?

In phrasing my question in this way, I am broadening the empathic field to include not only physical sensations and physical states, but also what it is like to live with the physical symptom. This will have many intricate aspects to it—his history, how it impacts his relationships, his daily living, and much else. I am opening up the possibility that the physical symptoms have an edge, which will become a *felt sense;* in other words, I do not assume that this is purely a physical state but that it can also carry meaning. I phrase my invitation such that he can move from just talking about the physical distress to noticing what it is like to live with the chronic bronchitis. This phrasing points him toward his *felt sense.*

Client: Well, I feel this tightness all up here (pointing to the sides of his nose) and I feel constrained here (placing arms over upper chest area) . . . It's hard to breathe. . . . (SILENCE with a focused attention on chest area) . . . And there is a kind of despair. I've had this problem ever since I was in junior high. It interfered with my playing sports . . . and . . . I just wish it would go away.

Therapist: So there is this acute awareness of the physical tightness and constriction in breathing and then there is a kind of despair about how long you've been struggling with this . . . how it affected you as a youth.

Client: (Nodding in silence, eyes closed)

Notice the movement that emerged as he attended in a nonjudgmental way to the physical symptom. He says: "And there is a kind of despair." Notice his use of "kind of"—this phrasing expresses that he can sense there is a "more" there beyond the single word "despair." This *more* that the word points to is the *felt sense.* This is concretely felt in the body but at first conceptually vague—there are no words yet.

Therapist: So we want to keep company with all of that.

This is important. You first have to just be with the *felt sense* —the whole feel of it without words. And then more begins to come.

Client: Yeah . . . and I think of my dad—he wasn't around much back then and now he is dead. (There is sadness in his face and some tears.) He died so soon after I felt we were getting to know each other better.

Therapist: So as you attend to your physical distress it brings up your dad . . . and sadness about his distance from you as a child and now about his death.

Client: Yeah . . . (Deep breathing)

He begins to connect his bronchitis to a longing for a better relationship with his dad as a child and now how his death is especially sad because they were finally becoming close. All of this is still just the beginning. What is felt on a bodily level still contains more than what has been said so far. I want to help him continue to stay with the bodily *felt sense,* not just talk. Asking an open question is one way to invite the *felt sense* to speak, to form into words or images.

Therapist: As you are sitting with your sadness and the tightness and difficulty breathing . . . perhaps you could sense into the tightness right now, asking inside what more is in the tightness and sadness now.

Client: (Silence)

Usually after asking an OPEN question, there is a time of waiting while attending to the *felt sense.* The *felt sense* opens in a slower time zone. The usual way we think fast does not enable a *felt sense* to open. A slowing down and just "being with," with no pressure for "answers" is necessary for something to emerge from this felt level of experiencing.

Client: Oh . . . (Deep sobs) . . . I'm remembering being in the hospital room and seeing how emaciated my father was. . . . (Sobs) . . . I didn't want to see that . . . he used to be so strong and big. . . . (Sobs) . . . I felt so scared seeing him like that. . . . This is my father. . . . (Deep sighs) . . . (Silence) . . . WOW! I can't believe all that came just now. . . . I had to hold all that back before while at the hospital. I knew I had to be strong for my family—my mother and children—so I blocked all that out.

Therapist: Such relief now to let yourself really acknowledge what you felt seeing your dad so emaciated . . . seeing him dying.

Client: Yes. . . . (Eyes brighten and for the first time he looks out at me) . . . I can't believe it. My sinuses are all clear now.

Here a whole new experience emerged into full consciousness—but this does not say it quite, because until it emerged just now, he had not really been able to live this experience. It had been carried in his body but not known. By letting it constellate as a *felt sense* and attending to it in such a way that language emerges directly, the body releases. He is living this deeper meaning and breathing freely.

Case Example: Spiritual Presence Interacts With *Felt Sense*

A very intelligent and sensitive 35-year-old woman with the pseudonym of Pam has been a practicing Roman Catholic since childhood. She is not a follow-the-rule Catholic. She is spiritually committed to her faith, but she is very aware of the problems of authority and positioning of men above women within the church. She was hired by her parish to coordinate educational programs. It was with great pride that she began her work in this capacity. She developed an outstanding program.

Pam came a long way since her traumatic childhood. Her father repeatedly abused her, physically and emotionally. During her high school years her father beat her every day. She was gang-raped twice. A football player she knew in high school beat her up. She abused alcohol and other drugs. When she graduated, she was determined to leave home. She lived in an apartment complex owned by a drug dealer. Over time she overcame her addictions, married, and had one child. Her abusive past continued to haunt her, however, and could be triggered by relationship dynamics that instanced an abuse of power.

Within the last 6 months a new priest was assigned to her parish. She immediately became alerted to his denigration of her authority. He seemed threatened by her independence and began going into her files at night. In public, he would challenge her authority. Then an event occurred in which he did not show up for a churchwide event she organized that required a priest to officiate. She realized that he was out to destroy her credibility and so she resigned. Other colleagues validated these perceptions and she received much acclamation for her work.

As you could imagine, the parallels to her prior abuse experiences did trigger past trauma, but as you will see, there was a spiritual journey embedded in this recent traumatic event.

Pam came to the session and immediately noticed the fresh bunch of lilacs sitting in a vase on a table in my office. She seemed pleased to see these flowers and said, "Oh, those are such beautiful lilacs. Lilacs are supposed to represent goodness."

By this particular session she had already "grieved" the level that seemed to fit the situation. She had to end many significant relationships and leave the work environment that she had created. But she was concerned because "the extent of my rage and grief seems immense and I don't understand why there is so much. I am still crying every day and find it difficult to talk about what happened." Here is an example of how intense emotion and the discharge of the emotion does not engender a process in which she really gains a fresh understanding of what all of this means to her. As she sits with the strong emotion I invite her to sense the felt edge.

Therapist: Take some time now just to notice how all of that grief feels in your body. Notice where in your body and the quality of the sensations. Stay right at that edge with your gentle attention and notice what comes.

Client: (Silence) . . . I know it goes way back. . . . (Tears) . . . I have gone to this church my whole life. . . . Even when I left home and was drinking every night. Somehow I managed to go to church every Sunday. I would wake up with a hangover and go to church. Then I would pray. This was my only home. This was where I connected with a sense of goodness. . . . Oh, I see . . . I have lost my true home.

Therapist: This true home was where you connected to your goodness.

Client: Yes. . . . Now that I look back I can't believe I managed to do that. I really wanted to go. . . . My best friend would pick me up. I would not have been able to get there myself. But she had to go out of her way . . . so I know I really wanted to go . . . otherwise she wouldn't have come.

Notice that even during her drugged states her organism found a way to move toward what was life-giving. There is a long time of silence here. The felt sense continues to open through a slowing down and just sitting with what is *felt*. Then she begins to speak again.

Client: My mother was very religious. Her faith was sincere. She would take me to church as a child. After she died I felt I could still find her there at church. . . . Now that I cannot return to my parish it is as if I am cut off from my mother as well. . . . I know I found my faith through her. . . . It is so scary now. It is like I have lost everything. . . . I cannot go back to the only home I had and I can't find my connection with my mother either.

As another silent pause begins, I notice the client's eyes searching and then resting on the vase of lilacs.

Client: But maybe I can, I can find her in what she loved to do. She loved flowers. She always tended her flowers.

Therapist: Your eyes are looking at the flowers on the table.

Client: In fact she loved lilacs. . . . (Laughs) . . . Oh my, . . . it is amazing to me that I came here and you have lilacs in your office. . . . I feel now that I will be OK . . . that God is still guiding me in my life. . . . I don't know what will come next . . . but I feel more assured now, and hopeful and a little stronger to go forward.

One may think of the *spirit* as moving through the body here. Her body is stirred to go to church. Her body resonated with the symbolic communication expressed through the lilacs. My body felt her noticing the flowers right at the point that she felt her deep connection to her mother and her mother's faith. Her body was moved to look at the lilacs as a *forward direction moving* from the felt connection to her mother to the spiritual symbol of the lilacs. Her body felt the meaning of the symbol (lilacs) and this transformed her spirituality. Now the meaning was within her, no longer dependent upon a particular form for it to manifest. My *felt sense* registered the profound nature of what happened between us. *We both were changed.*

Conclusion and Implications for Culture and Psychotherapy

In this chapter, I addressed how the relationship between experiencing and symbolization illuminates the function of cultural meaning in psychological process. More specifically, I have explored the ways in which the experiential focusing method challenges the cultures of Western medicine and secular psychology. A psychotherapy process that facilitates a direct engagement with the *felt sense* works with the whole person—mind, body, and spirit in interaction with environments of meaning—to effect physical healing, and personal and spiritual growth. This model offers a process definition of health. The Self is not treated as a content, a personality, a pattern, or a structure. Instead, the Self is the capacity to notice and be with whatever is emerging, while allowing new symbolizations to form. A capacity to hold concepts loosely, and to welcome movement and change in a nonjudgmental way, becomes a way of being and relating, rich with meaning and creativity.

This model addresses the limitations of the Cartesian Model and brings a new way of working with the whole person. It moves beyond the usual method of problem solving that relies upon logical thought processes, to an ability to access an intricacy of ordered knowing that is unique to the individual and more complex than we can think. There is a distinction between the emotion and the *felt sense,* a fuzzy edge around an emotion that carries meaning that has not been formed yet. The interactive nature of all human process is seen as fundamental, linking us to environment, cultures, and spirit as a dynamic whole, which engages life beyond particular form.

We live in a complex global village that cries out for better ways to communicate respect for differences among people. Inherent in the *felt sense* is a valuing process. It is not necessary to impose values from the outside as there is a desire to live from a sense of purpose that moves beyond the individual.

Focusing-oriented psychotherapy offers a process model of psychotherapy that enables an intricate differentiation of personal meaning as it emerges from the body in interaction with culture and spirit. Through developing this capacity to be with what is there and wait for the new meaning to form, one's ability to stand one's ground increases, and people are less likely to be controlled by political powers or repressive cultural forces. There will be a furthering of diversity and a nonhierarchical appreciation of differences for the purpose of further development of human potential. A deep empowerment of people becomes possible.

Psychological wellness is fostered through engagement with the *felt sense* level of human process. At this level, mind, body, and spirit are already one interactive whole through which deeply open and creative humanness can thrive and develop. As psychotherapists, we can facilitate the restoration of this inherently natural process within each person and nurture the capacity for each person to heal and continue living to the fullest.

Recently, I had the opportunity to explore the rain forest in Costa Rica. It was an incredible experience to witness the over 100,000 species of living beings all interconnected in such a way that each organism was enhanced by the other. Suddenly, it seemed absurd that Homo sapiens is considered one species. A new vision of social wellness became clear. I thought, this is what Focusing is all about—an ongoing process of symbolizing felt experience that enables the intricacy of personal meaning, beyond known forms and categories, to express and articulate through interaction with the diversity among us. Oppression, categorization, cultural bias, the violent control of other beings and nations all work against the inherent value of each human life.

Fundamentally, once we have put a person in a category we have lost this essential connection to the *felt sense* and the power of differentiating felt meaning. As the world learns of this process, we will evolve a way of being in which diversity and human dignity thrive together. Human relationships will be based upon valuing the intricacy and fresh creations that continue to emerge through an empathic understanding and inherent valuing of each other.

References

Gendlin, E. T. (1962). *Experiencing and the creation of meaning.* Toronto, ON: Free Press of Glencoe.

Gendlin, E. T. (1981). *Focusing.* New York: Bantam.

Gendlin, E. T. (1987). A philosophical critique of the concept of narcissism: The significance of the awareness movement. In D. M. Levin (Ed.), *Pathologies of the modern self: Postmodern studies on narcissism, schizophrenia, and depression* (pp. 251–305). New York: New York University Press.

Gendlin, E. T. (1991). On emotion in therapy. In J. D. Saphran & L. S. Greenberg (Eds.), *Emotion, psychotherapy and change* (pp. 255–279). New York: Guilford.

Gendlin, E. T. (1996). *Focusing-oriented psychotherapy*. New York: Guilford.

Gendlin, E. T. (1997a). How philosophy cannot appeal to experience, and how it can. In D. M. Levin & J. McCumber (Eds.), *Language beyond postmodernism: Saying and thinking in Gendlin's philosophy* (pp. 3–42). Evanston, IL: Northwestern University Press.

Gendlin, E. T. (1997b). *A process model*. New York: The Focusing Institute. (On-line at www.focusing.org)

Gendlin, E. T., Beebe, J., III, Cassens, M. J., Klein, M., & Oberlander, M. (1968). Focusing ability in psychotherapy, personality, and creativity. In J. M. Shlien (Ed.), *Research in psychotherapy, 3* (pp. 217–241). Washington, DC: American Psychological Association.

Gendlin, E. T., Grindler, D., & McGuire, M. (1984). Imagery, body, space in focusing. In A. Shiekh (Ed.), *Imagination and healing* (pp. 259–286). Farmingdale, NY: Baywood.

Grindler Katonah, D. (1991). *Focusing: An adjunct treatment for adaptive recovery from cancer*. Unpublished doctoral dissertation, Illinois School of Professional Psychology, Chicago.

Grindler Katonah, D. (1999a). Case study: A six-week training in focusing with someone who has cancer. *The Folio: A Journal for Focusing and Experiential Therapy, 18*(1), 6–42.

Grindler Katonah, D. (1999b). A journey of transformation and focusing when an illness threatens. *The Folio: A Journal for Focusing and Experiential Therapy, 18*(1), 56–62.

Hendricks, M. (1986). Experiencing level as a therapeutic variable. *Person-Centered Review, 1*,141–162.

Hendricks, M. (2001). Focusing-oriented/experiential psychotherapy. In D. Cain & J. Seeman (Eds.), *Humanistic psychotherapies: Handbook of research and practice* (pp. 221–251). Ross-on-Wye, UK: PCCS Books.

Hendricks, M. (2003). *A felt sense is not an emotion: It is a new human development*. New York: The Focusing Institute. (On-line at www.focusing.org)

Ikemi, A. (2001). Presence, existence and space: Key concepts in focusing-oriented psychotherapy. In A. Weiser Cornell (Ed.), *The Focusing Connection, 18*(1), 1–4.

Ikemi, A. (2003). Research themes and characteristic research methodologies in the Japanese *Journal of Humanistic Psychology* [In Japanese]. *Journal of Humanistic Psychology, 21*(2), 263–266.

Kanter, M. (1999). Clearing a space with four cancer patients. *The Folio: A Journal for Focusing and Experiential Therapy, 18*(1), 27–36.

Kirschner, E. (2004, October). Focus on: Atsmaout Perlstein. *Staying in Focus: The Focusing Institute Newsletter, 6*, 8.

Krycka, K. (1999). The recovery of will in persons with AIDS. *The Folio: A Journal for Focusing and Experiential Therapy, 18*(1), 80-93.

Lawrence, N. J. (2004). Focusing in Afghanistan. *Staying in Focus: The Focusing Institute Newsletter, 4*(2), 1–2.

Levin, D. M. (1997). Gendlin's use of language: Historical connections, contemporary implications. In D. M. Levin (Ed.), *Language beyond postmodernism: Saying and thinking in Gendlin's philosophy* (pp. 42–65). Evanston, IL: Northwestern University Press.

Lutgendorf, S., Antoni, M. H., Kumar, M., & Schneiderman, M. (1994). Changes in cognitive coping strategies predict EBV-antibody titre change following a stressor disclosure induction. *Journal of Psychosomatic Research, 38*(1), 63–77.

Merton, T. (1968). *Zen and the birds of appetite.* New York: A New Directions Book.

Rogers, C. R. (1951). *Client-centered therapy.* Boston: Houghton Mifflin.

Stern, D. G. (1996). *Wittgenstein on mind and language.* New York: Oxford University Press.

Tart, C. (2000). *States of consciousness.* Lincoln, NE: iUniverse.com, Inc.

Walsh, R., & Vaughan, F. (1996). Comparative models of the person and psychotherapy. In S. Boorstein (Ed.), *Transpersonal psychotherapy* (Rev. ed., pp. 15–30). Albany: State University of New York Press.

Wilber, K. (2000). *Integral psychology: Consciousness, spirit, psychology, therapy.* Boston: Shambhala.

Young, A. E. (1998). Ways of knowing respectful, powerful relationship. *The Folio: A Journal for Focusing and Experiential Therapy, 17*(1), 7–15.

5

Integrating the World's Psychologies

William L. Mikulas

In the first part of this chapter, according to the goals for the book, I discuss some personal influences and experiences that have shaped my perceptions and knowledge. These examples are vehicles to discuss some general issues related to gender/cultural differences, Eastern and Western psychologies, and the development of integrative therapies. I introduce my approach of Conjunctive Psychology, an integrated psychology that draws from all the world's psychologies. In the second part of the chapter, I show how aspects of Conjunctive Psychology apply to two cases. Buddhism is intertwined throughout.

A Modern Pythagorean

Pythagoras was a Greek who taught in Southern Italy from about 530 BCE to about 500 BCE, around the same time as the Buddha was teaching. For Pythagoras, number is the essence of reality and mathematics is the key to reality, a position I do not take literally, but to which I resonate on an experiential level.

Author's Note: Connie Works, my production assistant, was invaluable in the creation of this chapter.

For as long as I can remember, I have had a deep love for mathematics, which continues today. For me, an elegant proof is a thing of beauty and mathematics is a description of the manifestation of the fundamental ground. Among many other mathematical topics, I love number theory, logic systems, and recreational mathematics. I love music, which is totally intertwined with mathematics as Pythagoras was one of the first to demonstrate.

I think that my mathematical orientation has helped me see past form to essence. I can see the essence of a theory, meditation practice, or spiritual path, beyond the specific forms. For example, I can see the type of mental training that is occurring during meditation, independent of the meditation tradition, what the body is doing, the object of meditation, or the attitude toward meditation. Most of the current Western misunderstandings and prejudices about meditation confuse form with essence. And, it is at the level of essence where we can most easily and most effectively integrate disparate psychologies and therapies.

Also, starting about the age of 13, mathematics was my first serious introduction to alternative realities. For example, our consensus reality consists of three physical dimensions. But, perhaps this reality is a subset or cross section of a more basic reality of more than three physical dimensions. It is intellectually stimulating to consider a higher reality of four physical dimensions (time is not a physical dimension), and some people may have experienced this reality (Rucker, 1984). Current cosmologies in physics suggest universes with 10 to 25 dimensions.

I went to college as a math and physics major and gradually drifted into psychology. Here, the behavioral sciences in general, and learning theories in particular, most spoke to me and my mathematical/scientific view of things. Behavior modification was a logical extension.

Years later, when I was a young college professor, we brought Rollo May to our campus. May was the leading existential psychotherapist, and the two of us had a public dialogue comparing, contrasting, and combining existential and behavioral approaches. This led to a small friendship over the years. One time we reflected on what we had learned from our various conversations. His main point was how our personal backgrounds led us to the type of psychology we practiced and advocated. My math and physics background led to behavior modification. May, on the hand, was interested in art, philosophy, and psychoanalysis; and he was a minister for two years. He was introduced to existentialism by his mentor Paul Tillich, a Protestant theologian and existential philosopher, at a time when general interest in existentialism was at its peak. Tuberculosis put May in a sanitarium for 18 months, and the continual closeness of death made existentialism even more meaningful. Relative to a theme of this book, existentialists often come to see the arbitrariness of the culturally conditional reality, and then try to find or establish some meaning and authenticity in life.

Before Rollo May, I was certainly intellectually aware of how one's personal path influences one's view, but my interactions with May made this particularly clear. What had seemed obvious to me about psychology became less universal and complete. Michael DeMaria (2001) is my current friend in the existential/phenomenological domain.

According to May, anxiety is a result of a threat to one's existence as a self (e.g., May, 1967). In Buddhism, we talk about the anxiety that results from clinging to a sense of self and challenges to this self, and the basic desire to become and the desire not to become. Near the end of his healthy life, I asked Rollo if he thought Buddhism might provide a "solution" to some of the existential issues; he thought so.

Where Have All the Flowers Gone?

I was a student at the University of Michigan throughout the 1960s, where I got all my college degrees. I received a good education in classrooms and labs, and a better education in the surrounding social/political environment, including being a member of a fraternity and observing and playing many sports. It was a wonderful time and place for a person like me, a time of great social change and challenging of cultural and political assumptions. I was involved with many political action groups, at first focusing on civil rights and the Kennedy-Nixon election, and later the Vietnam conflict. Through the election of Kennedy, we brought Camelot to America and ended the political career of Nixon, or so we thought.

The 1960s were also marked by a resurgence of the women's movement, which I naturally supported; power to my sisters in their fight for equality and justice. I have stayed aware and supportive of women's issues ever since. Relative to this, I think we are now at a plateau of naive complacency. That is, there is a sense that we have identified almost all of the gender biases, although we still need changes in the marketplace. People who consider themselves moderately aware and politically correct in this area often are quite unaware of the prevalence of gender biases in their own thinking and perceptions. This naive complacency has slowed the women's movement.

Western psychology is filled with inadequately explored gender biases, related to such things as type of therapy, goals of therapy and personal growth, processes of development, and nature of the self (Mikulas, 2002). For example, self-actualization is often offered as a criterion or goal for mental health; but this is a Western White male value. In most of Asia and the

Middle East, individualistic self-actualization is a sign of mental illness and/or immorality, and it is not highly valued among many Western women and non-White minorities (e.g., Cross & Madson, 1997; Dwairy & Van Sickle, 1996; Hoshmand & Ho, 1995). Integrating the world's psychologies requires developing a perspective that is superordinate to, and free from, gender/cultural biases.

Largely unexplored are the gender biases in the whole scientific/experimental approach. I strongly value this methodology, but I also realize it is a restricted Western White male epistemology. It generates a certain type of data and knowing, which is very important, but incomplete. A more powerful and integrated psychology must include other types of knowing (Hart, Nelson, & Puhakka, 2000; Mikulas, 2002; Wilber, 1996). For example, in Buddhist psychology primary emphasis is given to the cultivation of prajna, immediately experienced intuitive wisdom, a nonconceptual form of insight. Experimental data and conceptual knowing certainly may be part of the antecedents for personal change, but they rarely, on their own, directly result in significant personal growth. Prajna, on the other hand, transforms and purifies one's being. For example, conceptually knowing that everything changes does not alter one's being, but experientially observing this change in an insightful way may reduce one's attachment to things as a source of happiness. An interesting question is how prajna relates to the type of insight postulated in some psychotherapies.

While I was a graduate student, some of the women students started developing ideas for courses and programs in women's psychology. I supported women's rights, but could not see the need for a whole course in women's psychology, until I talked with the women! I was shocked by my ignorance, and came to realize that women lived in a different reality than mine (Schaef, 1981). This view was reinforced by the consciousness exploration of alternative realities that many of us were engaged in at the time.

Also, while I was a student, behavior modification was coming together as a field. This was very exciting and controversial, as the basic assumptions of the powerful and dominant psychoanalytic positions were being challenged. At Michigan, like almost all such schools, behavior modification was a questionable to unacceptable topic in psychology. Clinicians considered it too experimental, and experimentalists considered it too clinical. When fellow student Bill Sheppard and I put together the first Michigan psychology course in behavior modification, we could not call it by that name; rather, it was called "Experimental Bases of Clinical Behavior." It would be a number of years before Michigan had another course in behavior modification. In addition to behavior modification being a logical extension of my interest in learning, it also fit my social/political agenda of empowering the people, in this case through behavioral self-control. I still strongly believe that therapies and personal growth programs that emphasize the development of behavioral self-control are usually the best way to maximize cooperation, generalization, maintenance, freedom, choice, positive self-concept and self-esteem, self-efficacy, and internal locus of control (Mikulas, 1986, 2002). It is also a good way to make the treatment program less expensive, and it facilitates consideration of therapeutic objectives and related ethical issues.

Hello World

A strong feature of the University of Michigan is the large number of international students, about 8,000 when I was there. This resulted in a very active International Center and many international clubs focusing on various cultural, religious, and political topics. I immersed myself in the international community in many ways. Near the end of my student days, I met and later married Benita, an extraordinary lady from Germany.

Since my first trip outside North America as an undergraduate, I have been an avid traveler. Benita's family gave me a door into the German culture and a base for us to explore Europe. We have now traveled through much of the world and lived in different parts for varying amounts of time. I have been a visiting professor in Ireland (University College of Dublin) and Thailand (Srinakharinwirot University), and am currently an honorary professor in Argentina (University of Flores) and a visiting professor in Thailand (Chulalongkorn University).

My association with two Thai universities and my continual involvement with Thai students and faculty has taught me much about the wonderful Thai culture. In addition, the king of Thailand is one of the world's great leaders. Living in Thailand was an extraordinary opportunity for me to learn about and practice the form of Buddhism that was most important for me at the time. In addition, I have had the good fortune to be involved with several international organizations concerned with integrating world psychologies, particularly the blending of Eastern and Western psychologies. Especially important for me was the Transnational Network for the Study of Physical, Psychological, and Spiritual Well-being (Mikulas, 2003). I learned much from this group and made a number of good friends. They also put out many books that are good resources for integrating psychologies and therapies (e.g., Kaku, 2000).

From an international perspective, what constitutes health, including mental health, is very culturally influenced. For example, a Western therapist might stress independence, assertiveness, nonconformity, competition, freedom, individual needs, expression of feelings, and self-actualization, while an Eastern therapist might stress interdependence, compliance, conformity, cooperation, security, collective goals, control of feelings, and collective actualization (Ho, 1985). Similarly, there are strong cultural biases in types of therapy. Consider the traditional Western talk therapy, where one tells a stranger personal details of one's life. This is basically a Western female therapy; Western men do not respond to it as well (a major issue in the men's movement), and it does not suit most Asians.

A Generalist in a Specialist World

I learned a lot while at the University of Michigan, but I never fit into the psychology department's very specialized categories. For example, one semester I was coteaching a course in behavior modification and helping in research with single-cell recording. Another semester, I was studying classroom learning and the biology of memory. This was great experience for me, but strange behavior to the Michigan specialists. My journey through the graduate program was much bumpier and more varied than for most students. But it all fit together for me under the domain of learning, including behavioral research, biological correlates, and applications in clinic, home, school, and workplace. Learning has stayed central to my academic understanding, teaching, and research (Mikulas, 1974, 1977, 1978) and is a major vehicle for integrating psychologies and therapies (Mikulas, 2002).

But back to the issue of specialization. The history of Western thought has generally been one of fractionalization and specialization. Religion and science battle and carve out their own domains. Science breaks into many separate disciplines, which develop their own terminology and programs. Psychology separates from philosophy and divides into two feuding camps: experimentalists and clinicians. Clinical psychology gradually disintegrates into a mass of contradictory theories and therapies. Academicians reward themselves for very specialized research and thinking.

This specialization has gone way too far in North American mainstream academic psychology (NAMAP). Within this approach, in order to do clean and unconfounded research on therapies, most investigators study a very simple form of "therapy" that is usually just a piece of the therapeutic package a sophisticated therapist would individualize for a particular client.

Therapists in the field usually require a treatment package that is much more complex and integrated than the therapies traditionally taught and researched in NAMAP. And for those of us developing integrated therapies, the overspecialized approach is missing many of the most important dynamics that take place at superordinate levels. Common and significant examples here include exactly how psychological attitudes affect biological health, how behavioral changes impact self-concept and conversely, the interrelationships between behavior modification and transpersonal awakening, and the true nature of happiness and peace of mind.

Within NAMAP, a popular question has been: What is the best treatment for depression—cognitive behavior therapy and/or antidepressant drugs? But from a generalist position, there are many possible causes of depression, including brain disorders, biological cycles, seasonal effects, positive ions, environmental allergies, food sensitivities, nutritional deficiencies, immune system suppression, inadequate reinforcement, conditioned emotional responses, problematic thoughts, low self-esteem, discrepancy between self and ideal self, and a wide range of beliefs and self-fulfilling prophecies (Mikulas, 2002). Different causes would require very different types of therapy.

Eastern Psychologies

Whereas the history of Western thought (Western Europe, North America) has been dominated by fractionalization and specialization, Eastern thought (primarily Asia) has remained more integrated. Eastern psychologies are totally intertwined with biology, sociology, and religion. In traditional Asian cultures, there is no word or role for a psychologist; it makes no sense to treat a person's mind and behaviors without also working with nutrition, life-force/energy, lifestyle, family relations, meditation, spiritual practices, and environmental influences. In fact, in most of the world psychological health is a subset of overall health. Eastern and Western psychologies are very different, including what constitutes data and research, how the individual is influenced by cosmic forces and central dynamics, such as those related to life-force, which is a concept fundamental to Eastern psychologies and marginal in Western psychologies. The two sets of psychologies cover different ground; one is not "better" than the other, and there are strengths and weaknesses to both. But integrating them yields a psychology that is superordinate to both, and integrative therapies that are much more powerful than can be found in either one alone.

Eastern psychologies have been influenced by, and intertwined with, Indian yoga, Chinese Taoism, and Buddhism. I am interested in and draw from all of these, but it is Buddhism that most speaks to me personally. Appealing to me is that basic Buddhism, as taught by the historical Buddha, is not philosophy or religion, and there is nothing to be taken on faith. Rather, it is a practical psychology in which one sees for oneself how the basic teachings (*dharma*) relate and work for oneself. It is a very direct way to reduce suffering and facilitate transpersonal awakening, by going to the essence of the relevant dynamics. Within the many forms of Buddhism are many rituals and devotional practices, which are good for some people, but not for me. My practice is the cultivation of awareness (mindfulness) as found in the *vipassana* literature (e.g., Goldstein, 1993), and I am inspired by Zen's direct pointing to the awakened perspective (e.g., Suzuki, 1970).

In traditional Buddhist cultures (e.g., Tibetan, Southeast Asian), Buddhist psychology is embedded in a religious cosmology of *reincarnation* and *karma*, which strongly influences the beliefs and actions of most practitioners. For example, most Thai people will do things to generate "merit" to improve the next incarnation of themselves or family, and many Tibetans cultivate compassion by reminding themselves that anyone could have been their mother in a previous life. Some people believe Buddhism should stay embedded in such cultural cosmologies, even though this was not the teaching of the Buddha. Others, like me, are working to separate Buddhist psychology and adapt it to other cultures. Also, in traditional Buddhist cultures, institutionalized Buddhism is usually patriarchal, hierarchical, and authoritarian. This has created limitations for women in these cultures and conflict when such approaches were brought to the United States. Currently, an American form of Buddhism is evolving, which is more democratic, more open to women and lay practitioners, and less bound to a specific Buddhist tradition.

Relevant to my personal social/political agenda, a strong feature of Buddhism is to freely give away the teachings to whoever is interested. It is common in many Buddhist retreats for there to be no charge, but people have the opportunity to make a contribution (*dana*) to support the organization and/or teacher. I regularly give free programs for the community on Buddhist practices and related topics. Also, on my university website are a number of my books that anyone can access for free. This is great for my work in economically poor countries, and a couple of the books are often accessed by community people and referred to clients by therapists (Mikulas, 1983, 1987).

What has had the biggest influence on Western culture and thought in the last 50 years? To me and others there are two answers: computer technology and the influx of Eastern thought. Eastern thought is influencing art, philosophy, religion, economics, ecology, and psychology. Probably, the vast majority of people reading this have had some exposure to an Eastern-based practice such as yoga, meditation, breathwork, tai chi, martial arts, acupuncture, or chi kung. Currently, in the United States, there are at least a million Buddhists, 7 million regular practitioners of hatha yoga, and 10 million regular practitioners of an Eastern-based meditation. Western psychology in the near future will have to be very different due to the interest and demand of these people, in addition to the overall power of the Eastern practices. At many psychology conferences in the last few decades, talks and workshops on Eastern practices usually draw the biggest attendance.

Despite all of this, Eastern psychologies are conspicuously absent in most of NAMAP's courses, curricula, texts, and journals. There are many reasons for this. First is that most of the people in power are unfamiliar with the Eastern literatures and often reluctant to learn. We need to wait for the next generation of psychologists coming in now. Second, since Eastern psychologies are intertwined with religion, NAMAP considers them religion and therefore irrelevant and/or inappropriate. In the United States, Buddhism is almost always in departments of religion and/or philosophy. But, basic Buddhism is not religion or philosophy, as the Buddha continually emphasized; it is psychology! (There is, of course, a wonderful set of religions and a rich philosophy grounded in basic Buddhism, and philosophers can argue that any psychology is an applied philosophy.) I teach a course in Buddhist psychology, and there may be a few others; but, from my point of view, this should be a standard course in most psychology departments. I think this will eventually happen because Buddhist psychology is so powerful and applicable.

What particularly saddens me is the arrogant provincialism that is very common in NAMAP, although often simply due to ignorance. For example, a very prevalent attitude is: Do not tell me about Eastern psychological concepts until you have Western-style research to support them. Through this attitude, one chooses to disregard a massive body of knowledge and research, collected over thousands of years, and across very disparate cultures (Kwee, 1990; Mikulas, 1991; Sheikh & Sheikh, 1996)! As another example, the main North American group focusing on developing integrative therapies currently restricts itself to only considering Western therapies. This is a very limited approach compared to the integration of Eastern and Western therapies that is happening at the international level. In the last few years, this group had a series of articles in their journal (*Journal of Psychotherapy Integration*) identifying mindfulness as a central component in therapy integration, which it clearly is. At this point, one should turn to Buddhist psychology, the world psychology that, by far, has the best understanding of the nature and cultivation of mindfulness. But instead of seeking out this information, or even being open to it, this group chose to simply ask each other what they meant and thought about mindfulness.

As a third example, consider meditation, which worldwide is probably the most used practice for improving the health of body, mind, and spirit. But, again, knowledgeable discussion of meditation is basically absent from NAMAP's texts and curricula. When meditation is discussed, it is usually just a paragraph or two, and most of the time it is described as one way to produce relaxation, often in the context of stress reduction. But relaxation is just one result of one type of meditation; there are many much more important results, such as *prajna,* opening the heart, and reducing attachments. Sometimes meditation is discussed relative to different states of consciousness, but some of what I have read appears to be inaccurate and confused relative to my knowledge of the literature. In addition to the inadequate knowledge about meditation, there is basically no formal training in various meditation practices and how they can be incorporated into therapy. In my ideal program for training future counselors and therapists, I would require all students to learn and practice meditation, to cultivate listening and empathy skills, among many other reasons.

Conjunctive Psychology

I am a member of NAMAP, which has treated me well; I honor this. Thus, I regularly do my best to facilitate NAMAP's evolution. But some time ago, I realized I did not have the time or patience to deal with the inertia and politics. So I made up my own psychology called Conjunctive Psychology (Mikulas, 2002), and teach a course with that name. This is not something I intend to recruit for; it is simply a pedagogic tool.

Conjunctive Psychology draws from all the world's psychologies and health systems, including Western psychology, Buddhist psychology, the yogic sciences, *ayurveda,* Chinese medicine, and Native American wisdom and practices. And it integrates this knowledge across the four levels of being: biological, behavioral, personal, and transpersonal. (For the transpersonal, see Cortright, 1997; Walsh & Vaughan, 1993.) Emphasis is given to heuristic models and implications for therapy and personal growth, ways of conceptualizing that most directly suggest practical interventions. It is definitely not postmodern in that it seems obvious to me that there are universal principles of existence and behavior, and these universals allow for the integration of world psychologies. For example, in Buddhism one of the fundamental "marks of existence" is that everything changes.

I believe that there are general principles by which the universe moves from one state to the next, principles described in part by our theories of evolution and learning, which are much more intertwined than are usually discussed (e.g., Skinner, 1975). For example, the operant conditioning principles of how reinforcement works are universal worldwide, but what is reinforcing and reinforced varies tremendously among cultures and individuals. Postmodern theorists focus on the great diversity found in the specific forms of behavior; I focus on the essence of the universal principles by which behaviors are learned.

Particularly important in Conjunctive Psychology are principles and practices that cut across levels of being. For example, I suggest that there are universal somato-psycho-spiritual practices that impact all levels of being, improving the health of body, mind, and spirit. That is, the same practice improves biological health, psychological functioning and well-being, and spiritual awakening. Four such universal practices are quieting the mind, increasing awareness, opening the heart, and reducing attachments (Mikulas, 1987, 2002). Attachments are mental clinging to things such as perceptions, rituals, expectancies, opinions, assumptions, images of self, and models of reality. I think therapists should, as much as possible, incorporate these four universal practices into their therapies and their own personal practices.

In Conjunctive Psychology the optimal therapist or counselor, what I call the integrative helper, works on all of these levels of being simultaneously, although one or more levels may be emphasized at a particular time. Also, the levels of being, from biological to transpersonal, describe some practical sequences. As a general rule, with many exceptions, biological issues should be moderately resolved before behavioral issues, behavioral before personal, and personal before transpersonal. Also, psychological development, including development of the self, tends to move from the biological to the transpersonal. There are interesting correlations here with Maslow's hierarchy of needs, the yogic *chakra* system (Mikulas, 2002), and the developmental stages of a therapy or personal growth group (Gilchrist & Mikulas, 1993).

Returning to Rollo May and one of the main things I learned from our conversations, I would say that existential therapies focus on the transition from the personal level to the transpersonal level. In my model, most clients are not ready to deal with existential issues until they have first dealt with biological, behavioral, and personal issues. Hence, behavior modification usually precedes existential psychotherapy.

Tantra

There are three major branches of Buddhism. First was Hinayana Buddhism, currently represented by Theravada Buddhism in Southeast Asia and Sri Lanka. Emphasis here is on ordering one's life along moral and practical guidelines, cultivating concentration and mindfulness, and reducing craving and clinging (quieting the mind, increasing awareness, reducing attachments). Later came Mahayana Buddhism, which added an emphasis on opening the heart. (Zen is usually considered a form of Mahayana, but I think it is closer to Hinayana.) Still later came Vajrayana Buddhism, as represented by Tibetan Buddhism, which incorporated *tantra*.

The word *tantra* in Sanskrit has meanings such as continuum, extend, context, and loom. In Vajrayana, it involves the recognition of the continuity of the enlightened state within the unenlightened state; they are not separate. This includes the profound understanding that one is already fully enlightened, even if the personal-level self does not realize it. In Conjunctive Psychology, I propose that the transpersonal level of being is always already present; it simply has to be uncovered. Essentially, there is no difference between the sacred and the profane; one can just as easily spiritually awaken while cleaning up dog poop as chanting in the temple. A full understanding of this is critical to anyone seriously involved on a spiritual path.

More generally speaking, what all this means is that the issues of daily living, such as conflicts with a coworker, are not only important for biological and psychological health, but also are the optimal opportunities for spiritual awakening. One can have success in the world and enlightenment, the main appeal of *tantra* when it first began as a major force in Asia. One can work on all levels of being simultaneously, as with the universal practices.

In the last few decades many Americans went to Asia to live a monastic life for a few years. While there some discovered very clear, calm, and centered states of consciousness. But when they returned home, they were disappointed to find how quickly they were thrown off by their old attachments. For example, a significant other could still push the buttons to make one angry. Creating a space where attachments are not elicited does not reduce the attachments. On the other hand, reducing attachments deals with issues of daily living, and simultaneously allows enlightenment to be uncovered. This parallels the Buddha's pre-enlightenment experiences, where he found that the yogic practices of the time could suppress defilements, but did not reduce them. Buddhist practices reduce defilements, such as anger and greed.

In my ideal world there would be no such sport as boxing. But when circumstances led my good friend Stanley Levin to become involved with amateur and professional boxing (e.g., he was the promoter and lawyer for Roy Jones, Jr.), I saw the *tantric* side of the sport. For example, there were many street kids caught up in heavy drugs who quickly headed for a life of crime and jail. But some of these kids got free from the drugs by coming into the gym and physically working out, punching on bags, and learning discipline from the trainer. Talk therapies, cognitive behavior therapy, and other therapies we teach would not reach or work for these kids.

In the United States, we college professors were very disappointed by the students of the 1990s. Compared to students of the prior 50 years, these students were less involved in politics, social issues, interpersonal relationships, and their own education; and they were often sarcastic about those who were involved. They were very passive and very easily bored, demanding that the external world feed and entertain them. They felt they had a right to be given a degree; they were not interested in actively becoming educated. Again, I am overstating things and there were many exceptions. But the absence of a *tantric* approach to life, a zestful engagement with life, is going to create many severe problems for many of these people, including effects on biological health, psychological wellness and happiness, marital and vocational relationships, and personal growth.

Finally, it has long been my intention to become as invisible as possible. I actively avoid academic fame, personal promotion, and autobiographical reference. I avoid having my picture taken and stay off of TV. For the early Pythagoreans one chose what type of person to be: lover of wisdom, lover of success, or lover of pleasure. The first was considered the best, which is my choice; but as a *tantric* practitioner, I have no problem with pleasure. So, when I was asked to write this chapter, my immediate response was of course not; I have no interest in writing anything autobiographical. But then my *tantric* side got me to agree, thinking it might be a good way to make some important points.

Case Examples

Below are two case examples that illustrate a Conjunctive Psychology approach to therapy. Both examples were chosen because of the inclusion of components from Eastern psychologies, one of the themes of this chapter. If a client has a spiritual orientation, I will talk and work within that tradition, such as Christianity or Hinduism. If not, I will utilize whatever conceptualizations fit the client. One property of behavior modification, as I approach it, is that it is less culturally biased than many other therapies, and thus easier to fit in with and show examples from a variety of spiritual traditions, including Christianity/Judaism (Lasure & Mikulas, 1996) and Buddhism (de Silva, 1984).

The two case examples are somewhat fabricated: Names and some details have been changed to protect the clients, the cases have been simplified and cleaned up for clarity of discussion, and a number of side issues have been deleted. The descriptions, however, are very accurate in terms of the dynamics of the processes and interventions. Other cases could be offered to make the same points.

Yoga

Michelle suffered from anxiety and depression. Drugs had provided some relief, but she was reluctant to up the level of this approach. Counseling helped her understand the causes better, but provided little relief. What she did like was a hatha yoga class, where the combination of exercise and relaxation seemed natural and helpful. She discussed her psychological problems with her yoga instructor, who referred her to me for further direction.

When she first met with me, she said she was interested in "yoga and meditation therapy." Further discussion and assessment, greatly aided by her previous counseling, identified a cluster of interrelated problems. First was her general inability to relax, which I could see in the tension in her body and her shallow breathing. Second was an agitated mind that regularly generated problematic thoughts outside of her control, thoughts that elicited anxiety, anger, and depression. Additional thoughts about these emotions compounded the problem, such as being anxious about being anxious or anxious about lack of control. Third were memories of when she had been mistreated by others, the most traumatic being memories of physical abuse by an uncle. Various situations and thoughts elicited these memories, which elicited anger or depression, which elicited anxiety, which elicited a feeling of helplessness, and so on.

I strongly encouraged her to continue her hatha yoga classes, and, because of her interests, all of our discussions were from a yogic perspective. I told her I would teach her meditation to control her mind, but this was not the place to start. I explained that in yoga we want to do things with the body to prepare for meditation, and breathwork was a place for her to begin. We discussed the yogic science of breath (*pranayama*) and its various benefits.

There are many reasons I began with breathwork with her. It was obvious from watching her breathing that this was a critical area. Breathwork is a good way to relax and an excellent lead-in to later meditation. It was something she could quickly learn and apply, thus increasing her sense of self-control and optimism about, and patience with, later interventions such as meditation. I have come to believe that breathwork is one of the most applicable therapeutic interventions, although seldom used by Western psychologists.

On the first treatment day, Michelle learned about the differences between chest breathing and diaphragm breathing, and how exactly to do diaphragm breathing. She was given related homework assignments with a heavy mindfulness component; that is, she was instructed to pay careful, detailed and nonjudgmental attention to the body sensations accompanying her breathwork. Some concentration practice was introduced, in that whenever her mind left her body sensations, she should gently and firmly bring her attention back.

On the second treatment day, she was given instructions on how to be more mindful of her breathing throughout the day. When she noticed shallow breathing, she would correct it. She also learned a basic thought-stopping procedure. Whenever an undesirable thought arose, she would shout "STOP" in her mind and mindfully take a few deep breaths. She understood that this was just a temporary practice until she learned stronger forms of mental control. The fact that this was something she could quickly learn and apply increased her optimism, motivation, and self-efficacy. On the third treatment day, I had her close her eyes, relax with deep breathing, watch her breathing, and realistically imagine situations that elicited some anxiety. She could watch her breathing change, and then use her self-control skill to alter her breathing and re-relax. I gave her related homework practice.

On the fourth treatment day, we began progressive muscle relaxation, where she learned to sequentially tense and relax various muscle groups. Again, mindfulness was emphasized, paying careful attention to body feelings, both during tension and relaxation. She practiced this at home, both with and without audiotaped instructions. Throughout the training she learned how to periodically mindfully scan her body for places of tension to relax. Particularly important for Michelle was learning to relax muscles in her neck and shoulders, where tension was a common source of headaches. All of this nicely dovetailed with her hatha yoga practice.

Gradually we combined her breathwork skills and muscle relaxation skills into one basic self-control skill. She learned how to notice in her body when she was upset, regardless of how this might be cognitively labeled (e.g., anxiety, anger) and then relax. Mindfulness training helped her to notice this earlier and earlier in the chain of events, and thus made it easier to change or avoid.

With this powerful self-control skill, she practiced at home with imagined scenes, as she had learned to do earlier just with breathwork. She started with scenes that produced a small amount of dis-ease, such as anger or anxiety, and then gradually moved into some that produced greater and greater dis-ease. Because of the range and variety of situations that elicited dis-ease, this was a more effective approach than developing structured hierarchies as in desensitization. Simultaneously, she was cultivating this self-control skill in real-life situations, as they arose, and some that she intentionally put herself in. For example, one time she visited a store where she had been cheated. She was very pleased that she could do this without being upset.

In parallel with this, a couple of weeks into therapy, we began meditation, which she was really looking forward to. In fact, the mindfulness and concentration instructions embedded in the breathwork and muscle relaxation training had already started this. Her hatha yoga classes often ended with some type of meditation, but this was usually a form of guided imagery, rather than the mental training we would do. In her hatha yoga class, however, she did learn how to comfortably and easily sit in the full lotus position. Although I do not recommend or require this of people I teach to meditate, I am delighted when one can do it and we can use it for meditation.

So her meditation practice was a basic concentration practice, with mindfulness as an important but secondary component. She would sit in full lotus with eyes closed and her attention on the rising and falling of her diaphragm. Whenever she became aware of her attention having left her diaphragm, she would gently and firmly bring it back. This type of meditation had two important interrelated effects for her. First, it helped her quiet her mind, which added to her ability to relax. Second, she eventually learned how to control her thoughts to a large extent. When a thought arose, she could stop it or let it go.

The attitude of meditation is the component of meditation practice that is least well understood in the West, but it is very important (cf. Mikulas, 2002). It is the mental set in which one approaches meditation, with optimal attitude including persistent dedication, a welcoming openness to experience, and being in the here and now. Meditation practice is a microcosm of living in general, in that one's attitude toward meditation is often one's attitude toward many other activities, but the attitude may be easier to observe during a "simple" activity such as a sitting breath meditation. For Michelle, learning how to make friends with herself during meditation helped her make friends with herself in all situations, an important component in reducing her depression.

Finally, Michelle learned to do lovingkindness meditation (cf. Salzberg, 1997). We constructed a hierarchy of people, beginning with her sister whom she loved the most and gradually moving through people she liked less and less, ending with the uncle who had abused her. She learned how to meditate on a person while feeling lovingkindness toward that person. She very gradually worked her way through the hierarchy, the last half being completed months after we had stopped meeting. To her great surprise, she was eventually able to think about the uncle without being thrown into anger or depression. Note that this does not mean she forgot or condoned what the uncle had done, but she freed herself from the memory continually hurting her.

This was the essence of Michelle's therapy. Five years later, the last I heard from her, life was still very good for her. She had pursued other things we had discussed, such as joining Weight Watchers and a health spa, and learning more about *ayurveda,* the natural healing system of India, which is heavily intertwined with yoga. She is now a yoga instructor.

Hinduism and Zen

Mia was raised a Christian in Midwest United States. Her spiritual quest led her to India where she found her guru and became a Hindu and a practitioner of *bhakti yoga,* the path of love, service, and devotion. Jarod was raised a Jew in the Northeast United States where he discovered Zen Buddhism and became an ardent Zen practitioner. Mia and Jarod met at an eclectic spiritual retreat in New York, discovered each other's central passion for spiritual work, got married, and later moved to northwest Florida.

Despite their central common interests in spiritual work, their first 2 years of marriage had many conflicts. They sought out marriage counseling, which was moderately helpful, particularly related to learning better communication. But the counselor's inability to incorporate the spiritual component they felt was too limiting. After attending one of my free community lecture series on universal spiritual practices, they came to consult with me.

Mia found Zen too cold and impersonal; she wanted to sing and dance with joy (figuratively and literally speaking), not sit in a corner. She felt Zen made Jarod distant, authoritative, and too detail-oriented. Jarod felt that Mia's practice was too superficial and "fluffy," and caused her to be irresponsible in the duties of daily living. We had wonderful conversations, sometimes as a trio and sometimes as a duo.

For Jarod, I helped him see past the level of form to the essence of Zen; that is, true liberating Zen practice should be just as applicable during Hindu chanting as during sitting meditation. There were many classic Zen stories that were helpful here (e.g., Reps, 1957), several of which he already knew, but came to understand more deeply as he applied them to his own marital life. For example, one story ends with the Zen master telling the student, "We don't need any more stone Buddhas around here."

For Mia, I reminded her of her belief that everyone is an incarnation of God, including Jarod, and of her guru's teaching that everyone's life is optimally designed for spiritual awakening. I also helped her understand that following one's heart does not mean being imprecise or irresponsible. We discussed yogic teachings on ordering one's life along moral and practical guidelines (*yama* and *niyama*), which includes nonviolence, not stealing, avoiding sexual excess, nonpossessiveness, truthfulness, cleanliness and purity of body and mind, contentment, and study of self and spiritual works.

As a trio, we discussed how a marital relationship, in addition to many other things, can be a shared journey of spiritual growth. Sparks and conflicts were now seen as opportunities for discovering and working with desires and attachments, which is central to both yoga and Buddhism. And they each came to see the other as a wonderful live-in guru, a knowing and caring teacher. We had a lot of fun brainstorming how to make various activities also vehicles for awakening, such as how the communication exercises they had learned from the counselor could also be a practice in meditation. Or, when one is upset, it is an opportunity to look for exactly who is this self that is upset. The four universal somato-psycho-spiritual practices (mentioned earlier in this chapter) became their general guidelines for this voyage, an approach which is superordinate to intervention at just one level of being.

The above was the key to therapy; everything else flowed somewhat easily after that. For example, one of my graduate students helped them do behavioral contracting relative to division of labor in their practical lives. Before, this had been a major source of conflicts. Now they approached it differently; the contracting helped them find a balanced reciprocity, and the formal contract could be released after a few weeks. I was also able to direct them to another marriage counselor for some minor issues. But now they did not demand that the counselor be spiritually oriented, because they could embed this counseling into their spiritual practices.

Last Qualifications

The above cases have strong Eastern/spiritual components because that is one of the things I am contributing to this book. But they are not typical or representative of general counseling cases. A person working in a community mental health center is going to be much more involved with issues at the biological and behavioral levels, and a counselor in a university center will be more involved with behavioral and personal level issues. Conjunctive Psychology provides a heuristic approach for all cases.

Since the two cases involved people with strong interests and backgrounds in Eastern approaches, that was our frame of reference, an orientation applicable to only some clients. For example, another case was an engineer with no such interests and who considered spirituality irrational superstitions. For him, humans are deterministic biological computers. Hence, in our work together we conceptualized what we were doing as reprogramming the biocomputer. For other cases, such as the drug addicts in the boxing gym, mentioned earlier, any conceptualization is an intrusion to be minimized or omitted, as the emphasis is a physical action. The goal of Conjunctive Psychology is to identify the essence of the principles of behavior change and personal growth, which take diverse forms and are conceptualized in many ways. The integrative helper, with a quiet aware mind and open heart, objectively assesses the client's strengths, weaknesses, and needs, and the way the client thinks about these and related issues. The helper can then suggest courses of action described within the client's language and cosmology. What is specifically done with different people will vary tremendously; there is no standard orientation or required therapeutic techniques.

There is no research data on the effectiveness of Conjunctive Psychology, such as an operationally defined conjunctive therapy compared to appropriate control conditions or other forms of therapy. What exists are many separate bodies of research related to various components that a Conjunctive Psychologist might utilize (cf. Mikulas, 2002). For example, relative to meditation, which is discussed in this chapter, in addition to the massive world literatures, there is also a very sizable Western research literature (Andresen, 2000; Murphy & Donovan, 1997).

To Your Health

In Conjunctive Psychology, psychological wellness is recognized as a subset of overall health across all four levels of being (biological, behavioral, personal, and transpersonal). These levels are totally intertwined; a change in one produces changes in the others. Thus factors that influence biological health (e.g., nutrition, breathwork, bodywork, life-force) also affect psychological health. Because of the nature of one's clients, an integrative helper may focus on the behavioral and/or personal levels, but she or he should be aware of biological and transpersonal influences that must be addressed first, later, or concurrently, perhaps via another helper. A unique strength of Conjunctive Psychology is identifying central dynamics at each level and how the levels interact. For example, very important at the personal level is the belief that one can do what is required in various situations and thus have some control. And usually the best way to affect such beliefs is through changes at the behavioral level, such as learning skills that give one control. Then the beliefs about control affect biological health.

Conjunctive Psychology is a *tantric,* action-oriented approach, in which the client actively does things, such as learning behavioral self-control skills or practicing meditation. On the other hand, one learns not to fight what cannot be changed and to unconditionally accept reality as it is, even while simultaneously doing things to change that reality. All of this empowers the person to be more effective, such as having satisfying and fulfilling relationships, work, and leisure activities.

In conjunction with empowerment is the psycho-spiritual freedom that comes as one gradually awakens to a broader or more fundamental reality, as through universal practices such as opening the heart and increasing mindfulness. This allows the person to gradually dis-identify with some cultural conditioning, including the conditioned sense of self, which then leads to existential freedom and peace of mind, called enlightenment in Buddhism.

I believe that these types of changes at the individual level are some of the most effective ways to promote positive change in a culture or society, as opposed to, for example, hoping politicians will create and lead the way. We are now at a point in history when, drawing from all the world's knowledge, we have very powerful somato-psycho-spiritual practices that everyone reading this can use to significantly improve her or his life and the lives of others, and in so doing also improve the culture in which one lives.

References

Andresen, J. (2000). Meditation meets behavioural medicine. *Journal of Consciousness Studies, 7,* 17–73.

Cortright, B. (1997). *Psychotherapy and spirit.* Albany: State University of New York Press.

Cross, S. E., & Madson, L. (1997). Models of the self: Self-construals and gender. *Psychological Bulletin, 122,* 5–37.

DeMaria, M. (2001). *Ever flowing on.* Pensacola, FL: Terra Nova Publishing.

de Silva, P. (1984). Buddhism and behaviour modification. *Behaviour Research & Therapy, 22,* 661–678.

Dwairy, M., & Van Sickle, T. D. (1996). Western psychotherapy in traditional Arabic societies. *Clinical Psychology Review, 16,* 231–249.

Gilchrist, R., & Mikulas, W. L. (1993). A chakra-based model of group development. *Journal for Specialists in Group Work, 18,* 141–150.

Goldstein, J. (1993). *Insight meditation.* Boston: Shambhala.

Hart, T., Nelson, P. L., & Puhakka, K. (Eds.). (2000). *Transpersonal knowing.* Albany: State University of New York Press.

Ho, D. Y. F. (1985). Cultural values and professional issues in clinical psychology: Implications from the Hong Kong experience. *American Psychologist, 40,* 1212–1218.

Hoshmand, L. T., & Ho, D. Y. F. (1995). Moral dimensions of selfhood: Chinese traditions and cultural change. *World Psychology, 1*(3), 47–69.

Kaku, K. T. (Ed.). (2000). *Meditation as health promotion.* Delft, The Netherlands: Eburon.

Kwee, M. G. T. (Ed.). (1990). *Psychotherapy, meditation, and health.* London: East-West Publications.

Lasure, L. C., & Mikulas, W. L. (1996). Biblical behavior modification. *Behaviour Research and Therapy, 34,* 563–566.

May, R. (1967). *Psychology and the human dilemma.* New York: Van Nostrand.

Mikulas, W. L. (1974). *Concepts in learning.* Philadelphia: W. B. Saunders.

Mikulas, W. L. (Ed.). (1977). *Psychology of learning: Readings.* Chicago: Nelson-Hall.

Mikulas, W. L. (1978). *Behavior modification.* New York: Harper & Row.

Mikulas, W. L. (1983). *Skills of living.* Lanham, MD: University Press of America.

Mikulas, W. L. (1986). Self-control: Essence and development. *Psychological Record, 36,* 297–308.

Mikulas, W. L. (1987). *The way beyond.* Wheaton, IL: Theosophical Publishing House.

Mikulas, W. L. (1991). Eastern and Western psychology: Issues and domains for integration. *Journal of Integrative Eclectic Psychotherapy, 10,* 229–240.

Mikulas, W. L. (2002). *The integrative helper.* Pacific Grove, CA: Wadsworth.

Mikulas, W. L. (2003). Conjunctive Psychology appreciates Yataka Haruki. *Journal of Constructivism in the Human Sciences, 8*(2), 133–135.

Murphy, M., & Donovan, S. (1997). *The physical and psychological effects of meditation* (2nd ed.). Sausalito, CA: Institute of Noetic Sciences.

Reps, P. (Ed.). (1957). *Zen flesh, Zen bones.* Garden City, NY: Doubleday.

Rucker, R. (1984). *The fourth dimension.* Boston: Houghton Mifflin.

Salzberg, S. (1997). *Lovingkindness.* Boston: Shambhala.

Schaef, A. W. (1981). *Women's reality.* Minneapolis, MN: Winston Press.

Sheikh, A. A., & Sheikh, K. S. (Eds.). (1996). *Healing East and West.* New York: John Wiley.

Skinner, B. F. (1975). The shaping of phylogenic behavior. *Journal of the Experimental Analysis of Behavior, 24,* 117–120.

Suzuki, S. (1970). *Zen mind, beginner's mind.* New York: Weatherhill.

Walsh, R., & Vaughan, F. (Eds.). (1993). *Paths beyond ego.* Los Angeles: Tarcher.

Wilber, K. (1996). Eye to eye (3rd ed.). Boston: Shambhala.

6

Hawaiian Psychology

William C. Rezentes III

Malia and her husband were the victims of a tragic automobile accident. Days later, Malia woke up in the hospital with severe injuries that would heal over time. Her husband, however, had died. Malia completed her physical therapy and had attempted to move on. Grief stricken, Malia was severely depressed. Her depression was soon complicated with psychotic-like symptoms as she made claim to "seeing her husband." After a year of not being able to shake her hallucinations, Malia thought to move from her rural residence to Honolulu, the largest city in Hawai'i. The "sightings" of her husband continued on a regular basis and she sought out help. Malia's first therapist diagnosed her with Major Depression with Psychotic Features. The second therapist added on a Post Traumatic Stress Disorder diagnosis. Medication was recommended and when that failed, Malia was referred for inpatient hospitalization. And while Malia's symptoms persisted and worsened, rendering her unable to work and properly parent her younger children, she did not want to be hospitalized for fear of going *pupule* or crazy. Malia withdrew into a private world of profound sadness, fear, confusion, and hopelessness. She continued to see her outpatient therapist weekly for grief therapy and psychiatrist monthly for medication. Her prognosis was poor according to her therapists. Efforts to qualify her for social security benefits based upon a psychiatric disability had begun. Malia and her therapists thought to have her younger children raised by a relative.

A friend suggested that Malia, being of Hawaiian heritage, inquire about free services at a Hawaiian social service agency that specialized in working with Hawaiian families in a culturally relevant and sensitive manner. The agency's seasoned social worker referred her to the consulting clinical psychologist. That would be me.

Malia presented as a very kind, reserved Hawaiian woman of aloha who was in a cloud of *kaumaha* or depression. She really did not think she was *pupule,* but rather feared that others would label her as crazy for seeing her husband. Still, Malia understood that her *kaumaha* was too heavy and interfered with her moving on. Many things were revealed in a Hawaiian psychological assessment. Malia is a traditional Hawaiian raised to understand and live traditional Hawaiian values, practices, and beliefs. One such belief was in *'aumakua,* or family relatives that have passed on who continue to love, guide, protect, and even scold us. Malia's husband was doing what many *'aumakua* do, which was returning to her in *kinolau,* or earthly form, as *pueo* or Hawaiian owl, uncommon on O'ahu and almost never seen in urban Honolulu. Her husband was trying to watch over her and their children.

What ensued in therapy was a mixture of Western grief therapy intertwined with traditional Hawaiian ways regarding death and dying, the grief process, and how to move on. As is customary, Malia agreed to the overall treatment goal of moving on with her husband as a loving memory. In the weeks that followed, Malia was able to make closure, Hawaiian style, knowing that she would again be with her husband when it was her time to pass over into the spiritual world. Malia was able to now move through the stages of grief. The Hawaiian grief work included *"pule"* or prayer, interpretation of *moe 'uhane* or dreams, and *akakū* or visions, and spiritual realignment of her husband in relation to her and her children and extended family. Malia's depression remitted and she was soon able to find employment and properly care for her children.

Clearly, treating Malia required cultural sensitivity and ideally, cultural competence. Malia's previous therapists are skilled, competent, and well intended in providing the highest quality of service possible given their training and experience. What was unfortunately missing was a working knowledge of and capacity to integrate Hawaiian culture in her therapy, and generally in the field. I am always pleased to receive many referrals for this purpose. Just as we all refer individuals and families whose presenting issues are outside of our areas of competence, we need to examine our own ability to work with those not within our cultural competence. For the purposes of this chapter, Hawaiian Psychology is the pursuit of finding a fit or, wherever possible, integrating the best of traditional Hawaiian culture and Western psychology in the therapeutic environment. And where not possible, how to remedy the divergent worlds, not only in the best therapeutic and healing interests of Hawaiians, but also it is hoped, by improving upon Western psychology.

My Hawaiian Psychology Development

Born of parents of Hawaiian, Portuguese, and Puerto Rican ancestry, I was raised in the *mokupuni* (island) of O'ahu, the *moku* (larger land district) of Honolulu, in the *ahupua'a* (district) of *Pālolo,* in the *'ili 'āina* (locale) of Wai'ōma'o. My "one *hānau*" or birth sands is nestled in a valley on east O'ahu's Ko'olau mountains and extends to Kalehuawehe, a section of Waikīkī. Reared in a hapa-haole manner, or a mixture of predominantly Hawaiian and what islanders call "local" traditions, I was also exposed to Western culture as some degree of assimilation was expected and as a means to survive, a necessity for most Hawaiians. I attended Catholic parochial school from kindergarten through the 8th grade, and Kamehameha High School for Hawaiian students, a legacy of Princess Bernice Pauahi Bishop, before heading to "America" for college. Kamehameha was instrumental in my formative years as I was schooled with Hawaiian students during the 1970s Hawaiian cultural renaissance. It was the first time in generations that it was "okay" and even "cool" to be Hawaiian, a time of cultural growth, identity development, reflection, expression, and more. Knowing at an early age that I would attend a "mainland" college, it was ingrained in my *na'au* or gut that I would return home to share with other Hawaiians and islanders the benefit of my opportunities.

After completing a year of study at Drake University in Des Moines, Iowa, I transferred to the University of Southern California (USC) in Los Angeles. With good intent, I was largely treated as a model minority and was once told that I "make my people proud." I responded to the person's well intended but naive statement by saying, "you must make your people proud too." Understanding his unintentional slight, we *ho'opono* or set things right and became friends.

My training and bachelor degrees in Psychology and Gerontology at USC prepared me for graduate school at the University of Hawai'i's Clinical Psychology program. I have the uneasy distinction of being the first Hawaiian graduate of this program according to some faculty persons. The oversight of my Portuguese and Puerto Rican ancestry was perhaps due to the perceived improved image of, and thus focus on, Hawaiians in the cultural renaissance. Anyway, I thoroughly enjoyed the academic and professional challenges and opportunities to grow in the program. Calm on the exterior, sometimes anxious inside, I felt drawn to the knowledge, wisdom, insights, talent, and skills of professors and peers in psychological theory, research, and practice. I was a curious and determined young man allowed access to keys of the Western science and art of psychology.

There was, however, another side to my immersion into Western psychology. I felt as though I was navigating in a subcultural labyrinth in which I was expected to learn the values, practices, beliefs, and mores that felt different, foreign, and incongruent with my own. While graduate school is difficult for many students, I noticed that many persons outside of mainstream culture had additional challenges with their navigational compasses and radar. I lacked sufficient power and position and could not always effectively and proactively navigate in this new and often foreign academic world with its particular culture. Here are some examples.

I was told by a faculty person who sat on the admissions committee that given my academic profile, particularly my modest GRE test scores, "even if I tried my very best, I'd be lucky to barely pass and make it out of the program." *Pū'iwa* or surprised, I thought this to be *hō'upu'upu* (thought implantation or the power of suggestion). My efforts to reassure the faculty person—given my undergraduate successes, the poor reliability and validity of GRE test scores for minorities, and my determination, drive, motivation, and discipline—were not successful. I had no power to negotiate. Fortunately, I was able to obtain a strong GPA that was noticed by several faculty persons. This and *pule* (prayer) helped me to overcome the negative *hō'upu'upu.* I often went to the ocean to *kapu kai* (cleanse) and thank *Ke Akua* (God) and my *kūpuna* (ancestors) for their support.

Later that semester, another faculty person said, "Bill, we're going to turn you into a real psychologist yet." When I inquired what was meant, I was given a diatribe on the kinds of changes I had to make, ranging from my dialect, walk, and attire to how I was to learn a new worldview as a scientist-practitioner. Fully intending to help me, the faculty person had no idea how it was experienced as invalidating my identity and cultural practices and beliefs. I continued to *pule* and *kapu kai* to fend off negative influences.

At the start of graduate school, I was told that I needed to have a clinical advisor. I cautiously approached a well liked and respected professor who had heard of my dilemma and graciously added me to her already bulging advisee list. While I wondered why I was not initially *ho'okipa* or properly invited as is customary and expected in my culture, I was very thankful for having an advisor of great intelligence and *na'au* (heart). She taught me how to understand the subculture of psychology and to survive, negotiate, and thrive in graduate school. We freely exchanged cultural perspectives and worldviews that were sometimes very different, but we always shared in an atmosphere of mutual learning. The professor is now a lifelong friend and colleague of much aloha and respect.

As previously noted, I lacked the power and position in graduate school to negotiate my cultural identity with the subculture of psychology, sometimes landing upon unforeseen land mines. A few examples of what I found difficult include

- The Western value of rugged individualism reflected in most psychological theory and practice.
- Being openly challenged in class by a self-admitted atheist professor for being a practicing Catholic Christian who also valued Hawaiian spirituality. The professor could not understand and argued vehemently how any person of intellect could subscribe to the Catholic opium of the masses and pagan Hawaiian spirits. I wondered how the professor dealt with clients who commonly have spiritual/religious convictions.
- A mainstream culture classmate in an oral presentation openly refuting and dismissing the notion that *ho'oponopono*, the traditional Hawaiian practice of group problem resolution, was no different from Western forms of family therapy.
- A thesis committee member refusing to approve a completed project because I did not videotape the subjects, knowing that the Hawaiian subjects declined consent as it made them feel very uncomfortable. Unable to negotiate, I chose to drop the nearly completed thesis and honor the research subjects' feelings as is culturally *pono* (proper) and ethical.

Silently, I held steadfast that negotiating my cultural identity, values, and practices was never an option, and I paid a social-cultural price. When I look back, these experiences are common among oppressed Hawaiians, that of being shot down before beginning an endeavor, or being told directly or indirectly that Hawaiians were "less than" and stupid, dumb, and lazy. This is a fairly common theme in therapy with Hawaiians as the stereotyping and prejudice continue to exist. In my case, I managed to learn the value, wisdom, and limitations of psychology's subcultural beliefs and practices. What was once strange and foreign is now largely understandable, but I continue to evaluate how its application is of benefit or harm to myself, my clients, and the Hawaiian community.

To extend the lessons learned, how does a dominant culture therapist, or one who operates from the professional subculture of Western psychology, work with minority clients? As I was judged as being marginally fit for graduate school, do we typecast and label with limited assessment and diagnoses those not of our culture and ethnicity? Are nontraditional clients only partially heard or not heard at all? Do we stereotype their experience of pain and suffering? Are clients silently chastised for their spiritual beliefs and persuaded to think more in line with Western psychological beliefs? And if so, who really benefits? My concern is that minority clients' cultural identity, beliefs, and practices might be negated, minimized, chastised, or ignored so they better fit the dominant cultural expectations of what they should be. Perhaps this feeds the mental health stigma and contributes to apparent noncompliance, no-shows, and premature terminations commonplace in therapy.

I submit that we are ethically bound and are capable of honoring the identity and cultural views of minority clients. My question is whether negotiating culture and identity is an option for minority-culture clients when working with a dominant-culture therapist or even a minority-culture therapist who overly operates from the professional subculture of Western psychology. Cushman's (1995) examination of psychotherapy as a cultural enterprise is apropos as therapists and clients all bring their individual and collective cultures to the therapeutic setting. Good intentions and belief in one's subcultural worldview often blind one, particularly when mixed with arrogance or limited worldviews. Are the "best clients" (like "best students") those who best reflect our values? Many of my nonmainstream colleagues in Hawai'i quietly say that therapists who primarily operate from the subculture of Western psychology with minorities provide "White, middle-class therapy." Although trained to actively listen to our clients, I wonder how well we actively reflect on our own beliefs and biases. Are we prepared to learn, share, and even give up power and position in the therapeutic enterprise in the best interest of the client, effectiveness of therapy, and for other moral goods?

Hawaiian Psychology is a way to allow Hawaiian clients to better negotiate and be at home with their identity and worldview, which is often crucial for therapeutic success. This is surely a better alternative to complete assimilation that ignores the identity, history, culture, and spirit of a person for the well intended, blind, and sometimes arrogant issuing forth of westernized therapy. The mutual assimilation or bridging of cultures in therapy does of course apply to other cultural groups.

Becoming a Practicing Hawaiian Psychologist

After meeting the challenge and academic rigor of graduate school and passing the state license examination, I fulfilled a promise to myself—to further explore, learn, and live Hawaiian culture as I spent much energy on Western education. This journey also included becoming more fluent in the Hawaiian language, becoming an *'olapa* (dancer) in a traditional *pā hula* (hula school), learning *haku mele* (song and chant composition), and playing and later recording traditional Hawaiian music and chant. In these varying traditions, I was immersed in traditional Hawaiian cultural protocol, worldview, beliefs, values, and spirituality, learning from excellent *kumu* (teachers), including a very special *kupuna* (elder). With the necessary foundation and careful mentoring, it was a blessing to be selected to learn traditional healing practices. Many long and inspirational discussions on the differences and similarities between Hawaiian and Western cultures in psychotherapy and life were a true blessing. The *wili* or weaving of my Hawaiian and Western cultural lei continued in professional and personal life. Soon, the term Hawaiian Psychology came to mind. How did I attempt to integrate these two worldviews as a Hawaiian Psychologist? Here are some examples.

My original research for my master's degree had to do with the effect dialect had in psychological assessment. I administered the WISC-R intelligence test to a sample of Hawaiian youth in English and in the local Hawai'i dialect called Pidgin English. There were significant differences in the four subtests where there was substantial verbal instruction and content. Thus, in this early pilot study, the impact of language and dialect was important in intelligence testing. There was more to be discovered beyond the research findings. I was also introduced to the culture and politics behind research and how the pressures and rewards to publish or perish can sometimes result in unethical compromising of research subjects and rendering valid research findings. I further learned how Hawaiians were studied for decades by a variety of researchers across many fields resulting in many theses, dissertations, and lucrative research grants with little or no benefit, and in some cases, harm to the Hawaiian community. This has fortunately been curtailed in recent years as Hawaiian community leaders and advocates routinely question and discern the quality and usefulness of research for our communities.

My doctoral dissertation had two studies (Rezentes, 1988). After an exhaustive literature review of the health statistics of Hawaiians, I developed and validated a pilot Hawaiian acculturation scale entitled *Nā Mea Hawai'i,* or Hawaiian Ways (Rezentes, 1993). Hawaiian acculturation as measured by this scale and socioeconomic status were found to be significant predictors of stress in the second study, whereas the common measure of blood quantum of percentage of Hawaiian ancestry (admixture) was not. This sparked a number of similar research studies to include the development of acculturation scales by three of my dissertation committee members. In collaboration with a research psychiatrist and statistician, the *Nā Mea Hawai'i* scale continues to be used in my own research (Rezentes, 1993; Streltzer, Rezentes, & Arakaki, 1996; Streltzer, Rezentes, & Arakaki, 2000), student theses and dissertations, as well as funded research projects. Working with another Hawaiian psychologist, the *Nā Mea Hawai'i 'Elua* (Revised) scale was also developed. As the *kahu* or guardian of this scale, it is my *kuleana,* or responsibility, to review research proposals and provide free consultation so that the scale is used properly in culturally valid research studies that will benefit Hawaiian communities. Assisting other researchers in culturally competent research with Hawaiians is one aspect of Hawaiian Psychology. I am honored when asked to consult with other promising transcultural research projects involving Hawaiians.

My career journey has taken me thus far to places and settings that I had never expected. From being a school counselor, to a 5-year tenure as a police psychologist, to surprisingly being asked to join an established private practice a year out of graduate school, there were numerous opportunities to grow as a Hawaiian psychologist in a multicultural world. In the "professional building" where my practice was located the other friendly business owners and employees would remark, "I can usually tell your patients . . . they look different from the rest." The practice I had joined was in an affluent neighborhood in eastern Honolulu. Hawaiians came and were referred from all over the island in part because there were so few Hawaiian therapists. I later relocated to windward O'ahu and have a home-based practice that includes home visits to serve the underserved and poor. They are rich in life, spirituality, and culture in spite of their poverty and psychosocial problems. Much to learn and share. In every setting, there was an implicit calling for adaptation of Western psychology within the cultures of Hawai'i, and particularly that of the Native Hawaiians.

Native Hawaiian Identity

Although every person here is a resident of Hawai'i, only those with *koko* or Hawaiian blood and ancestry are Native Hawaiian. This emphasis on ethnic and cultural identification over geographic and statehood identification is apparently different from other states. For us, a native Texan or Californian or New Yorker refers to one's spiritual cousins, the indigenous tribal peoples that Christopher Columbus mistakenly labeled as Indian. Further, Hawaiians do not understand why anyone would make claim to any native ancestry other than their own. While a largely immigrant nation understandably needs a national identity, the coveting of others' identity is not *pono* or proper. There is a growing handful of *malihini* or newcomers to Hawai'i who insist on calling themselves Native Hawaiians because they have made Hawai'i their home. Some of them simply want the apparent benefits of being Hawaiian (e.g., Hawaiian trusts, lands, assets, and the idealized image of a Hawaiian) without assuming the responsibilities of our history, culture, and spirit, particularly the aloha spirit. It is never proper to covet another identity as it insults both your own true identity as well as the people whose identity you usurp.

What results is a common feeling among Hawaiians of being overwhelmed, crowded, overlooked, and outright displaced. The 2000 census revealed that 50 percent of persons identifying themselves as Hawaiian lived outside of Hawai'i (U.S. Department of Commerce, 2000). The primary reason is economic as Hawai'i has one of the highest costs of living combined with lower wages for working persons. At present, wealthy persons from all over the world are buying up the remainder of developable lands and constructing multiple, affluent homes and businesses that skyrocket property values effectively and sadly forcing Hawaiians to leave. For Hawaiians, there is a continued and shared sense of spiritual, cultural, as well as physical displacement. For a migrant, immigrant, or refugee, there are reasons to leave and usually a knowing that they have a homeland. We have no other homeland. For us, Hawai'i is our "mainland." Our roots in the land and love of the ocean are difficult to explain on paper. As an ancient people, with deep interconnection and ties to the land and sea, we do not transplant well. Just as beachside coconut trees swaying in our *moa'e,* or trade winds, would not grow well or at all if uprooted, shipped, and planted in the extreme dry heat of the Las Vegas desert or in the cold rain of Seattle, likewise, it is very difficult for Hawaiians to remain Hawaiian in spirit and culture away from our "one *hānau,*" or birth sands. Our name "Hawaiian" comes from the root, Hawai'i, our traditional word for our land and people. We are one and the same.

Kaumaha

These and other historical and current losses and the stripping of our culture have led to what I called the "*Kaumaha* Syndrome" (Rezentes, 1988). Following the visits of Captain James Cook, our population declined by an estimated 95 percent, primarily due to Western diseases for which Hawaiians had no previous exposure or immunity. Depopulation from disease epidemics (e.g., venereal disease, tuberculosis, measles, smallpox, cholera, bubonic plague) devastated the Hawaiian population from an estimated 800,000 at James Cook's first visit in 1778 (Stannard, 1989) to 134,925 in 1823, to a mere 39,504 Hawaiians and part-Hawaiians in 1896 (Schmitt, 1968). In the first of his series of publications entitled *The Hawaiian Kingdom,* Kuykendall (1938, p. 386) states that "During the years 1848–1853 the future of the Hawaiian race looked especially dark, for in those years epidemic diseases, like a gigantic scythe, cut great swaths through the native population and its ultimate extinction came to be quite generally thought of as inevitable." The survivors were left with great *kaumaha* or sadness and loss (Kame'eleihiwa, 1992; Lili'uokalani, 1990; Rezentes, 1996).

Kaumaha literally means "weight" and figuratively means heavy, downcast, and dreary (Pukui & Elbert, 1986). Recently, it has taken on the connotation of melancholy and what Western psychology terms depression. Amidst the population decimation, great social and political change has occurred and continues. Some further examples include the exploitation by foreigners of the 1848 *Māhele* (division of lands) that led to Hawaiians' land dispossession. Another is the 1887 "Bayonet Constitution" that forced our King Kālakaua at gunpoint, to sign a new constitution that stripped his powers and the rights of Native Hawaiians. Perhaps the saddest example is the 1893 overthrow of our Queen Lili'uokalani and our internationally recognized government by American businessmen in an act of treason backed by the United States Marines Corps that put the final nail into the coffin of Hawaiian self-determination (Kame'eleihiwa, 1992; Lili'uokalani, 1990).

Further examples include the 1898 illegal annexation of Hawai'i to the United States based on Congress' simple majority vote versus the required two thirds majority vote and statehood itself in 1959, which Native Hawaiians opposed. With American expansionism and colonialism came the pressures and outright coercion to assimilate. Children were beaten for speaking Hawaiian in school. To improve their chances for employment, Hawaiian adults changed their names to English ones, sometimes simply by taking on an English titled street name. It was illegal for a Hawaiian child to be given a Hawaiian name without a Christian/English one. Native customs, beliefs, practices, and worldviews were strongly put down and often ridiculed and abused. Once an extremely healthy and vibrant people, Hawaiians now have the lowest life expectancy in Hawai'i and are typically at the bottom of most indices of health and well-being (E Ola Mau, 1985; The Kamehameha Schools/Bernice Pauahi Bishop Estate, 1983). Ironically and hypocritically, efforts to address Hawaiian rights are currently being challenged in state and federal courts as being racist. Examples include the Kamehameha Schools, a private school on three islands that was founded and willed by Princess Bernice Pauahi Bishop from her personal land and other assets while Hawai'i remained an independent nation, and the 1920 Hawaiian Homestead Act. The former drew some controversies as it is associated with considerable resources. The latter, sponsored by a Hawai'i congressman and prince, Jonah Kūhi'ō Kalaniana'ole, to provide some displaced Native Hawaiians with a place to live, is also being challenged. The persons behind these lawsuits and other continued acts to further strip Hawaiians of their remaining rights are the same recent visitors to our shores that covet our identity. The result is that Hawaiians remain the only native people that lack official federal status, and similar to Native Americans, also lack sufficient recognition and redress. Our lands, governance, health, education, economy, housing, and even cultural identity and rights remain in the hands of our wardens, the federal, state, and local governments of the United States.

There is a strong survival instinct in all humans. When faced with extinction, the instinct intensifies. Some are able to survive while others continue to tragically whither, suffer, and die. Those of us who descend from the survivors of biological and social genocide are humbled and feel much *'eha* or pain for our fallen brothers and sisters while continuing to struggle to survive. So, as I go on with examples of Hawaiian Psychology, I ask that you remember the historical and current backdrop that was summarized, and encourage you to research it further (Ii, 1959; Kahananui, 1984; Kamakau,1991; Kamakau,1992; Kame'eleihiwa, 1992; Kuykendall, 1938; Kuykendall, 1953; Kuykendall, 1967; Lili'uokalani, 1990; Malo, 1951).

Case Examples of Hawaiian Psychology

One historical account of Kānaka Hawai'i or Hawaiian People tells us that we are the descendants of *kalo* or the taro plant. *Hāloanaka,* the first child of *Wākea,* the sky father, and *Papa,* the earth mother, was born premature and died. He was buried in the ground and after a while a *kalo* plant arose from the child's body. The leaf was given the name *Laukapalili* (quivering leaf) and the stem was named *Hāloa.* He is the mythical ancestor of all the indigenous people of Hawai'i and earth (Malo, 1951). *Kalo* remains as the staple food for Hawaiians. Sharing this *mo'olelo* or story with orphaned children in therapy reconnects them with our ancestral parents that can be seen, touched, and felt. Having a Hawaiian sky father who provides rain for our earth mother who bears fruit to taro and other life-bearing sustenance can be very healing. They are provided with taro to plant, nurture, and maintain. Some have decided to start their own taro patch. The literal and metaphoric healing in the context of Western grief therapy and Hawaiian *ho'oponopono* (Pukui, Haertig, & Lee, 1972; Rezentes, 1996) is apparent. Further, Hawaiian family systems are shared. The children learn that there is no word for orphan or illegitimate child as all children and life are *kapu* or sacred. They also learn that there is no word for "uncle" or "aunt" but rather, *mākua* or parent generation that along with *kūpuna,* or grandparent generation, provide earthly parenting and nurturing to all children. It is akin to the African proverb that it takes a village to raise a child. Connections with the orphans' earthly village *'ohana* or family are fostered, including those who have passed on to the spiritual world and even to those yet to be born. These connections are physically, emotionally, and spiritually fostered with these children who eventually learn how to move on with healthy, happy memories of their birth parents.

Persons with tremendous losses frequently come for therapy. With the death of a loved one, a Hawaiian Psychological approach assists Hawaiians in helping them through their *kaumaha* or grief process in a number of ways. For example, many persons in their *kaumaha* are saddened by a lack of closure: never having the opportunity to say goodbye, to speak to the deceased one last time, regretting that their last words were spoken out of anger, hurt, or negativity, and so on. When reminded or taught the Hawaiian traditional belief that the spirit remains near the corpse until burial, many Hawaiians can see the cultural opportunity for earthly closure. As in times past, they learn or remember it is one of our ways to express aloha, to ask for forgiveness, to vent a disagreement and set matters to right. Others make promises to the deceased or their family members. For many Hawaiians, feelings of "talking to a spirit" often come naturally. For others, it is an awakening of something ancient in modern times. Through the grief process, they are okay with talking, relating, and connecting spiritually through their *na'au* or center of emotion with deceased ones. Many speak of their dreams of loved ones and even having temporary sightings that are culturally appropriate and not at all pathological. Still others smell the departed person's favorite fragrance or essence of a flower. Intuition and even predictions of the passing of loved ones emerge in therapy. The hosts of emotions are worked through in a respectful and loving manner in a Hawaiian Psychological therapeutic context. Overall, healthy, loving, and balanced relationships with loved ones in this and the spiritual world are developed, enhanced, and maintained. Typically, the Hawaiian person already has a good understanding of these relationships and shares how they relate to others, once trusting that they will not be clinically judged. Even when psychopathology exists, the treatment continues to respect their spiritual and cultural beliefs that, even if distorted, are often instrumental in realigning their worldview to a healthier one.

A woman was referred to me for having visual and auditory hallucinations. She also had a rich history of predictive dreams, seeing and interpreting *hō'āilona,* or portents, and in communicating with family ancestors. The referral question was whether her current symptoms were due to psychological or cultural determinants. After a careful assessment, I referred her to a Hawaiian cultural healer who knew the woman and her family. In collaboration, we determined that she had Bipolar Disorder with psychotic features. Concurrently, and of equal importance, we also concurred that she was a *haku* or medium, traditionally trained and gifted, with a long history of assisting others, particularly family members. She received Western treatment and Hawaiian healing. In addition to therapist, my role was akin to a Hawaiian Psychological case manager. The woman was relieved and accepted her "dual diagnoses" and worked well with her physician, psychiatric consultant,

Hawaiian healer, and myself. She progressed nicely in treatment and was able to carry out her *kuleana* or responsibilities as a *haku*. It is possible and not uncommon for persons to have a Western-based diagnosis and Hawaiian spiritual/cultural array of symptoms. As is done in mental health and medicine, consultations and case management are necessary. The key here is the acceptance, respect, and cooperation by both the Western practitioners and traditional healers with each other and, most of all, the patient.

I have had the privilege of working with several Hawaiian veterans who primarily served in the Vietnam War and had moderately severe or very severe Post Traumatic Stress Disorder (PTSD) and other significant disorders (e.g. major depression, substance abuse, etc.). One of the common therapeutic threads, if not ropes, was their cultural dissonance in being a Hawaiian, fighting for America against a people they did not know. Specifically, the dissonance and outright conflict centered on representing and fighting on behalf of the very country that overthrew the Hawaiian constitutional government decades earlier in 1893. Further, they came to understand that most of the Vietnamese soldiers were common folk such as farmers who had done nothing to Hawaiians or to Hawai'i.

In working with their PTSD, it was essential they resolve this dissonance and conflict that was sometimes hidden in their traumatic experiences, and they had to overcome their difficulty in adjusting to civilian life. An example is a Hawaiian veteran in his homeland having a flashback to Vietnam, where the terrain is not too different from Hawai'i's. Some would literally head for the hills and mountainside in an attempt to escape their traumatic recollections, only to feel the comfort of an environment similar to their war zone memories. Imagine their psychological "jam up" as some call it.

Some of these warriors knew little of traditional Hawaiian culture as they were raised in the decades of assimilation to American ideals and culture. Treatment included traditional Western-based therapy for PTSD that was necessary but insufficient for most. Individually and sometimes in a group, they teased out and arrived at a fundamental truth that they are Hawaiian warriors, drafted as "boys" in someone else's war. As patriotic as they may have felt, there remain deeper, ancient ties to their ancestors and homeland. They found their metaphorical homeland was right under their noses. In various ways, via Hawaiian language, history, customs, practices, beliefs, and worldview, they discovered an identity of old that better fit the assimilated identity. As Hawaiians, they rooted themselves in traditional Hawaiian culture and learned how to adapt and better cope with contemporary society. As one warrior put it, "War couldn't kill the aloha in me." Another said, "I always knew I was Hawaiian, just never knew it was okay to be it." And yet another warrior stated, "It's in our *koko* [blood] and in our *na'au* [gut], stronger than genetics, our spirit, our Hawaiianness."

Clearly, knowing the historical and present experiences of Hawaiians and other cultural groups greatly assists the therapeutic process. There is evidence that knowing a person's culture enhances, and can often make or break, the therapeutic process (Handy and Pukui, 1972; Pukui, Haertig, & Lee, 1972; Rezentes, 1996). Some relevant concepts include:

- *Akakū* (visions), their significance and interpretation.
- *Hoʻoponopono* (literally "setting things to right"), a traditional process to prevent, treat, heal, and plan healthy family and group cohesion.
- *Inoa* (name), how names influence, guide, direct, and assist one in knowing oneself in healing and general life direction.
- *Kūʻauhau* or *Moʻokūʻauhau* (genealogy), an utmost traditional value, that assists one in finding and knowing one's identity, potential gifts, reference groups, and more.
- *Moe ʻUhane* (dreams), their significance and interpretation.
- *Moʻolelo* (stories), traditional manner to convey messages, lessons, and cultural views on how to live healthy and in a balanced way.
- *ʻŌlelo* (words), the traditional belief in the power of the word to be an indirect and direct cause of positive and negative change, feelings, thoughts, and behavior. This belief was illustrated in the *ʻōlelo noʻeau* (proverb), *i kaʻōlelo nō ke ola, i kaʻōlelo nōka make,* or In the word there is life, in the word there is death.
- *ʻŌlelo Nōʻeau* (wise sayings, proverbs), simple and profound wisdom from ancient times and how they may assist healing.
- *Pīkai*, also called *Kapu kai* and *Hiʻuwai* (ocean, water cleansing), to heal one of *pilikia* (troubles), *ʻeha* (pain), *hopohopo* (anxiety), *lepo* (literal and figurative filth), and so on.
- *Pule* (prayer) and *Oli* (chant), prayer sometimes in chant form being common in all traditional healing.
- *Wehiwehi I Ka Paipala* (literally, open Bible), a relatively contemporary tradition for Hawaiians whereby Bible passages are selected after prayer for guidance, insight, revelation, reflection, and so on.

The potential contribution of Hawaiian Psychology extends beyond the integration of Hawaiian, Western, and other approaches for Hawaiians to the very selection of therapists as healers.

Western and Hawaiian Approaches to Recruiting and Training Healers

We are familiar with how psychologists are recruited, trained, and eventually licensed to practice the science and art of psychology. Student trainees are typically chosen based on academic prowess, standardized testing scores, and recommendations. With some exceptions, psychologists who choose clinical applications of the psychological sciences are selected and trained by professors who are typically academicians. It is assumed that internship supervisors will provide mentoring and training as they learn the clinical application of theory and research in rigorous and demanding applied community settings.

Our profession, as in the related professions of psychiatry and social work, does little to directly examine a person's intrinsic capacity and gifts to work, assist, and yes, heal others. Requiring students to participate in psychological evaluations and intensive therapy to ensure they are stable and suited for clinical work used to be done. This practice, however, brings about much liability and poses ethical concern. At best, academic advisors and committees screen out students clearly not suited for clinical work. More often, the screening falls on internship supervisors and directors. Given the years of study and training invested to become a clinician as well as the economic incentives in becoming a licensed psychologist, it is very difficult for anyone to decide to self-select out of the profession. And once licensed, the profession's continued ability to evaluate clinicians' continued healing competence relies upon continuing educational requirements and the avoidance of ethical and legal challenges that risk licensure suspension or revocation.

How do we "know" who would make a good therapist/healer? Although this is not the forum for a comprehensive discussion of the current system of selecting and ensuring culturally competent therapist/healers, let us examine how traditional Hawaiian healers are chosen. In contrast to the typical ways in which future therapists are recruited into psychology training programs, *Kāhuna,* or priests/experts, who performed holistic Hawaiian healing were carefully selected when young and thoroughly trained by one or more mentors for 20 years or more to develop and be recognized as possessing the necessary skills and attributes (Hewett, Alailima, Kamakea-Ohelo, & Mann, 2000; Ii, 1959; Kamakau, 1991; Larsen, 1946; Malo, 1951; Pukui, Haertig & Lee, 1972; Rezentes, 1996). The mentors knew and often *hānai* or adopted/raised the students whose aptitude for healing was assessed, shaped, supported, tested, and advanced at an early age.

The qualities of a healer are discussed in the writings of Samuel M. Kamakau (Kamakau, 1992), one of the most prominent and enlightened Hawaiian scholars and authors of the 19th century. And Hewett, Alailima, Kamakea-Ohelo, and Mann (2000) derived criteria for traditional Hawaiian healers. According to Kamakau, Hawaiian healers are characterized by three distinct qualities:

1. *Ma'ema'e o waho*—the outward purity of the healer, that in appearance, manner and practice the healer emulates purity that was visible and understood by the people who looked at him or her.

2. *Ma'ema'e o loko*—the inward purity of the healer, understood in all that the healer said, the healing was done through his or her work, and the continual success of the healer.

3. *Haipule*—the piety of the healer, conceived as a direct relationship with *Akua* (God, higher power), an important quality shown in the aura of the healer.

In view of these criteria, the similarities and differences between Hawaiian and Western healing are apparent. Whereas the qualities of outward and inward purity are not commonly used to describe Western healers, their meaning has potential application. A therapist should have a healing manner, ethical character, and wisdom—all qualities that should be emphasized in admission screening and the clinical development of trainees. Our reputation within our professions and in the community is in part due to our outward and inner appearance and persona.

On the other hand, *haipule,* or the important quality of piety based on a relationship with God or a higher power, is probably not a characteristic of a Western healer with the possible exception of pastoral counselors and others who integrate spirituality with mental health expertise. Nonetheless, it may give us pause as to consider how we attribute our clinical skills and successes. How well do we connect with and affirm our healing connections and commitments, whether ascribed to a higher power, code of ethics, science, other sources, or our individual self?

Traditional healers have additional qualities:

1. *Mo'okū'auhau*—the genealogy of the healer. That a healer can verify his or her lineage, from an established lineage of healers, as traditionally believed chosen by the ancient gods, is sacrosanct as he or she is the embodiment of the *mana* (authority and power) of that lineage. Although there are families with generations of therapists, most Western-trained healers probably do not think of clinical skills and healing as running in the family. The United States is a society that emphasizes individualism. A Hawaiian healer also can be taught through *Mo'o Kahuna,* or the teachings of a lineage. Western healers have rich traditions through their professors, mentors, schools of study, and theorists. In this way, it is very similar to traditional Hawaiian healers.

2. *Ulu Pono*—the success rate of the healer. Most therapists, including those with strong empirical foundations, do not have an established success rate. Aside from provider feedback reports from insurance companies and health maintenance organizations, how might we approach knowing our success rates in our practices? We should start with asking our clients and the community.

3. *Hana mau ana*—the years of commitment to healing. We all know about the investment of time, energy, and money that goes into our training. The key

is what initially established, and now sustains our commitment over time. Again, how would those we serve describe our commitment?

Psychological Practice in a Cultural Enterprise

I want to next comment on how we may ensure our therapeutic effectiveness by integrating our connections with culture and community. Seeing psychotherapy as a cultural enterprise in Cushman's (1995) terms, and as developed by Lisa Tsoi Hoshmand in this book, is the polite challenge. In reality, most of us are taught to view patients and their life experiences from a pathological viewpoint. The medical model superimposed on what I regard as our *cultural healing exchange* limits much of our vision to disease, pathology, inner conflict, destructive behavioral patterns, negative cognition, dysfunctional and abnormal relationships, and so on. Although there are strength-based approaches, how do we factor in culture and community in understanding well-being?

We can begin with *ho'olohe* or listening to our patients for their cultural and community models of health and well-being. An example in Hawaiian Psychology is *Lōkahi* (balance and harmony) of self, *'ohana* (family), *'ohana nui* (greater family, community), nature, and with *Ke Akua* (higher power). To understand how integrating *lōkahi* as a model of health and well-being would facilitate the healing process, see Pukui, Haertig, and Lee (1972) and Rezentes (1996).

I respectfully suggest that we need to integrate our culture and community in the cultural healing exchange of psychotherapy. As we learn from our patients, admire their courage, empathize with their losses, and celebrate their victories and healing, what do we *bring* to this cultural exchange? Is the therapy deemed "successful" only if the client manages to cross over to our subcultural world and walk, talk, see, and act like us? Or do we mutually decide upon the healing foundation, process, and outcome? The remittance of pathology and achieving treatment goals and objectives is good, but insufficient if we do not share the power and responsibility of the cultural healing exchange. I pray that we see our "10 o'clock appointment" as a dynamic, cultural healing exchange with a real person. *Aia nō iā mākou*—it is up to us.

One of the main purposes of this chapter was to demonstrate, encourage, and reinforce cultural sensitivity, and, really, cultural competence. We already have done so in some ways as in other specialty areas. Using a systems model, we can move from the micro and meso levels to macro-level perspectives.

There are other applications in how one integrates traditional Hawaiian culture with Western psychology that can be adapted to other cultural traditions (Rezentes, 1996). Some considerations include:

1. *Who are the people?* Hawaiians are an ancient people and their import in therapy and life has been discussed.

2. *What are their indigenous values?* Traditional Hawaiian values such as aloha, *'ohana* (family), *'āina* (land), *lōkahi* (harmony) are gateways of understanding the Hawaiian individual and group psyche.

3. *Traditional and Contemporary Models of Mental Illness.* How do we apply Western diagnostic classifications (such as the DSM IV and ICD 9 CM) and models of mental illness to traditional and contemporary Hawaiian society and culture in this case? Traditional causes and manifestations include *hō'upu'upu* (thought implantation), *hā'upu* (self-thought implantation), *hua 'ōlelo* (the power of words), *ānai* (curses), *'anā'anā* (sorcery), and *noho* (possession). Contemporary causes and manifestations include Kaumaha Syndrome (collective, cultural depression) and the Hā'ole Syndrome (deficits of aloha, without inner breath).

4. *Traditional Healing Practices.* What are some of the psychologically related healing practices that potentially can be helpful in therapy? Traditional Hawaiian examples include *ho'oponopono* (setting to right, group/family therapy), *moe 'uhane* (dream, dream analysis), *akakū* (visions), *wehiwehi i ka paipala* (open Bible), *pule* (prayer), and *oli* (chant).

5. *Therapist/Healer Issues.* What do we as therapists bring to the therapeutic setting that assists, detracts, and in some cases sabotages healing? How does a therapist integrate himself or herself into the family structure and protocol for effective healing?

6. *Client Issues.* What might one reasonably expect from Hawaiian clients in therapy? What are their models and views of healing and expectations from healers?

7. *Therapeutic Setting.* How might the therapeutic setting be an optimal venue of healing for Hawaiians? What are effective self-disclosure, protocol, communication, and circumspection to enhance respect, trust integrity, and healing in the Hawaiian context? How might one bridge Western and traditional Hawaiian therapy with regard to language, center or focus, expressiveness, communication, openness and intimacy, cause and effect, views on wellness, family structure, time schedules, and treatment goals?

8. *Acculturation.* How does one assess the interface of traditional Hawaiian culture with those of Western/American, Asian, and other cultures? How does one assess the level and pattern of acculturation of a Hawaiian and its implications for therapy?

9. *Bicultural Healing Methods.* Which Western-based therapies, when adapted and modified for the Hawaiian client, are generally successful and unsuccessful? What bicultural therapeutic methods and techniques are effective (e.g., Hawaiian values clarification, use of metaphor, legend, history, and

proverbs)? What "cultural homework" might be suggested to generalize and enhance therapeutic gains in a Hawaiian's everyday life?

10. *Conception of Psychological and Social Wellness.* In traditional Hawaiian culture, our understanding of the ebb and flow, waxing and waning, and cyclical nature of the universe in which humanity exists suggests that our individual well-being is never in isolation outside of the therapeutic setting. We exist and are forever interconnected to our own past, present, and future being; to our *'ohana* (family) and *'ohana nui* (communities), to the *'āina* (land), *kai* (ocean), and *lani* (heavens), and most important, to *Ke Akua* (God, higher power). Psychotherapists need to recognize that for Hawaiians, psychological and social wellness is separated only in compartmentalized theory, thought, and comfort zone. Thus, wellness is an ever-present choice to attain *lōkahi* or balance with self, others, community, nature, and some belief in a power beyond what we can physically sense, measure, and even totally comprehend. Knowing who you are, where you come from, your group(s) of origin, historical and present challenges and successes is part of that essential choice. Learning what is *pono* (right, righteous) and *hewa* (wrong) through *kūpuna* (elders) teachings as well as trial and tribulation is also integral. Learning your rightful and valuable place individually and collectively in the world community further enhances well-being. This includes knowing that power is an illusion and that oppression works against the oppressors as much as the intended victims due to negative *mana* (power) that wastefully drains and sucks life from all. I have termed this the Hā'ole Syndrome and strongly suggest that we chose to live with *aloha* and *mana* (Rezentes, 1996). In summary, therapists need to respect and optimally understand in their *na'au* (gut) that psychological and social well-being is a process, lifestyle, and way of being, in which people strive for *lōkahi* in the *pono* Hawaiian and human spirit of *aloha* and *mana,* not an outcome measure.

Further Reflections and Conclusion

We are often encouraged to think outside of the proverbial box. While knowing the fundamental roots of our traditions, it is usually a healthy endeavor for a person of any tradition to consider alternative schools of thought and tradition. As said in the *'ōlelo no'eau,* or Hawaiian proverb, *'A'ole pau ka 'ike i ka hālau ho'okahi*—not all knowledge is taught in one school (Pukui, 1983). For cultural sensitivity and competence, these alternative schools of thought are often outside of Western psychology.

While very holistic, traditional Hawaiian healing arts and sciences are first and foremost spiritual. Everything about healing flows from our connection with *Ke Akua* via prayer, meditation, introspection, observation and interpretation of dreams, visions and portents of nature, *kūkulu kumuhana* (the pooling of our spiritual resources), and so on, which allows for all forms of healing to manifest. Although psychology and other related healing arts and sciences might not adopt the same spiritual emphasis, I sincerely suggest we attend to the spirit of how healers examine themselves and the profession. For it is in the spirit and not in the letter of said examination that one finds truth and wisdom for a special, and for some sacred, life work.

Hawaiian Psychology is the integration of traditional Hawaiian culture with psychological theories, practices, beliefs, and customs for healing. It is with humble passion that I encourage dynamic thought, feeling, and action leading toward effective psychotherapy and healing. This chapter is an attempt to describe my continued personal and professional journey in this life endeavor. Living it, the spirit of cultural competence in servitude to Hawaiians, is embedded in my *na'au.* I believe that the discussion of Hawaiian Psychology can be a template in working toward cultural competence with other cultural groups as well. Why not? There is so much in common in the spirit and manner in choosing to bridge cultural differences.

I have certainly asked psychologists and related professional practitioners to further examine themselves. It can be sensitive and evoke reaction. While it was sincerely meant to assist, support, encourage, and perhaps even enlighten others, I extend my humblest apologies to anyone I may have unintentionally offended. *E huikala kākou, na Ke Akua*—May the higher power release all transgressions. Aloha.

References

Cushman, P. (1995). *Constructing the self, constructing America: A cultural history of psychotherapy.* Cambridge, MA: Perseus.

E Ola Mau. (1985). *Native Hawaiian health needs study: Medical task force report.* Honolulu, HI: Alu Like.

Handy, E. S. C., & Pukui, M. K. (1972). *The Polynesian family system in Ka-'u Hawai'i.* Tokyo, Japan: Charles E. Tuttle.

Hewett, K., Alailima, C., Kamakea-Ohelo, K., & Mann, K. (2000). O Ke Aloha Ka Mea I Ho'ōla 'Ai–Compassion is the Healer: An indigenous peoples healing conference. *Pacific Health Dialogue, 8*(2), 417–422.

Ii, J. P. (1959). *Fragments of Hawaiian history.* Honolulu, HI: Bishop Museum Press.

Kahananui, D. M. (1984). *Ka mo'olelo Hawai'i.* Honolulu, HI: University of Hawai'i Press.

Kamakau, S. M. (1991). *Ka po'e kahiko* [The people of old]. Honolulu, HI: Bishop Museum Press.

Kamakau, S. M. (1992). *Ruling chiefs of Hawai'i.* Honolulu, HI: Kamehameha Schools Press.

Kame'eleihiwa, L. K. (1992). *Native land and foreign desires.* Honolulu, HI: Bishop Museum Press.

Kamehameha Schools/Bernice Pauahi Bishop Estate. (1983). *Native Hawaiian education assessment project.* Honolulu, HI: Kamehameha Schools Press.

Kuykendall, R. S. (1938). *The Hawaiian kingdom: Vol. I. Foundation and transformation, 1778–1854.* Honolulu, HI: University of Hawai'i Press.

Kuykendall, R. S. (1953). *The Hawaiian kingdom: Vol. II. Twenty critical years, 1854–1874.* Honolulu, HI: University of Hawai'i Press.

Kuykendall, R. S. (1967). *The Hawaiian kingdom: Vol. III. The Kalakaua dynasty, 1874–1893.* Honolulu, HI: University of Hawai'i Press.

Larsen, N. P. (1946). *Medical art in ancient Hawai'i.* Honolulu, HI: Hawaiian Printing. (Reprinted from the 53rd annual report of the Hawaiian Historical Society for the year 1944)

Lili'uokalani, L. (1990). *Hawai'i's story by Hawai'i's queen.* Honolulu, HI: Mutual Publishing.

Malo, D. (1951). *Hawaiian antiquities.* Honolulu, HI: Bishop Museum Press.

Pukui, M. K. (1983). *'Ōlelo no'eau* [Hawaiian proverbs and poetical sayings]. Honolulu, HI: Bishop Museum Press.

Pukui, M. K., & Elbert, S. H. (1986). *Hawaiian dictionary.* Honolulu, HI: University of Hawai'i Press.

Pukui, M. K., Haertig, E. W., & Lee, C. A. (1972). *Nānā i ke kumu* [Look to the source] (Vols. I–II). Honolulu, HI: Hui Hānai; Queen Lili'uokalani Children's Center.

Rezentes, W. C., III. (1988). *Nā mea Hawai'i* [Hawaiian ways]: *Development and validation of a Hawaiian ethnicity scale to examine intraethnic differences in stress among Native Hawaiians.* Unpublished doctoral dissertation, University of Hawai'i.

Rezentes, W. C., III. (1993). *Nā mea Hawai'i: A Hawaiian acculturation scale. Psychological Reports, 73,* 383–393.

Rezentes, W. C., III. (1996). *Ka lama kukui* [Hawaiian Psychology]: *An introduction.* Kailua, HI: 'A'ali'i Books.

Schmitt, R. C. (1968). *Demographic statistics of Hawai'i: 1778–1965.* Honolulu, HI: University of Hawai'i Press.

Stannard, D. E. (1989). *Before the horror: The population of Hawai'i on the eve of Western contact.* Honolulu, HI: University of Hawai'i, Social Science Research Institute.

Streltzer, J., Rezentes, W. C., III, & Arakaki, M. (1996). Does acculturation influence psychosocial adapation and well-being in Native Hawaiians? *International Journal of Social Psychiatry, 42,* 28–37.

Streltzer, J., Rezentes, W. C., III, & Arakaki, M. (2000). Lack of association of psychological variables with natural killer cell activity in a Native Hawaiian population. *Transcultural Psychology, 37,* 80–99.

U.S. Department of Commerce. (2000). *Census of population: general social and economic characteristics.* Washington, DC: U.S. Census Bureau.

7

Toward a Feminist Ecological Awareness

Dana Becker

Although I wore the uniform of the late 1960s counterculture—long hair, tie-dyed mini dresses—and was as enthusiastic a fan of its music as any of my friends, as a college student I was oddly untouched by the political essence of the times. Like my friends, I was adamantly opposed to the Vietnam War, but unlike some of them I never took part in antiwar rallies or in any of the acts of civil disobedience so common in the late 1960s. In the early days of a marriage that followed closely upon college graduation, I was dimly conscious of the fact that some women who were a few years older than I were talking about themselves in a way that was new to me. At the time, however, it was the stereotype of women with hairy armpits in peasant blouses more than feminist ideas that captured my attention.

Because the world had seemed to open up to my generation of White, middle-class women—because education and career opportunities seemed freely available—I viewed my peers and myself as unconstrained by the social and economic strictures that had dominated the previous generation. We had attended a prestigious women's college and we expected to be taken seriously. Our mothers might have had to measure their worth in the glossiness of their Jell-O molds and the sheen of their china, but we knew better. Their lives looked dull and unpromising whereas ours appeared full of stimulation and possibility. I did not yet appreciate the societal expectations those lives fulfilled. That the cultural transformations we embraced with such optimism were far less than all-encompassing I likewise failed to see. When men in the Manhattan advertising agency where I worked during the summer of my junior year made remarks to me full of sexual innuendo, I felt only slight discomfort. When, as a brand new college graduate, I was told that I had been rejected for a teaching job at a private school because the administrators were concerned that a woman my age might leave to have children, I was deeply disappointed but not angered. These incidents did not prove the making of a feminist.

On the Way to an Ecological View of Change

The ongoing saga of my development as a feminist and a therapist is a multi-textured one. My experiences as a teacher of young children, as a social worker, as a developmental psychologist, as a family therapist and trainer of therapists, as a researcher, and as a professor have given me the advantage of many ways to look at my own and my clients' problems, causing me to cross and re-cross the same paths in different ways and by different routes. At times, I have felt lost, and as painful as this confusion has been, I have come to know it as important and fruitful. I have gradually learned not only to live in a sort of resigned uneasiness with my own doubts, but also to value them. For all its circuitous ways, my journey has led me gradually from a microsystemic to a larger sociocultural view of human problems. And that broadening of perspective has led me of late to chafe at the limitations of therapeutic answers to social and political questions, as I will discuss later. But it was not ever thus.

It was in the years after I gave up a doctoral fellowship at Yale and, with it, the perquisites of the classical education I had enjoyed for many years that I began to learn a great deal about myself and the world that had been hidden from my view. Only after I took up my first "real" full-time job as a teacher in an inner-city public day care center in Philadelphia did I come to be introduced to the mysteries of class and race. For me, having moved frequently with my family within the United States and lived in Italy for many years as my father was ascending the academic ladder, the sense of being an outsider was not new. I had, however, never experienced an "otherness" as profound as the one that greeted me as the only White adult working in a day care center located in the basement of the Bright Hope Baptist Church. Encountering the fact of my own Whiteness and privilege was a stunningly uncomfortable experience, but an important one.

As I continued to teach and, eventually, to train other teachers, my increasing interest in the psychological worlds of the children led me to consider applying to graduate social work programs. From a therapist my ex-husband and I went to see in the late 1970s, I had learned that many family therapists were clinical social workers. I can credit this therapist, whom I will call Ellen, with more than introducing me to one of my chosen professions; she also gave me a disturbing introduction into the perils that can accompany a "gender-neutral" couples therapy. At the time, I did not know what to make of her approach. Now I realize that some of the techniques she applied to our "case" were based on family systems theoretical ideas about the reciprocal and complementary behavior of people in dyads—for example, the idea that he drinks because she nags; she nags because he drinks. All I could see at the time was that the therapist appeared to be holding me equally responsible for my husband's binge drinking. There is no question that I was overfunctioning and he was underfunctioning in our relationship, and I do not mean to suggest that I did not have a hand in creating the problems in our marriage. The constant suggestion on the part of the therapist that I let go of certain responsibilities I had taken on in the interest of my husband's taking firmer hold of them, however, felt uncomfortably blaming as well as unworkable. I had been handling the money, not out of any desire to do so, but because things had gone badly wrong under his fiscal stewardship. When I mentioned to Ellen (rather unassertively, as I recall) that I was worried about what might happen if I gave up control over the finances—that when my husband had last been in charge of the bills, our electricity had been cut off—she was not receptive. Once again, we went home and I tried hard to follow her advice.

As our marriage continued to slip away, I blamed myself for stepping in when I saw a potential problem ahead—an unpaid bill, an unfixed shelf. Perhaps my husband *did* drink because I was overcontrolling and a nag. I did not know then that women whose partners abused alcohol were likely to be labeled by practitioners with their own "disease" of codependency, or that feminist therapists were to point out in the years ahead how such a label furnished yet another means of blaming women for the caretaking ways into which they had been socialized as girls. Even without this knowledge, however, it became harder and harder for me to believe that the therapist was doing us any good. The marriage ended, and as unaccustomed as I was to criticizing those in authoritative positions I decided, uncharacteristically, to make an appointment with Ellen to let her know how I had experienced the therapy. Our discussion was bland and unsatisfying. And although I was unaware of it at the time, my belief in the value of therapeutic transparency had its origins in this experience.

I eventually learned what feminist family therapists had to say about complementarity: that it was a construct based on the illusory notion that power in male-female relationships is equally shared. When held up to the light, the idea, say, that "he batters because she criticizes" does not make sense in view of the power differential between men and women within marriage. But this understanding was to come later. It was not really until I became a single mother myself in my early 30s, a woman with very little money and less time, that I began to read and think seriously about the continuing struggles of women in our culture, and even then my awakening was sluggish. The period of single parenthood that began in the early 1980s opened my eyes to systemic injustices faced by single mothers, and to any who would listen I advocated for that group.

I was trained in family therapy during the period when feminist family therapists like Rachel Hare-Mustin (1978) were just beginning to transform practice in that field. The Philadelphia Child Guidance Clinic, bastion of structural family therapy, had not yet gotten the feminist word, and like all the trainees in my cohort I unquestioningly accepted the thesis that middle-class mothers' overinvolvement ("enmeshment") with their children contributed to the children's psychological problems. I was encouraged by my supervisors to play up to distant ("peripheral") fathers in these families to encourage them to take on more active parenting roles. I would like to say that I was sensitive to the mother-blaming that pervaded the theorizing and practice of that time, but I cannot. Despite the joy I took in much of my work with families at the clinic, I found the manipulative coyness of paradoxical interventions disturbing and the sterile precautions taken against delving into feelings and histories off-putting. Having been raised to believe that honesty is integral to human relations, I could not abandon that principle here, nor could I accept the implicit assumption that human feelings and memory can be divorced from other aspects of human experience.

Just as I did not feel comfortable with paradoxical interventions, I did not trust "big bang" theories of change. I have never been very good at concealment, and some family therapy techniques championed at the time that required therapists to work outside the awareness of families were difficult for me to pull off. Working with guy wires and explosives behind the scenes was not what I had entered the field to do. I now believe that greater transparency with respect to process yields a stronger collaborative relationship between therapist and client. The theory of change I espouse is not a "big bang" theory, but one based on the idea of successive approximations, a notion that Howard Liddle, my mentor in family therapy and head of the Center for Research on Adolescent Drug Abuse, has so well articulated. Years ago I read a statement—an understatement, really—by the psychoanalyst David Rappoport to the effect that personality has a "slow rate of change." Having struggled to alter some entrenched aspects of my own personality and watched clients engage in that same struggle, I believe this to be the case. Clients, however, are not always looking for a personality overhaul and, as we know, they can often reach their goals without an interminable course of therapy. A multidimensional view that focuses not merely on personal determinants but on family and sociocultural factors influencing problem development facilitates, overall, a briefer therapeutic encounter as it calls upon the client to enact change in several domains simultaneously.

In my first social work job as a psychotherapist at a family service agency in the city of Chester, Pennsylvania, then the fifth poorest city in the United States, a community with a largely African American population and an unemployment rate hovering around 50 percent, I was to gain a broader view of those social and cultural forces. As part of a collaboration between the agency and the county, I became the first social worker to be attached to the county's emergency food centers. There were days when the press of bodies and the palpable sense of need seemed suffocating, days when I would leave the site taking in huge gulps of fresh air, guiltily grateful to be returning to my office. As was the case at the day care center, I knew that I had the option of escaping the visceral effects of poverty and oppression whereas those inside—literally and figuratively—could not. But I could not escape my awareness of those effects, nor did I want to; I had been privileged to go where many White, middle-class Americans do not go and learn what some never have a chance to learn about racism and poverty in our country.

Waking Up to Gender Socialization

It was my encounters with patients and staff as a social worker at a private psychiatric hospital a handful of years later that compelled me to consider gender inequities within the mental health system. Working at the hospital, I found myself smack in the middle of a medical model "sandwich" that was layered hierarchically in the following order: psychiatrists, social workers, psychiatric nurses. The psychiatric unit was a model of patriarchy. Nurses, involved in the day-to-day management of the unit and the patients, scurried to meet physicians' requests. Patients, particularly young women, eagerly awaited the visits of their male doctors. Some of the doctors, psychoanalysts for the most part, were preening narcissists not above treating nurses and social workers as their handmaidens. And most were ingloriously unaware both of the dynamics of the client's family system and women's place in it, such that mothers were frequently devalued, if not ignored. Social workers, on teams with doctors and nurses as well as with patients and families, were in a sort of professional no-man's land (or perhaps "all-men's land" would be more descriptive).

Many nurses on the young adult unit where I worked were frustrated with what they interpreted as the manipulativeness of the female patients, particularly those labeled "borderline" and those with eating disorders, and I could not help noticing that they expressed a great deal more animus toward the mothers of the patients than they did toward the fathers. In working with some of the more demanding patients, I struggled to understand what fueled their need for attention and what maintained their self-destructive behavior. I was less worried that I would be taken for a fool by these patients, a phenomenon some staff cautioned against, than I was interested in finding ways to talk to them and think about their problems. What I was beginning to understand in my work with "borderline" patients at the hospital was that the common ascription of certain motives to these women—that they were merely seeking attention or manipulating others, for example—was a major barrier to creating a relationship. I felt greatly validated when I read Daniel Wile's article, "Kohut, Kernberg, and Accusatory Interpretations" (1984). For decades, psychoanalytic psychotherapists had explained clients' angry or negative responses to the therapist and the therapist's interpretations as predictable indications of resistance or negative transference. According to Wile, however, it might be the pejorative nature of the interpretations themselves that played a part in evoking the reactions.

During these years, in considering possible subjects for my dissertation, I returned over and over again to the theoretical complications of the borderline personality disorder. I had found the descriptions of "borderlines" and their treatment in the psychodynamic literature problematic. Even when major theorists discussed only female "cases," they never mentioned gender. What I had read of Mahler, Kernberg, and others on the subject did not help me understand why most of the borderline patients who came onto our unit were women. I began to consider the possibility that sex bias (we did not call it gender bias in those days) might account in part for the prevalence of this diagnosis among women and that the socialization of girls might predispose women toward the constellation of the symptoms we now call "borderline." Although I had seen up close the very real distress women with borderline symptomatology experienced, I found clinicians' interpretations of their symptoms also to be increasingly troublesome. As, to my fascination, I began to learn more about the historically uncomfortable relationship between women and the psychiatric profession, I developed what has become an abiding interest in the historical and cultural construction of our conceptions of disorder and of psychotherapy practice itself.

My education as a clinician was proceeding apace. One day when I was meeting with a young female patient on the young adult unit with whom I seemed to be developing something of a good relationship, she suddenly turned to me and said with some venom that she wished I would not talk about myself all the time. I was completely taken aback, although I endeavored mightily to conceal this. In my practice, I had been experimenting with judicious self-disclosure, in keeping with my desire as a burgeoning feminist therapist to reduce the distance between therapist and client in the hierarchical order of things. From this young woman I learned that some individuals need everything that one has to offer, and that to receive anything less feels like a theft.

My understanding of "borderline" anger came not just from an exploration of books and articles but also from my own experience with anger expression. I began to consider the triggering effects of certain events on certain vulnerabilities—for example, the fact that a relatively minor incident could activate a vulnerability to separation. Both my personal experience and my clinical experience were teaching me that the knowledge of these potentially triggering events might enable people, with patience and practice, to manage the sense of emptiness and the rising swell of desperation that can lead to blinding rage in the moment. My clients seemed to feel understood when I asked them if the sensation they had at times was of an uncontrollable "geysering" up of emotion. Wile's (1984) perspective and my own observations pointed to the origin of the "tantrum" behaviors of so-called borderline women in women's fear of their own anger and their desire to avoid it to the extent possible. The reactions that looked so outsized to others had, in Wile's terms, an "underlying normality" (p. 361). Reading 19th century accounts of hysteria as well as contemporary feminist discussions about how women's anger is often expressed in strangulated forms (e.g., the manipulativeness of which women have often been accused) convinced me that, for women, a continuum of problems with anger expression runs the gamut from what is perceived by others as "overreaction" to an emotional reactivity that can lead to self-destructive and even suicidal behavior (Becker, 1997). Of course, in these cases we must consider histories of abuse and neglect as well as constitutional factors that may make certain individuals vulnerable to problems with emotion regulation, as Marsha Linehan (1993) has discussed. "Borderlines" are not so different from many other women, I concluded; women's problems with anger and anger expression are a matter of degree. I would not quickly forget Jean Baker Miller's (1991) maxim that "any anger is too much anger in women" (p. 185).

In the early years of my private psychotherapy practice, I saw a fair number of professional women in their 30s who were feeling anxious, sad, and confused. I recall how shocked I was when one young woman told me that she had had a "pity party" over the weekend. She had ended a more than 10-year relationship the previous year, had left her hometown, and had taken on a new job and a new life in the city. She seemed to be acting tremendously uncharitably toward herself, given the enormity of the losses she had so recently undergone. This was the first time I had heard the expression "pity party," and it brought home to me how the historical perception of women as hyperemotional has frequently led women and those close to them to be critical of their own emotionality, in light of the social requirement that they focus on the emotional well-being of others. I also saw in many of my clients the same phenomenon I had noticed in myself at times—anxiety related to the experience of sadness.

In reading the work of Carol Gilligan (1982) and Nancy Chodorow (1978) as well as the writings emanating from the Stone Center for Developmental Services and Studies at Wellesley College, I developed an interest in the ways in which women's socialization promoted relationality and connectedness. Gilligan and others (Gilligan, Rogers, & Tolman, 1991) spoke to the gradual erosion of a girl's sense of agency during the period of adolescence—how this sense of agency was supplanted by the perception of herself as one who must suppress her own needs to put others first. Dana Jack (1991) had talked about how depression in women stems from a "silencing" of the self. I began to ask female clients what they had learned about caring for others as well as what they had—or had not—taken in about the relative value of taking care of themselves. Eventually, I was to see how the purveyors of popular psychology as well as many clients and therapists were using the work of these feminist theorists to buttress the idea that relationality is ingrained in women—that it is part of their "true" nature—a notion that I now believe helps to maintain a gendered status quo. But first acquaintance with these works did not yield questions either about the essential "nature" of woman as relational or the universality of women's experience.

Although in my research on women and psychodiagnosis I was focusing primarily on the history and experiences of White, middle-class women, as part of a team at the Center for Research on Adolescent Drug Abuse, I was doing clinical work with African American, inner-city families, many of them mother-headed. The Multidimensional Family Therapy model that was being compared against cognitive-behavioral therapy for adolescent substance abuse is an approach that honors parents as the centrally important figures in their teenagers' lives. Therapists frequently meet alone with parents to help them process their thoughts and emotions in ways that facilitate their talking differently with their children. I was drawn to the approach for many reasons, not the least of which was that it put some "meat" (e.g., history, emotional content) on the bare bones of a structural family therapy model I had found too lean. This model seemed far more respectful of women's contributions to families and did not follow the historical precedent of viewing mothers as potential saboteurs of therapy. An approach that values women's care of and for their children and appreciates the difficulty some low-income single mothers have in finding and maintaining employment while taking responsibility for familial, social, and personal well-being had a great deal to recommend it to me. Encouraged by Dr. Liddle, I was able to bring my developing knowledge of women and single parenthood to working with families who were referred to the Center's clinic. By this time, I thought I knew something about women and about single-parent families, but, as I later discovered, there was still much to learn.

Case Example: Learning From Ms. Jackson

Ms. Jackson's appearance at the Center's clinic for her first appointment with her son Troy did not go unnoticed (the clients are given fictitious names here). She had no sooner sat down in the waiting room than she asked rather imperiously for coffee, and I was told that a student had gone off to procure it. Ms. Jackson, an African American woman in her 40s, who had worked as a nurse until she had had a heart attack 2 years before, had sought help for her son Troy because she felt he was acting too "grown." He was coming home at all hours; he was several years behind his age-mates at school because of repeated truancy; and she believed he was using drugs. Ms. Jackson had not waited until her son got in trouble with the law before going for help; she wanted to see her only child graduate from high school and find a career or trade for himself. But despite her obvious concern for Troy and his future, she was fatigued and in the initial phases of therapy frequently expressed a wish to be done with the onerous business of parenting this difficult teenager. Prickly and, by her own admission, quick to anger, Ms. Jackson tended to blow up at Troy when he upset her. Following such an explosion, he would usually leave the house. She did not pick her battles carefully; they ranged from fights over the way Troy wore his pants (they were too low on the hips to suit her) to major problems such as school truancy and unexplained late nights out.

Real possibilities for the two to engage in reasonable conversations emerged as Ms. Jackson revealed a capacity to reflect on her behavior and emotional states, and Troy showed an interest in sharing with his mother some of his experience of their relationship. At least in part as a result of my expressing interest in her life and respect for her feelings and ideas, Ms. Jackson began to show some trust in me, relating how she had been sexually abused as a girl, something she had never before told anyone. As a result of our discussion, when Troy asked her why she had never hugged him, she was able to tell him how fearful she had been about injecting any possible sexual element into their relationship because of her own early experience. With some help, she was able to hear her son describe the fear and anger he had felt when, in her addiction, she had left him with relatives who did not care properly for him; how frightened he was that she might have another heart attack; how he had always worried about *her* as she now worried about him.

By most measures, the case of Troy Jackson and his mother could be judged a success. It was an unexpected event, however, that was at least in part responsible for that accomplishment. Midway through the course of the twenty-odd sessions that were allotted to each family in the program, Troy got into some serious trouble with some men who said he owed them money, and one had held a knife against his throat as a warning. There was no need for more threats; Troy was not about to try to prove his manhood by tangling with armed thugs. He hid out at home, much to his mother's relief. Now at least she knew where her son was at night. The out-of-town residential vocational program that Ms. Jackson, Troy's social worker, and I had been touting, one in which Troy had shown little interest until now, began to appeal to him. Plans were quickly made for Troy to enter the program. The last weeks of therapy were spent helping Troy ready himself for this new venture and helping mother and son to talk about how the gains they had made in their relationship would be sustained.

In most models of psychotherapy, although the therapist does not determine client goals, she or he *does* determine the mechanisms by which change is achieved. It is more difficult to consider alternative pathways to change when things work out well in a case than otherwise. Ms. Jackson was by no means dissatisfied with the work we had done. And yet I started to wonder whether it would have been more helpful to have focused more on Troy and his problems than on her or on the relationship, as Ms. Jackson had often asked. At the same time, I questioned whether either Troy or his mother would have been able to manage that agenda without the building of trust in each other and in the therapeutic relationship that had been accomplished.

For all her prickliness, Ms. Jackson was the more able and willing of the two to change, and perhaps I exploited her softness toward her son, insufficiently trusting her ability to hold him consistently to the limits she had set or trusting that she could tolerate what would inevitably come in the aftermath—Troy's anger and, possibly, some short-term acting out. She had consistently given me mixed messages—that she wanted Troy to take her seriously and to respect her authority, but that she was too worn out to be bothered.

I was aware that many family therapists believe that the single most important task in working with female-headed, single-parent families is to shore up the parent's "executive" authority and tighten up boundaries between the generations (Fishman, 1988; Jung, 1996). Using this rationale, therapists often introduce skills and help engineer behavioral contracts between parent and child with little if any exploration of how overwhelmed and helpless the parent feels or any assessment of her readiness to take on the tasks of monitoring and limit-setting. In the Multidimensional Family Therapy model, a delicate balance needs to be struck between hearing the mother's story and validating her burdens and helping her monitor her teenager's activities and set age-appropriate limits for him or her (Liddle, Rowe, Dakof, & Lyke, 1998). Here, the therapist need not make a forced choice between two equally valid alternatives (Becker & Liddle, 2001). My concern about setting a problem-solving agenda with Ms. Jackson before she was ready may have led me to err on the side of exploring the mother/son relationship. Had I been avoiding pushing her and Troy in ways that might have shown us all the real difficulty of the task ahead?

Even at the time, I wondered what the outcome would have been had Troy not gotten into this final whirl of trouble. Although he and his mother had talked about much that had transpired in their lives and this had seemed to help their relationship, the dangers to which Troy was exposed on the street and at school remained. His life never did become an open book to me. Troy was not one to talk readily. When he did, it was easier for him to relate the injuries to which his mother's drinking had exposed him than to narrate a story of his own day-to-day existence that might have revealed more of its dangers, and I may not have pushed as hard as I could have to bring that experience forward. Despite my contacts with the school, the truancy officer, and the city social worker, it is clear that more intercession into the world Troy inhabited would have been necessary to help pull him back from the lure of the street. Looking back on the case, I cannot doubt that my absorption of a particularly American individualistic orientation toward the examination of the interior of people and relationships led me in the culturally accepted direction of promoting therapeutic discussion over social action.

Ms. Jackson had been prone to indulge Troy when she was not infuriated with him, and there were times when, as important as it had been to have him talk with her about his early experiences, I believe I did indeed trade on her motherly indulgence toward him, leaning on her more than I leaned on him. There is an old adage in the African American community that African American mothers "raise their daughters and love their sons." Perhaps I could have used this maxim to jump-start a discussion with Ms. Jackson about the difficulties she had in holding the line with Troy. In her seminal article, "Feminism and Family Therapy," Virginia Goldner (1985) has discussed the "ambiguous alliance" a mother makes with the family therapist. The woman needs the therapist to "legitimize her grievances" and get family members to change (p. 39); the therapist often needs the mother to bring the family in for therapy and to sign on to a vigorous change process. And yet the mother's and the therapist's ideas about how change should be achieved can differ vastly. The fact that women's socialization convinces them that they have, in Marcia Westkott's (1986) terms, an "imperative to nurture" often renders them particularly sympathetic to others' feelings. They can generally be pushed to make more compromises than other family members and to capitulate more often to the requests of the therapist (Goldner, 1985). As I have shown tapes of sessions with the Jacksons at conferences or in the classroom, I have asked myself more and more questions about the choices I made.

From working with mothers like Ms. Jackson, I learned a good deal about the central preoccupations of African American single mothers, and gender was not at the center of them. I certainly became convinced of what Elizabeth Spelman (1988) has so compellingly argued: that even when we routinely take account of race and class as well as gender, if we persist in claiming that—Black, White, poor, or rich—we "are all the same as women," we imply that differences among women exist in some part of us that is not "woman." If we do this, then despite the appearance that we are talking about women's differences, we are actually maintaining our own privileged position in society. I have learned—and discussions with my African American students have reinforced this—to be suspicious about conversations about race and class that do not include discussion of Whiteness and privilege, and to be skeptical of discussions of women's differences that focus primarily or exclusively on the experiences of poor and non-White women.

Listening to the Discourse of Difference

Of course, although most of us who are White never stop to consider *Whiteness* "difference," the dominant culture has made much of *male-female* difference from the 19th century debates over the "Woman Question" to contemporary discussions of gender distinctions in such popular books as John Gray's *Men Are From Mars, Women Are From Venus*. Many clients come to therapy having read self-help books and having been exposed to endless psychologizing by "experts" on television, in magazines, and in other media. Reading the work of Rachel Hare-Mustin and Jeanne Marecek (1990) alerted me that, by and large, psychology has constructed gender as difference, and psychological theories more often exaggerate male-female differences than de-emphasize them. In addition, there appears to be what Laura Brown (1994) calls a "dynamic tension" between the idea of gender as an innate, "natural" attribute and the notion of gender as a social construction. In feminist psychology, the bias has clearly been in the direction of essentialism, a bias that contributes to keeping women in their place (Bohan, 2002).

Now that I understand the social construction of difference, I hear the discourse of difference everywhere. I hear it, for example, in very bad advice middle-class White men and women clients frequently say they have received from their friends of the same gender about relationships, much of which centers around denying or camouflaging one's desires and feelings. For example, the injunction not to tell a man early in a relationship that he has done something that is distressing to them is one that many women often follow. The fear that *he* will cut and run if *she* speaks up is based on the belief that this will make the relationship too "real" for the man's liking, or that he will view her as making a "big deal" over something fairly minor because women are "too emotional," or that his ego is delicate and he will feel criticized and not be able to "handle" a request to do anything differently, or that he, like most men, cannot discuss subjects that have a high emotional valence. Clinging to these stereotyped notions of difference, the woman denies herself the opportunity to discover who this man is and what this relationship can sustain. Of course, if a man is not capable of hearing his partner ask for something from him or talking about something that upsets her, he may react poorly, and in some cases he may cut and run. But then, had the woman spoken up sooner, she would have had this information at the outset and spared herself significant pain. When, after months of trying to suppress her feelings, she finally expresses them, the man may come to believe—and rightly so—that he did not really know this woman, thus confirming the stereotype of women as duplicitous and manipulative.

A White musician in his late 30s, whom I will call Sam, had come to therapy following the breakup of a long-term relationship. He was depressed and said he wanted to look at the part he had played in that relationship so that he would not recapitulate in the future. After a number of months, Sam began dating again. I noticed how as he talked about his reentry into the dating world, he continually repeated that he did not want anything "serious." Sam was what women these days would call a "sensitive guy," and I had a familiar sense that he was often denying his dependency needs in order to project a more "macho" image. During one session, Sam mentioned that he had gone out with a woman he liked, but said he was not quite sure about her; he thought she might try to "nail my feet to the floor." This provided an opportunity for me to talk with Sam about stereotyped "locker-room" notions of women as grasping, clinging, and manipulative, a conversation I never could have envisioned holding in my early days as a practitioner.

The Working Mother Blues: Considering Middle-Class Gender Arrangements

A few years ago, a young divorced professional woman I will call Theresa came in for her psychotherapy session saying that she was feeling particularly bad that week. She said that when she had mentioned to her boyfriend Bill that she might need to go into her office to do some work on one of the days of a 3-day holiday weekend, he had questioned her decision on the basis that she should spend the entire holiday with her son Peter. She knew that Bill's ex-wife had primary custody of his own children and that Bill always managed to make plenty of time to play tennis and "unwind" from work while she, who had primary custody of her son, was still struggling to "make it" in the same male-dominated profession within which he had already made his mark. She also knew that her employers had little interest in accommodating the needs of a single mother. Theresa felt angry when she heard Bill's remarks, but at the same time she was overcome with guilt. Because caring and affiliation are motivated by gendered expectations, particularly by the pervasive sense that men's needs have more importance than women's (Westkott, 1997), Theresa's vulnerability to guilt was not surprising. When she was growing up, like so many girls, Theresa had accepted the naturalness and inevitability of motherhood. At this point in her life, she experienced daily the grinding worry about how well she was balancing work and family life that assails many middle-class working mothers. She clearly had trouble mobilizing herself to respond to Bill's remarks at the time he made them because her emotions were in such a muddle. Despite the immense thought and energy she had always put into the care of her son, Theresa constantly agonized over how Peter was doing and how she could improve her parenting. She had tremendous difficulty summoning up the sort of righteous outrage that would have enabled her to validate her own position in a discussion of this kind with Bill, since she herself did not believe she was a good enough mother. At the same time, she was frequently angry with Peter's father who, she felt, was often inconsiderate in his handling of some aspects of their parenting arrangements.

I cannot imagine talking with a woman like Theresa about her sadness and anger without discussing what she has learned about how to "do gender," to use Candace West and Don Zimmerman's (1992) phrase. This would involve considering in what particular ways she has taken in societal expectations of what her role should be and how she should mother, and how these figure into her vulnerability to criticism of her parenting. And, as a family therapist, neither can I imagine failing to help a woman like Theresa think about what kind of discussion she and her partner might have about his criticism and her vulnerability to it.

Arlie Hochschild (1989), originator of the term "second shift," contends that although one might think that the societal need for women to contribute to the family economy and for men to perform domestic chores would lead us toward "an egalitarian gender ideology" that would transform the division of labor at home, the pay differential between men and women and the high divorce rate, taken together, militate against the equality of domestic responsibility. In addition, these factors contribute to the construction of very conventional notions of gender, and individuals' reactions to them point women in the direction of supermomism and create men's resistance to accepting an equal share in domestic life.

These days, many therapists validate the domestic and emotional work that women do in families, but not all are committed to helping women and men to achieve equity in their domestic arrangements. Although I have found encouragement in the feminist family therapy literature for examining the locus of power in families, the longer I stay in the field, the less idealistic I am about whether psychotherapy can empower women in this domain, absent societal change. For empowerment to be achieved, challenges must be made to power-unequal policies, practices, and relationships, and these cannot be wrought through psychotherapy alone. For family therapists, the range of intervention options is at least a bit broader than it is for individual therapists. We now know that we can challenge the dominant power structure in couples therapy, for example, by having couples talk openly about money, sex, work, parenting, and household chores. Family therapists like Betty Carter insist that middle- and upper-middle class couples examine their values around these issues. In her work with these couples, Carter is not shy about giving her own opinions on these matters, telling a father, for instance, that he cannot be the kind of father he states he would like to be if he is working 70 hours a week, and asking parents who aver that their children are their "number one priority" to consider whether maintaining a summer home and a boat is worth the price of less time with the children. These dialogues strike at the very heart of American capitalism and consumerism and speak to the increasing importance some practitioners attach to making their values overt. There is no such thing as value-neutral psychotherapy. Whether we do or do not state our personal or political opinions, psychotherapy is a political enterprise. It is impossible to separate "the private," "the political," and "the social" when power relations pervade all three realms, not just the political (Cruikshank, 1999).

The Medical Is Personal: Learning About Women and Medicalization

Something I have taken away from my study of women and psychodiagnosis has been an awareness that in medicalizing women's problems we can end up attending to their behaviors and symptoms (Lerman, 1996) at the expense of understanding the social, relational, and historical contexts within which those problems are embedded. When I met Mary, a White woman in her early 60s who had been referred to me for psychotherapy, she told me that she had recently had several panic attacks. For some time before the first panic attack, she had been sleeping very poorly and had been experiencing a great deal of anxiety. As she described her symptoms, I assumed I would be referring her to a behavioral psychologist. Her symptoms seemed quite severe and I was well aware of the limitations of my expertise. As I continued to talk with her—as the social and cultural roots of her anxiety began to be revealed—it seemed that in addition to medication and the use of some behavioral techniques, exploration of her sense of her role as daughter, sister, wife, and mother could also prove valuable in alleviating her symptoms.

I learned that Mary's father had abandoned the family when Mary was quite young and that she had been the oldest daughter of an immigrant mother who spoke little English. As a girl, Mary had taken on many household responsibilities, including helping to care for her siblings. When she moved out of her mother's home and into her husband's, Mary assumed the duties of wife and mother with an equal sense of obligation. Now, with her children grown, and just as she had begun to envisage a less encumbered life ahead, a younger brother who had always leaned heavily on her had become sick and expected her to be very involved in his care. At around the same time, one of her daughters-in-law had had another baby and required more help. Mary had been driving on the highway to the daughter-in-law's house to baby-sit her grandchildren when the first panic attack occurred, and she had experienced subsequent panic attacks when she was driving on the highway. For Mary, as for many women, particularly those of her generation, saying "no" to the people who depended on her was not something to which her socialization had accustomed her. Nonetheless, although she was aware that she often felt angry about how many demands those close to her made upon her and how little they gave back, she never expressed anger toward them or asked others for help. Her panic attacks made it unnecessary for her to disappoint her family, to set limits, or to express anger; she simply could not fulfill her former role obligations (although I am not a psychoanalytic type, I cannot help recalling here what Freud had to say about symptoms as compromise formations). Unfortunately, however, neither could Mary enjoy her life. Learning to validate her own needs, express her anger, and set limits with her family began to prove an antidote to the anxiety attacks.

Conclusion and Further Reflections

Some critics who argue that the *personal* has formed the nucleus of feminist politics believe that the problem with the women's movement is that it took the idea that the "personal is political" too literally, thereby eschewing the struggle over "real" political questions. I would not disagree that the personal has wildly trumped the political over the past several decades. But one way to understand the contemporary relationship of the personal and the political is to take the slogan the "personal is political" *so* literally that we can begin to see how, as a society, we are reconfiguring altogether the level on which we become *able* to deal with political problems (Cruikshank, 1999). In my view, therapeutic discourse has become an important medium for addressing these problems, and the therapeutic culture has offered "solutions" that have not always proven helpful to those it has sought to benefit.

In a liberal democracy the "conduct of conduct," in Michel Foucault's terms, has led to psychological intervention as a form of recruitment into self-governance:

> "[The professionalization of being human]" . . . does not pit the interests of the experts against the interests and self-knowledge of the people. Rather, [it] . . . seeks to unite the interests of the individual with the interests of society as a whole. . . . Instead of excluding participation or repressing subjectivity, [it] operates to invest the citizen with a set of goals and self-understandings, and gives the citizen-subject an investment in participating voluntarily in programs, projects, and institutions set up to "help" them. (Cruikshank, 1999, pp. 39–41)

The "professionalization of being human" occurs increasingly at a time when the therapeutic realm is becoming more exclusively the domain of women. Of course women have historically been engaged in teaching others how to be human; now, as a result of their "expert" positions as psychotherapists, they can become the agents for transmission of society's teachings about the gendered self.

As many have done before me, I have asked myself whether psychology and psychotherapy are compatible with feminism. Although feminist psychology *could* be a vital political and intellectual arena, it seems constrained by a discipline that is "designed to flatten, depoliticize, individualize" (Fine & Gordon, 1992, p. 14). Many feminist ideas have been incorporated into the mainstream of the psychological professions, creating barely a ripple on the smooth surface of those professions or a profound disturbance in the consciousness of most of their members (Kitzinger, 1991).

Many therapists locate mental health problems primarily within individuals rather than in their environments (Caplan & Nelson, 1973), and feminist therapy has been thought to present a corrective to the dichotomization of private and public (Brown, 1994). But I cannot conscience the notion that therapy can "subvert patriarchy one life at a time, one therapy hour at a time," as some believe (Brown, 1994, p. 45). My skepticism is a constant itch. What if, as Laura Brown speculates, when "a feminist therapist . . . bravely describe[s] herself . . . as engaged in acts of resistance and revolution, . . . all we are witnessing is a feat of verbal legerdemain in which heroic-sounding justifications are advanced by a (usually) White and middle-class woman about the manner in which she makes her living" (p. 32)?

If we define power as control over resources and access to key institutions (Goodrich, 1991; Unger, 1986), it is difficult to claim that therapists can truly empower women. When I think about how feminist psychotherapists engage in the discourse of women's empowerment, I cannot help wondering if our attempts to empower our clients merely assist women in *experiencing* greater control over their lives while the oppressive context of their lives remains unchanged. I admire Judith Myers Avis's (1991) insistence on telling her clients plainly that therapy cannot transform the larger context of their lives, a position not often articulated by therapists.

Some years back I thought I knew what to do when very attractive White women who are by no one's definition wildly overweight (and some are not overweight at all) want to discuss their concerns about their weight in therapy. Now, I am not so sure I know. Yes, I have read Naomi Wolfe (1994), Susan Bordo (1993), and others on the sociocultural significance of women's hungers and society's vested interest in women's regulation of their appetites. And yes, I have talked with these women—and with myself—about unattainable contemporary societal standards for women's beauty. Those unrealistic standards, however, are still in force. I believe there is no discussion of "self-esteem" that can be of use here, and this is where we have placed the problem, culturally speaking—within the discourse of self-esteem. We ask the "self" to do a great deal in our culture. It is through the notion of the self that American individualism is most often expressed. And given my present interest in the legacy of individualism, I place the discourse of self-esteem and self-empowerment in the context of that historical tradition (Becker, 2005). So it gets more and more difficult to conceive of purely individual solutions to what are, after all, cultural dilemmas. Any examination of our "selves" is not a disengaged, objective analysis; it has the potential to transform the self that it examines (Woolfolk, 1998). I have come to understand that clients come to us not merely with problems, but with culturally formed *problematizations*—the kinds of problems for which psychological expertise is thought to have answers and which the therapeutic culture has deemed particularly troublesome (Rose, 1998).

Unfortunately, it is often through these problematizations that the status quo for women is maintained. In the 19th century, as middle-class women were beginning to move out of the home and the "Woman Question" was being debated, nervous "diseases" such as hysteria were thought to be strictly somatic in origin. The concern over hysteria points to the increase in the medicalization of women's problems at times of particular stress in gender arrangements. Today, when few would argue that tensions in gender arrangements do not exist, "stress" has become a significant problematization for women (Becker, 2005). It is often said that middle-class working women experience more stress than men do because of the multiple role occupancy dictated by their allegedly "natural" roles as nurturers. A woman more easily accepts a view of herself as "stressed out" than angry. Middle-class working mothers like Theresa, of whom I spoke earlier, can, if they are "stressed out," turn to therapists, medication, or consumer goods and services (yoga, massage, scented candles). Alternatively, they can "opt out" of the workplace altogether, as the contemporary vernacular has it, to care for their children. Of course, poor women will not have all of these options, but since poverty is also stressful, we can now begin to consider medical solutions to the stress-related depression and diseases that afflict them (Becker, 2005). I think I sound angry here, and the pull of my socialization would seem to encourage my deleting any words or sentences that smack of anger, but I have spent a lifetime trying not to retreat, so I will push ahead, in the spirit of Thelma Jean Goodrich's (1991) imprecation that we "not dampen the fire in order to soothe ourselves" (p. 32).

I frequently ask myself of what help therapy—even feminist therapy—can be in a world that affords women a very small menu of choices for solving problems intimately connected with a static social and political environment. Those things that I value as a therapist—doubt, the ability to take multiple perspectives, a socio-historical context for understanding human problems—lead me to believe that if women can locate their problems not just in themselves but in the social, political, and historical surround, if we can live with contradiction and complexity, perhaps we will be able to sort out inside therapy what is worth fighting for outside of it. I guess I am in for the long haul. I believe that when humans are willing to inhabit a more existential universe, when we are more accepting of ourselves and of the limits of possibility, we acquire the resilience and flexibility necessary to live our lives. This may not be a typically American view, given our historical emphasis on the vista of a good life as a straight diagonal upward, but that vision of progress can lead to a sense of personal failure for all of us who fall short of attaining it. Goodrich (1991) has expressed my sentiments on the score of doing feminist therapy better than I when she said that "knowledge of the limits [of therapy] grants us no solace; nor does it let us resign. Too many come to us and nowhere else. We cannot be victorious, yet we dare not be defeatist. We commit not to oversimplify, not to mystify, not to temporize, not to back away. We ready ourselves for the squeeze play" (p. 32).

References

Avis, J. M. (1991). Power politics in therapy with women. In T. J. Goodrich (Ed.), *Women and power: Perspectives for family therapy* (pp. 183–200). New York: Norton.

Becker, D. (1997). *Through the looking glass: Women and borderline personality disorder*. Boulder, CO: Westview.

Becker, D. (2005). *The myth of empowerment: Women and the therapeutic culture in America*. New York: New York University Press.

Becker, D., & Liddle, H. A. (2001). Family therapy with unmarried African American mothers and their adolescents. *Family Process, 40*(4), 413–427.

Bohan, J. (2002). Sex differences and/in the self: Classic themes, feminist variations, postmodern challenges. *Psychology of Women Quarterly, 26*, 74–88.

Bordo, S. (1993). *Unbearable weight: Feminism, Western culture, and the body*. Berkeley: University of California Press.

Brown, L. (1994). *Subversive dialogues: Theory in feminist therapy*. New York: Basic Books.

Caplan, N., & Nelson, S. D. (1973). On being useful: The nature and consequences of psychological research on social problems. *American Psychologist, 28*(3), 199–211.

Chodorow, N. (1978). *The reproduction of mothering*. Berkeley: University of California Press.

Cruikshank, B. (1999). *The will to empower*. Ithaca, NY: Cornell University Press.

Fine, M., & Gordon, S. M. (1992). Feminist transformations of/despite psychology. In M. Fine (Ed.), *Disruptive voices: The possibilities of feminist research* (pp. 1–25). Ann Arbor: University of Michigan Press.

Fishman, H. C. (1988). *Treating troubled adolescents: A family therapy approach*. New York: Basic Books.

Gilligan, C. (1982). *In a different voice: Psychological theory and women's development*. Cambridge, MA: Harvard University Press.

Gilligan, C., Rogers, A. G., & Tolman, D. L. (Eds.). (1991). *Women, girls and psychotherapy: Reframing resistance*. New York: Harrington Park Press.

Goldner, V. (1985). Feminism and family therapy. *Family Process, 24*(1), 31–47.

Goodrich, T. J. (1991). Women, power, and family therapy: What's wrong with this picture? In T. J. Goodrich (Ed.), *Women and power: Perspectives for family therapy* (pp. 3–35). New York: Norton.

Hare-Mustin, R. T. (1978). A feminist approach to family therapy. *Family Process, 17,* 181–194.

Hare-Mustin, R. T., & Marecek, J. (1990). Beyond difference. In R. T. Hare-Mustin & J. Marecek (Eds.), *Making a difference: Psychology and the construction of gender* (pp. 184–201). New Haven, CT: Yale University Press.

Hochschild, A. R. (1989). *The second shift: Working parents and the revolution at home.* New York: Viking.

Jack, D. C. (1991). *Silencing the self: Women and depression.* Cambridge, MA: Harvard University Press.

Jung, M. (1996). Family-centered practice with single-parent families. *Families in Society, 77,* 583–590.

Kitzinger, C. (1991). Politicizing psychology. *Feminism and Psychology, 1*(1), 49–54.

Lerman, H. (1996). *Pigeonholing women's misery: A history and critical analysis of the psychodiagnosis of women in the twentieth century.* New York: Basic Books.

Liddle, H. A., Rowe, C., Dakof, G. A., & Lyke, J. (1998). Translating parenting research into clinical interventions for families of adolescents. *Clinical Child Psychology and Psychiatry, 3,* 419–443.

Linehan, M. M. (1993). *Cognitive-behavioral treatment of borderline personality disorder.* New York: Guilford.

Miller, J. B. (1991). The construction of anger in women and men. In J. V. Jackson, A. G. Kaplan, J. B. Miller, I. P. Stiver, & J. L. Surrey (Eds.), *Women's growth in connection* (pp. 181–196). New York: Guilford.

Rose, N. (1998). *Inventing ourselves: Psychology, power, and personhood.* Cambridge, UK: Cambridge University Press.

Spelman, E. V. (1988). *Inessential woman: Problems of exclusion in feminist thought.* Boston: Beacon.

Unger, R. K. (1986). Looking toward the future by looking at the past: Social activism and social history. *Journal of Social Issues, 42,* 215–227.

West, C., & Zimmerman, D. H. (1992). Doing gender. In J. S. Bohan, *Seldom seen, rarely heard: Women's place in psychology* (pp. 379–403). Boulder, CO: Westview.

Westkott, M. C. (1986). *The feminist legacy of Karen Horney.* New Haven, CT: Yale University Press.

Westkott, M. C. (1997). On the new psychology of women: A cautionary view. In M. R. Walsh (Ed.), *Women, men, and gender: Ongoing debates* (pp. 362–372). New Haven, CT: Yale University Press.

Wile, D. B. (1984). Kohut, Kernberg, and accusatory interpretations. *Psychotherapy, 21*(3), 353–364.

Wolfe, N. (1994). Hunger. In P. Fallon, M. Katzman, & S. Wooley (Eds.), *Feminist perspectives on eating disorders* (pp. 94–111). New York: Guilford.

Woolfolk, R. L. (1998). *The cure of souls: Science, values, and psychotherapy.* San Francisco: Jossey-Bass.

8

A Woman's View of Clinical Trauma Theory and Therapy

Susan H. Gere

I am not sure when I thought I might be interested in doing psychotherapy, or even when I had any idea what that word meant. My family was not culturally sophisticated in that way but I did have a delightful encounter with a school psychologist who administered the WISC intelligence test as the gateway to my exciting Sputnik-era advanced science and math classes. I liked the personal attention he gave me and the way he gave me an opportunity to show my stuff. As an oldest child and a musician, I certainly always felt curious about others and responsive to the "music" of life. I think I may also have been a native developmentalist, having had the privilege of participating in caring for people from birth through death in my family. I imagine my exposure to the full-spectrum of life opened and tuned my heart. That included learning to relate to the variety of "odd" and mentally ill members of my extended family and rural community. Early on, I learned how to deal with difficult and, sometimes, frightening people. I imbibed an accepting, nonjudgmental and, often, humorous view of human nature. I do remember reading Freud's *The Psychopathology of Everyday Life* in high school and thinking, now here is something I can relate to.

When I got to college, I thought a psychology major would be a good idea, but by the time I had completed all the requirements for the only available psychology major—experimental—I thought better of it and switched to a major in French, which was much more humanistic. Actually, the connection between literature and human behavior was much closer than between laboratory rats and human behavior. I started graduate school in French but soon realized something was still missing. It was not until I got a job in the psychotherapy-rich environs of Boston that I began to understand what I really wanted to do and went to graduate school in clinical social work. Among other things, being in a mostly female learning environment was wonderful for me. I had not had any female professors in college and, in retrospect, felt that I never quite spoke the right academic language. In social work school, children and love and death and suffering were part of the curriculum and I was inspired by female professors who even talked about themselves from time to time.

The culture of psychotherapy has changed dramatically over the past 30 years in which I have been practicing. When I was trained as a very young social worker in the early 1970s, psychoanalytic psychotherapy was the dominant psychotherapeutic model, male psychotherapists were the norm, and social workers were considered the "handmaidens" of psychiatrists. Male dominance in theory and practice was even the norm in family and systems therapy (Hoffman, 1990) in which I also was trained, as well as in community approaches (Caplan, 1970). I was 23 years old when I started working in public and private agency settings. I was fortunate to have social work as my selected discipline at that time because there were some female clinical role models in social work. Even those women, however, had internalized their marginality in the psychotherapeutic enterprise such that terms like "penis envy" and "frigidity" were acceptable clinical language. I remember the numerous case conferences in which female clients were frequently referred to by both male and female clinicians as "histrionic" and "seductive."

Sexual drive theory as a dominant paradigm in psychotherapy was attacked (Masson, 1983) as inadequate a decade later in the 1980s by feminist theorists and clinical researchers who began to call attention to the rampant sexual abuse of children (Russell, 1984), domestic abuse of women and children (Walker, 1984), and the sexual abuse of women by their psychotherapists (Gartrell, Herman, Olarte, Feldstein, & Localio, 1986). In addition, to my great relief, directive models of family therapy were questioned by prominent female clinician/researchers (Hoffman, 1990) who saw those models as disempowering to parents, especially to the single mothers who were frequently seen in public clinics. I found this shift a relief because I had always been uncomfortable with the "I know better" attitudes in the strategies of early male family therapists, and more comfortable with Virginia Satir's reflective, joining, and wondering style. Also, I was on the quiet side as a clinician—spending more time on empathy, listening carefully, and looking for the right question(s). I did not so much question my own ability to be authoritative. I was simply more interested both in developing a mutual understanding of the material with the client and in more of a textual analysis of what people presented rather than telling them what they were doing wrong. I would guess that my rural values contributed to liking and respecting people "where they were" and my creative side got hooked by working with what clients were actually saying. Also, I am not natively very anxious about making sure people behave properly—perhaps another part of my rural, working-class roots. I can identify with people who are very angry or socially inept. Luckily, the Milan school (Hoffman, 1990) of therapy also validated a more questioning, less knowing approach to systemic work that is more compatible with my native style.

The community consultation model, with its emphasis on community empowerment and its utilization of the strengths of indigenous caregivers and paraprofessionals, was another natural orientation for me. Though, again, I gravitated toward more collaboration in consultation than toward externally imposed change strategies. My first job in the public mental health system was in the Department of Training, Planning and Research, helping to facilitate the transition from the male-led mental hospital "fiefdoms" to more diffuse and—intentionally—more egalitarian community-based models that incorporated the views of consumers and their families. Again, a natural arena for women's ways—certainly mine. I enjoyed the clinical freedom to move between the institutions and the community in the service of the work. We did not have to keep track of our direct contact hours and worked with logical support groups in homes and communities. While these services were statutorily required by the Community Mental Health Act of 1963, the 1980s saw a weakening of their influence as funding for these initiatives at the national and state levels moved from the public to private sectors (Werner & Tyler, 1993), and interpersonal approaches were replaced by more medically oriented, biologically based interventions. The dominant treatment paradigms moved back toward the more directive, "can do" models favored by predominantly male psycho-pharmacologists and cognitive-behavioral clinicians.

My first jobs in the mental health system were in mental hospitals, court clinics, and community mental health centers. In each of those settings, I saw the pervasive influence of adverse economic, social, and health factors on people's lives. I saw children who were beaten at home and discriminated against in school, drug-addicted parents who had no social supports, young people who had no social opportunity and many people who were victims of interpersonal and systemic violence. The psychotherapeutic tools that were available were grounded in the paradoxical assumptions that social and familial systems could be "fixed" and that external events were less important than intrapsychic structures. What was missing was a therapeutic construct to link social, systemic, and interpersonal violence with its effects on the beliefs, behaviors, and abilities of victims. Also, the moral link between the clinician and the client was virtually ignored. In response to my crying about the plight of one of my clients, an early supervisor said to me, "From this we make a living." While the tough love aspect of his response did not escape me, in retrospect I think there was no language available in psychotherapy at the time to capture the empathy and moral connection one feels with suffering and terrible life experiences.

Currently, in my work with clinical students, it always impresses me that the introduction of the trauma paradigm—with its acknowledgment of terrible life experiences, their expectable sequelae, and secondary trauma in clinicians—brings a great sigh of relief in students and an exclamation of "Why didn't anyone tell us about this before. Now many things make sense!" In my own training, I remember feeling terribly dissatisfied with intrapsychic interpretations of human behavior and longing for a way to acknowledge suffering that connected the client and the clinician rather than distancing us from each other. How could we all be in the same boat as human beings if suffering was pathologized? How could my suffering in relation to the client be legitimized? The notion of countertransference was useful but seemed to leave out so much about the normal resonance of the clinician to the client's experience. Perhaps our culture defines suffering as aberrant rather than expectable. If it is nonnormative, then it becomes dangerous to acknowledge.

Clinical Views of Trauma

The 1980s saw a lively and much needed development of clinical trauma theory through the ascendance of intellectual and political work by prominent feminist clinical researchers such as Judy Herman (1981), Laura Brown (1994), and Diana Russell (1984). How such relatively frequent and deleterious experiences as father-daughter incest and other forms of domestic abuse were viewed clinically changed dramatically depending on the psychotherapeutic research and theory available. By the 1980s, assumptions that father-child incest was rare, only minimally harmful to children, and should not be the focus of clinical intervention were questioned. Judith Herman's (1981) groundbreaking study of father-daughter incest concluded

> It would be an exaggeration to state that victims of sexual abuse inevitably sustain permanent damage. There is nevertheless considerable evidence to

> suggest that child victims, as a group, are more vulnerable to a number of pathological developments in later life, and that a considerable number of victims suffer lasting harm. (p. 29)

Feminist theorists and researchers also joined with a post-Vietnam-era group of male researchers (Figley, 1985; Finkelhor, 1984; Keane, Fairbank, Caddell, & Zimering, 1989) who challenged the cultural model of the imperturbable tough guy and acknowledged the debilitating effects of war on many vulnerable veterans and of the physical assaults experienced disproportionately by boys and men. Together, they developed the current self-help and empowerment-based "recovery" model that provides a skeletal structure for treatment of trauma survivors. It assumes that the person could use more knowledge about the effects of violence on him- or herself, is having difficult post-trauma psychophysiological reactions, psychological disorganization, distortions in interpersonal functioning, and is possibly using a variety of substances to manage the aftermath of traumatic experience. The goal is to help victims develop a sense of moving from seeing themselves as "victims" of trauma to "survivors" of trauma, more accurately assessing their responsibility for the event(s), and (re)constructing a positive sense of self and the world.

The important stages in the trauma "recovery" model laid down then provide the overall framework we use today: (a) using careful assessment, psycho-education about trauma, and, possibly, psycho-pharmacology to help the traumatized client stabilize and establish personal and interpersonal safety; (b) helping the person construct a narrative account of the traumatic experience from physical, sensory, and visual memory fragments that are generally available in rather "undigested" or temporally disorganized forms; and (c) using primary relationships, natural healing environments, therapeutic support, and recovery groups to help people find authentic connection with themselves and others that incorporates an acknowledgment of the traumatic experience and what it has meant to them. Underlying this model is the assumption (Janoff-Bulman, 1992) that there was a prior (pre-trauma) state of grace to return to psycho-spiritually in which the self and others were perceived to be essentially benign. Further, it is the working through of the memories and feelings about the trauma that is seen as key to recovery. This assumption seems most clearly to fit relatively discrete trauma experiences and many case accounts point to excellent recovery using this model.

In his book about his own experience and recovery, Michael Patrick MacDonald (1999) finds that joining with others and creating a gun buy-back project in the city of Boston helps him combat the personal sense of helplessness he felt when several of his siblings were killed due to gun violence and organized crime in his beloved "Southie." While most people probably "reconnect" to others in less public and politicized ways, the importance of validating one's experience, acknowledging the external traumatic stressors that were beyond one's control, and processing enough associated guilt and shame so that one's life no longer need be fundamentally "secret" (Blume, 1990) is assumed to be the platform that allows meaningful reconnection to one's life.

Feeling connected to one's self, to a community of people, and to a larger sense of purpose in life is consistent with my own outlook. Coming from a strongly connected family and community with an investment in making the world a better place for everyone, I find the trauma recovery model grounded in valid assumptions about what makes life bearable. The part of the work that does not have a home in my cultural experience is acknowledgment of the connection between adverse life experience and later adaptation. I believe I was strongly attracted to the enterprise of psychotherapy precisely because I believed that behavior has meaning. I still believe, however, that it is culturally radical to connect adverse life conditions with one's sense of identity in a culture that insists on relentless self-assurance. Herman's work (1997) refers to the "culture of denial about traumatic events" that sustains the repetition of violence in its many forms.

Psychotherapy and Trauma Recovery

In the 1990s, "integrative, stage-oriented" models of treatment incorporating clinical trauma theory, biologically based therapies, group psychotherapy, community-based traumatic stress debriefing, and body-oriented therapies ripened into a sophisticated set of interlocking assumptions about the nature of psychosocial trauma and healing. It includes the understanding that significant psychiatric symptoms evolve as a logical consequence of an individual or group's interaction with a violent, often unmanageable world (Esper, 1986). Central to definitions of Post Traumatic Stress Disorder remained references to "events that were outside expectable life experiences" (American Psychiatric Association, 1994, p. 424), and an assumption that traumatic experiences could be essentially viewed as discrete and distinct from "usual, expectable" experience. Analysis of large-scale surveys of community populations (Finkelhor, 1984; Russell, 1984) and epidemiological health studies (Felitti et al., 1998; Kessler, Sonnega, Bromet, Hughes, & Nelson, 1995), however, cast doubt on the "unusualness" of traumatic events, including adverse childhood events. Cross-cultural studies confirm the prevalence of traumatic events and their sequelae around the world and among all populations (Marsella, Friedman, Gerrity, & Scurfield, 1996; Shalev, Yehuda, & McFarlane, 2000).

In a groundbreaking, random-sample telephone survey of 1,000 women in the San Francisco area, Diana Russell (1984) found that one third of the women had been sexually abused before the age of 18. David Finkelhor (1984) found that 80 percent of college students had experienced one or more traumatic events. In the most extensive study of a community sample to date, the U.S. Department of Health and Human Services, Centers for Disease Control and Prevention surveyed almost 10,000 members of the Kaiser Permanente health plan (Felitti et al., 1998). The authors found that the majority of people surveyed experienced at least one, and 25 percent experienced more than one, extremely adverse experience in childhood including abuse, parental mental illness, suicide, incarceration, addiction, and domestic violence. Societal violence, poverty, and war have contributed to further trauma for whole populations (Marsella et al., 1996; Shalev et al., 2000).

Current attempts to integrate basic research with clinical practice (van der Kolk, McFarlane, & Weisaeth, 1996) question the bias of early clinical trauma theory that suggests that traumatic experiences are discrete, nonnormative, and disturb a person's underlying assumptions (Janoff-Bulman, 1992) about a "benign universe." As an example of what I would refer to as "life-span trauma," Gilfus (1999) describes a culturally inclusive "survivor-centered epistemology" honoring the strengths of survivors and what she calls the "wisdom of victimization" (p. 1239). It aims to include the social and cultural context in which multiple sources of trauma can be acknowledged. She argues that to do culturally sensitive work, the "symptoms" of trauma survivors need to be reframed and appreciated as "smart survival (and resistance) strategies" (p. 1244). One of these survival strengths she labels "world-traveling"—a concept borrowed from Maria Lugones (1990)—for those who live outside the "mainstream U.S. construction or organization of life" (p. 390). Survivors of pervasive childhood and life-span trauma are unequally represented in places with few economic and political resources (Marsella et al., 1996). They are often subject to "racially-based psychological trauma" that includes the historical genocide and ongoing struggles of Native Americans, the World War II internment of Japanese Americans, and the historical enslavement and race-based injuries experienced by African Americans (Gilfus, 1999).

Recent work by African American clinicians such as Poussaint and Alexander (2001) has suggested that for subjugated minorities, the pervasive experience of racism is its own category of psychosocial trauma. Clinical researchers and mental health advocates have lobbied the American Psychiatric Association's Diagnostic and Statistical committees during the past 10 years for some form of diagnostic category that goes beyond "Acute Stress Disorder" (which describes the aftermath of a traumatic event within the first month) and "Post Traumatic Stress Disorder" (which describes the longer-term sequelae of relatively discrete traumatic events). Chu (1998), Herman (1997), van der Kolk et al. (1996), and others have argued for a diagnostic category that more usefully describes those states that could be described as "chronic," "complex," or "pervasive."

The positionality demanded of the clinician dealing with culturally based trauma includes an appreciation for the psychological demands of "world traveling." It entails an emphasis on facilitating the acknowledgment and integration of the multiplicity of selves necessary for this going between worlds. It includes the recognition that, for many whose survival depends on defending oneself creatively in a violent world, a "just world" and a "safe home" are out of reach. It is the clinician's responsibility to acknowledge both the historical antecedents of the client's identity formation and the ongoing reality of a threatening world for many. One of the clearest examples can be seen among gay clients whose psychological work includes deconstructing internalized cultural homophobia while maintaining self-protective vigilance against violent gay bashing. It is the clinician's responsibility to position herself both in the past and in the present as an ally in the client's developing relationship to self and culture. In this regard, a female clinician may be psychologically and morally well-equipped to help if she has achieved an understanding of her own internalized sexism while recognizing that women continue to be at risk physically and economically.

Gilfus (1999) posits that those who suffer decades of traumatic experiences develop worldviews and coping capacities that *always* accounted for the reality of unmanageable and sometimes overwhelming social interpersonal violence. Such environments would necessitate *adaptive* worldviews in which violence is expectable and significant resilience is not unusual but is required for survival. Practitioners need to develop a realistic view of the social conditions and cultural practices that cause traumatic experiences, respect the understandable defensive strategies victims have developed, and create therapeutic alliances that allow the holding and sharing of both suffering and hope for a better future.

Placing Myself in the Field

As a clinician and teacher, I have practiced with individuals, families, and communities and have trained clinicians over the past 30 years. I have learned that theory grows to match our clinical and cultural ability to perceive and cope with reality. It seems to me that we American clinicians, as a cultural group, have begun to acknowledge insurmountable stresses such as poverty, war, discrimination, and social violence in their many forms that brought our immigrant ancestors to the "new world" and that continue to affect many people here and throughout the world. My own developing worldview has been greatly influenced by the truths that I have learned from my survivor clients and from the growing body of epidemiological and clinical research about psychosocial trauma. As a community of practitioners, we clinicians need to be careful about imposing worldviews that are inadequate or harmful. A savvy trauma client I interviewed in 1987 asked me if I would have thought she was psychotic had I seen her 10 years previously. In fact, she carried several severe mental illness diagnoses other than Post Traumatic Stress Disorder (PTSD) by the time we met and began successfully working together within the trauma recovery framework.

Just as I have found the trauma recovery framework useful, I have also recognized the need for a more integrated clinical theory to adequately describe the cultural reality and treatment of chronically traumatized individuals and communities. I would add that, for those who suffered from chronic trauma in the early decades of their lives, there is not necessarily any relief in adult life. Economic and health problems, and the "pile up of losses" (Harvey, Barnett, & Overstreet, 2004) continue even in the context of healing from earlier life events. Recovery-oriented models have been more successful with clients whose traumatic experiences can in some way be distinguished from their non-traumatic experiences. Psycho-education, supportive psychotherapy, adjunctive psycho-pharmacology, narrative reconstruction, cognitive-behavioral exposure and desensitization, and group therapies all help reduce suffering and promote growth. I use all these strategies.

With people who have lived in the context of constant disruption and violence, however, "recovery" has seemed an inadequate and, for some, an insulting clinical model. *Recovery from what, exactly?*—chronic and ongoing abuse and neglect by mentally ill parents, multiple sexually exploitive experiences, impossible choices about which dysfunctional set of relatives to live with to ensure survival, ongoing isolation and narcissistic injury, impossible demands to raise siblings when one has not been parented oneself, homelessness, and so on. Indeed, when applied to people who have survived ongoing trauma in their lives, even positive concepts such as "resilience" in the face of extraordinarily difficult circumstances (Rutter, 1987), "stress-hardiness," which allows people to believe that they can meet challenges personally (Kobasa, Maddi, Puccetti, & Zola, 1985), "optimism" (Scheier, Weintraub, & Carver, 1986), and "sense of coherence," which allows people to understand events in the service of managing them (Antonovsky, 1987) are *necessary* for survival, but not always *sufficient* to "keep them afloat" in the face of chronic sociocultural stress. One client who has had multiple personal losses and health problems complained that she just could not "get her head above water" to cope on a day-to-day basis. Even the concept of "post-traumatic growth" (Harvey, Barnett, & Overstreet, 2004; Neimeyer, 2004; Tedeschi & Calhoun, 1995) seems an affront when one is barely treading water and there is no definable "pre trauma" to compare with "post-trauma."

In response to working with clients who seem to move very slowly through recovery, I often feel that I am simply not doing it right. At the same time, I wonder if my own socialization as a woman makes me vulnerable to internalizing and feeling "responsible" for unresolved trauma work in much the same way that my clients feel "responsible" for what has happened to them. I wonder if the clinical expectations may simply be too broadly defined and that our tools are still not fully matured. In addition, though psychotherapy could be a powerful healing practice, we cannot expect psychotherapy to solve problems that require systemic social and political interventions.

I am fortunate to have been a member of two trauma supervision groups of female clinicians for the past 10 years. Our collective experience is often of working with people who have developed in the context of decades of adversity that can have personal, familial, sociocultural, and economic sources, as well as sequelae. "Sitting" with the legacy of horrible previous and ongoing stressors demands tough-minded scientific thinking, respectful "moral solidarity" (Herman, 1997; Marin, 1981), and existential alliance-building. The alliance-building that is most authentic for me is an I-Thou position in which the pain and aggression that reside in my soul find a resonance in that of my client. This is not to say that I am the same as my client or that my experience is the same, but that the same *vulnerabilities* exist in each of us. So the rageful feelings and the terrified feelings a client brings find an "Aha!—I know that feeling" in myself, rather than a distancing response.

Interestingly, research on counselors-in-training suggests that their own histories of adverse childhood experiences may be positively correlated with their capacity to be empathic with their clients (Wilcoxon, Walter, & Hovestadt, 1989). In my own research (Gere, 1999) on training student trauma survivors in social work and mental health counseling, I concluded that the most significant factor in helping relationships is not any particular personal history but the capacity to *reflect* on that history. This may be the most important therapeutic factor in psychotherapy in general. The taking of the self as the object of attention and reflection allows for both healing and transformation. I deeply believe in this power for myself as well as for my clients. In that way and existentially, we are genuinely "all in the same boat." In addition, current trauma recovery models favor reflection on the narrative meaning of traumatic events over abreaction. Narrative self-interpretation allows for an empowering *selection and choice* process about which negative events to remember and how to contextualize them to maximize the good that can come from acknowledging them.

Because the current culture of psychotherapy reimbursement is oriented to short-term, biological and cognitive behavioral models, and measurable outcomes, however, both engagement with suffering and its narrative meaning are not fashionable. Happiness and positive thinking (Seligman & Csikszentmihalyi, 2000) are currently more in favor and may mirror our national preoccupation with "optimism" and "toughness." It seems that a "negative" or "depressive" candidate cannot win an election in our current political climate. Those experiences attributed to women—vulnerability and depression, not to mention emotions such as anger, even if justified—seem to have become taboo even in the therapeutic literature.

As a female clinician, being willing "to go there" with suffering—demonstrating genuine empathy, understanding of worldviews, and offering compassion for great difficulty—seems to me the essence of a de-pathologizing and respectful position. Empathy has been shown to be a contributing factor to positive outcomes in psychotherapy. It is a relational capacity shared by both men and women, but I would say that my own capacity to bear suffering in a relational context has certainly been honed in the caretaking relationships with family members as well as with the many clients I have sat with over the years. Empathic alliances lend hope for healing and growth. I keep three photos of one of my children and myself nearby to remind me of this. We were caught in a sequence of moments that has continued to be emblematic of how I understand "suffering in relation." In the first photo, my 3-year-old is in tears over some mishap, but I am peaceful. In the second photo, we have our arms around each other in a comforting pose. In the third photo, my child has left my arms, is in motion, and I am sorrowful, having absorbed some of her pain. I do not mean to suggest that clients are tantamount to my children, but that the "holding" of suffering still seems valuable to me as a therapeutic activity and critical in the gradual transformation of relational capacity with survivors on life-span trauma.

The internalization of someone who cares and is willing to listen carefully and share painful emotions and ideas serves as a platform for the development of a different self. In a recent interview (documented in *Strong at the Broken Places* by Cambridge Documentary Films, 1998), clinician Marcia Gordon shares that her own life of despair from chronic childhood abuse and adult prostitution and drug abuse changed when one person showed her she cared. Gordon recounts her emergent understanding that she used drugs to cover the pain of being chronically beaten, exploited, and abandoned, and her sense that she was bad and ugly and brought the abuse on herself. She talks about self-destructive behaviors and the repetition of abusive patterns over years of violent relationships. In her own recovery, she talks about the importance of realizing that she could be of value to others and help them too.

I believe it is a much underrated truth that helping serves the clinician as much as the client. Often, new clinicians in training or those outside the field will say, "How do you stand to hear all those awful stories?" The answer, of course, is that sitting with a client's pain, even when it is of great proportions, is a privilege that nurtures our own humanity and relieves our own isolation. Recently, I held an administrative position that required a great number of meetings and, what seemed to me, a draining level of interpersonal detachment. I found myself going to my clinical practice one evening after a long administrative day, and feeling with surprising force how grateful I was to be in emotional contact with another person. I, myself, needed the solace of caring for someone and cherishing the life she was struggling to save in the face of a life of trauma that included late-stage cancer. When I think of what I bring as a woman to working with psychosocial trauma in its many forms, it is the recognition of the deep value of the holding environment (Winnicott, 1965) in trauma work. The holding environment allows for the recognition and integration of both sorrow and aggression. This is not a new concept, nor is it a gender-bound concept; but it is certainly at the heart of what we recognize as "maternal thinking" (Ruddick, 1980), whether practiced by a man or a woman.

Case Example: Mira

Mira was born to a Euro-American mother and a Japanese American father whose family had spent World War II in an internment camp. She was 18 months old when her mother was hospitalized with schizophrenia the first time. She already had a little sister and three more children were born by the time Mira was 7. Over time, during her mother's long absences, Mira was substitute mother, wife, and, eventually, sexual surrogate to her father. Her Japanese family helped care for the children and they rotated among their aunts and back to their parents each time their mother was released from a hospital. Their mother was never really symptom-free. She would alternate between catatonia and violently delusional states. Mira was simultaneously protective of her mother and very afraid of her. In that miracle of human altruism, she understood that her mother was ill and could not be held responsible for her behavior. It is not clear how much she adopted the substitute maternal role out of love for her siblings and how much it was forced on her. She says she did not want her siblings to know life without a mother, but her father also demanded that she behave as an adult woman. She describes always being an excellent student while having to manage a household and never having any time for herself. Because of the family's frequent moves and her status as the only minority child in her many schools, she felt alone and isolated and had few friends though kind adults provided various temporary safe havens for her.

Despite overwhelming odds, Mira managed to go to college while living at home and found work to help support her family. She was not satisfied with the work because she knew she was capable of doing something more interesting, but her hope for self-fulfillment was always tempered by her father's control of her choices. His mantra to her ambitious wishes was: "Dumbheads who think they're smartheads are really shitheads." What she took from this was that it is stupid to want anything and that she should not think too much of herself or push herself into the limelight. She said, "The way I got through difficulty in my childhood was to decide always to do the right thing because I will be above reproach and will never accidentally be selfish." Her father's domination also interfered with any romantic relationships she had, and he continued to be the central figure in her life until his death when she was in her 30s. A year later, her mother also died.

I began to see Mira after her parents died. She was working in an academic setting, doing ceramics for her own pleasure and trying to make friends while remaining deeply involved with her siblings and aunts. She had no religious affiliation in her childhood but joined a liberal protestant congregation as an adult. In spite of her father's interference, she had managed some significant relationships with men and sought treatment with me when the most recent one had failed.

Mira's initial concerns were about her deep sorrow at losing an important relationship and her fear that no one could ever love her. She freely gave a history of her family relationships, including her mother's mental illness and the abuse by her father. She also said she had briefly seen another therapist who had tried to focus on working with her about the sexual abuse. Mira said she recognized that the sexual abuse was wrong but she did not consider it the most important thing about her and did not want to focus on it. Instead, she wanted to focus on current relationships and her lack of ease with both men and women. She said, "Where do you go when your mom was crazy? I pick my pleasures. I like to make things with my hands, I like to cook, I like to clean and organize things. I do want a relationship but I don't care about sex or about being cherished. I like to be collaborative—that is my religion—but I always end up being too responsible. There is always too much work to do and I get exhausted. I'd like the simple peace of knowing that I make someone happy, but I feel like I bother people and make them yell at me or reject me. They tell me they love me and then they leave me. I'm not like other people." She was also overworked and undervalued in her work life. I soon learned that Mira was also vulnerable to viral infections and accidents and was often sick and in physical pain.

Our early work together focused on Mira's self-punitive work style. She would literally work herself sick both on her job and in her church life. She enjoyed the satisfaction of feeling she was competent and accomplished, but she could never set a limit on the amount she worked. She was in an endless cycle of exhaustion, illness, fear of punishment for not finishing work quickly enough, and anger with those to whom she owed work—bosses and members of her church congregation. Even though we talked continuously about self-care, Mira believed that it was wrong to think about herself, that she was "bad," and that her father was right. She said, "I feel I can't win because my father made me feel if I'm not good to him, I'm bad, and the things I care about will be taken away from me." She was chronically in despair about not being able to succeed and afraid of letting people down.

When we explored her relationship with her father, Mira shared that she both loved and admired her father and was nauseated by him. He was the only consistent adult in her life and was intelligent. But, he made her watch pornography and consistently molested and raped her, telling her it was her duty to take care of him sexually and making her feel "dirty and contaminated." Her father was depressed and periodically suicidal, putting her at risk for being abandoned by him as well as by her mother. She blamed herself for the sexual abuse and, as an adult, found herself getting angry and self-destructive when men made sexual advances. She would tell herself over and over again how stupid and ugly she is.

Mira had relatively little difficulty creating a narrative of her traumatic life. She never really forgot the details and had constructed a partially heroic self-identity as a person who could endure and work through anything. This moral construction of herself helped her keep moving forward and helped her bind the aggression that could have threatened her only reliable relationship with her father. She also made real choices to act in an altruistic way with great competence for the good of the family. Given the paucity of meaning she was offered, Mira made existentially important choices to organize her universe in a moral way. But she certainly never allowed herself to mourn the many losses of her childhood or to forgive herself for her victimization. In fact, at a narrative level, she was more identified with her father (the aggressor) than with her mother (the victim). She loved her siblings but referred to "a hole in my life where a real family would have been." The family she created sustained her in providing a sense of coherence to her life but did not nurture her own developmental needs.

Concomitant to her self-definition as a caretaker, self-care was a frightening concept. To genuinely care for herself, she would have to face the massive losses and violations and this could overwhelm her. Therefore, she could not really connect with people in satisfying ways; she could only serve them. She was afraid to invest hope because "only stupid people think things will turn out all right." She also had a pervasive meaning-making question about the nature of "truth." She observed her parents "making up their own self-serving reality" all their lives. This poor relationship to reality really infuriated Mira, but she also felt sympathetic toward her parents with a remarkable wisdom born of compassion: "I knew who my mother and father were when they were sick is not who they were originally as people."

Unlike some trauma survivors, Mira never agreed to take antidepressants to help with her despair. She protested that she "depended on her brains for survival" and feared drugs would affect her most trusted asset. She also never accepted any overt solace from me nor would she participate in a trauma recovery group. But, she came to use our relationship to share her worries and to mourn deeply. Gradually, Mira was able to mourn for her lost childhood and grieve the loss of parenting and the death of her parents. She eventually found a partner with a comparably difficult childhood who appreciates her deeply. I saw them once together to congratulate them on their marriage and to meet him. Mira stopped her meetings with me, quit her job, and focused all her energy on making her husband happy and enjoying their relationship. She was uneasy with her husband's moodiness but, with characteristic determination, decided to make the best of it with him. With great ambivalence, she agreed to try to have a baby with him and after failed IVF (in vitro fertilization) attempts, adopted a daughter. In a horrible turn of bad luck, that child turned out to have signs of significant mental illness and restimulated Mira's sense of helplessness and hopelessness at ever finding happiness. She felt rejected by her child as she had by her mother and the child's behavior put stress on the marriage. Mira reengaged in therapy with me and a child and family therapist is working with the family.

While the clinical trauma recovery frame is certainly a useful backdrop in the work with Mira, it has not been adequate. Mira's suffering is so deeply rooted in formative relationships and cultural realities that it demands an integrative approach that includes close examination of her relational template (Prior, 2004), a recognition of the cultural factors in her development and treatment, and a "survivor-centered stance" that acknowledges her as a competent person with experience that makes her an "expert" in her own right (Gilfus, 1999, p. 1253).

Using the trauma recovery frame, I have worked to validate and normalize her adaptations to the many levels of violence and adversity she coped with and the reliving, hyper-arousal and avoidance issues evidenced in her anxiety, depression, hopelessness, and fear of the demands of authority figures and of sexuality. Psycho-education around psychosocial trauma and developing social support around her traumatic life have been less successful, however, and, perhaps, less relevant for both cultural and intrapsychic/relational reasons. She is strongly identified as Japanese American. This includes a reverence for family, a certain stoicism in the face of adversity, and emphasis on identity in relation to others. Kleinman (1987) observed that while mental health symptoms are often regarded as universal, some critics see constructs such as PTSD as more American and Eurocentric. I have come to work with Mira more from her own point of view around issues of trauma.

Actually, one of my Asian trainees helped point me in the right direction culturally. She was very disturbed by the definitions of trauma and recovery models I was teaching because, as she said, defining responses to natural disasters, war, and domestic violence as post-traumatic had no relevance in her home country. She explained, "This is just everyday life to us. . . . We do not see this as out of the ordinary and have no public health or mental health resources for responding." This observation has relevance for working with Mira because she has said, "In my neighborhood, getting hit was not a big deal. . . . Many parents kicked their kids around, molested the kids, went to jail, attempted suicide, expected the oldest daughters to take care of the younger ones."

Bhui and Bhugra (1997) point out that when client and clinician do not share the same culture there can be a gulf between them. In this case, I actually do share gender, class, and family values similarities with Mira (I am the big sister of a number of siblings in a working-class family that needed my labor). At the same time, I am not of Japanese heritage, do not have a seriously mentally ill parent, have not been required to be a surrogate wife, and have been encouraged to lead my own life. Therefore, my expectations for Mira's development of self-care and finding her place in the world may be very different from hers. Mira's worldview includes the expectation that enormous demands on her, relentless criticism, little support, and few resources are normative. Even though she may experience a longing for things to be better, she resists the betrayal of her roots that hoping and achieving represent. Also, without the resources and in the face of ongoing demands that are not of her choosing, there is real substance to her persistent question, "Is this [void] the human condition?" Her mother's mental illness, her father's abuse, overwhelming work and little support, her husband's moods and her daughter's special needs add up to a life that makes her feel she is "in jail—with no exit—exhausted and unhappy," that she is "a bother to people." She evidences the classic symptoms of PTSD, but traumatizing relationships were so pervasive in her development that the dread of things going wrong is almost completely ego-syntonic. Bad luck *is* reality. She has no shattered assumptions because this grim universe has been hers since she can remember. One might say that she struggles more with a shattered but resilient soul.

In working with Mira's suffering and existential question, learning about her sense of self and others is core to the work. Numerous clinicians and object relations theorists have addressed the mechanism of internalization by which the abused child replicates the pathological family relationships in her own image. Fairbairn (1952) spells this out: "The child will develop rigid, self-negative beliefs to account for abuse or neglect by the parents. In the child's view of things, the causal and moral responsibility for the painful relationship lie entirely with [her]" (p. 65). On a moral level, the clinician is responsible for reminding the client that, as a child, she could not have been responsible for what was done to her and expected of her. On an intrapsychic level, however, this can be experienced as challenging the introjected aggressor and altering the dominant narrative of the powerful child who can control a frightening interpersonal universe. This leaves the clinician with the moral responsibility to offer alternative self-supporting narratives and alternative sources of strength as old dissociated identities are integrated. The weak, terrified, dissociated child can be overwhelmed without a robust relationship to a strong, self-loving identity. In Mira's case, I have always asked her to imagine alternative, less abusive self-talk when her abusive introject threatens to overwhelm her authentic sadness.

In his work with severely abused boys, Stephen Prior (2004, p. 62) summarizes the basic psychodynamics of chronically abused and neglected children as including (a) relentless reliving of abusive relationships; (b) reliance on identification with the aggressor as a basic mode of psychological defense; (c) self-blame or unshakable conviction of being the cause of the abuse, deserving the abuse and being utterly bad; and (d) seeing interpersonal contact as being physically and/or sexually violent. Mira's internal object world includes all of the above dynamics. She becomes involved in relationships that replicate the impossible demands of her childhood. She believes she was to blame for her abuse, the loss of her mother as a mother, and everything that goes wrong in her adult life. She identifies with her father's abuse of her and sadistically drives and criticizes herself. She refers to herself as a "warrior" and her father as a "broken warrior." Even so, she says, "I can't win, it's hopeless. I'm going to be destroyed. I'm facing a whole battalion but I'm going to kill as many as I can before I go down." She is constantly afraid that she will be hit or sexually abused in her intimate relationships. As a result, she says, "I need to keep moving, find some aspect of my life that is important to me, and work on it—something to help me feel less loathsome. . . . I feel my husband is angry with me all the time and I have to keep a leash on myself."

In working with this defeated and self-defeating Mira, I have found that no amount of fighting the warrior is useful. She is, in fact, more tenacious and fierce than I. She is more skilled at this fight and *is* like an old battered general. I can, however, hold my ground and be unafraid of her power and let the aggression she contains be contained in our work. She keeps coming back to the work. Sometimes she is in so much pain that all I can do is just sit there and silently empathize with her suffering. Sometimes, like the abused elf servant, "Dobby," in the Harry Potter series (Rowling, 1999) she flagellates herself emotionally and all I can do is ask if there is any other way she might think about herself or anything she could call herself other than "stupid, bad, and ugly."

Our relationship actually became less tense and more intimate feeling after an experience that could have ruptured it. Some time ago, Mira chose not to come to our session and called me an hour before the scheduled hour to cancel. When I called her to reschedule, she sheepishly and somewhat defensively said she did not think she should have to pay me for the missed session. When I suggested that this was a situation that she had chosen, that was not beyond her control, and that she should pay me, she railed at me and felt "incredibly hurt, betrayed, and violated" with an emotional force that even astonished her. This was notable because it was unusually relational—she often treated me as if I were not there—and because she had allowed herself to be "bad" for once and felt she should be understood and not punished. We had a few telephone exchanges before she agreed to see me again, and when we met it was as if we had weathered a storm and both the relationship and Mira's sense of self seemed strengthened and, somehow, more relaxed. The healthy experience of nonviolent aggression that could be contained within a relationship and that did not lead to abandonment or annihilation was reparative for Mira. I actually see this experience between us as having been a step in allowing Mira to entertain the possibility of an intimate relationship with a man. In fact, she and her husband have tried to "contain" many issues on which they differ. She neither avoids nor vilifies him when she is angry, but fully engages.

Conclusion and Final Thoughts

In this case description, I have not sufficiently conveyed Mira's competence and creativity. There are two Miras who function simultaneously. One is what we call "Super-Mira"—the woman who helped her family survive, who made it through college, who is highly accomplished, enjoys making beautiful ceramics, and is fearlessly in touch with her truth. There is also the sick, lonely, and self-hating little girl who tries her hardest to please bullies so that she will not be abandoned.

The socially skilled Mira can muster a "good face" when she needs to—she has internalized the American cultural demand for a relentless cheerfulness and she understands the culture of psychotherapy enough to know that there are limits on how self-destructive she can be. Our relationship is a subtly respectful one. She keeps coming to meet with me out of acknowledgment that I honor her worldview, that I am smart enough to accurately assess her pain, empathic enough to hold it with her, and persistent enough to find out if she can see things differently to get some distance from her internalized oppressor. I do not pretend to have effected any kind of cure. I keep being there because she is a tough survivor I respect and I value sitting with her. Is it important to worry about how long she will need our conversations or whether I could be more clever and skilled or move her along faster in the work? Probably not. I just hope I can be there for as long as she needs me. It is a privilege to be there.

It also is a privilege to be in a field that has such high aspirations for contributing to the well-being of others. I am encouraged by the changes in the field of psychotherapy and by the integration of feminist principles and clinical trauma theory into our knowledge base. Women clinicians and researchers have made enormous contributions to the moral dimensions of how we work with people and to the ethic of caring (Noddings, 1984) that I believe are essential. It is caring that motivates us to form working alliances with our clients in therapeutic relationships that invite life's bad luck and suffering into the space where it can be held and understood together. I often experience a relieving sense of psychological and social and spiritual wholeness when I am in the midst of the clinical work. The mutuality of the experience cannot be overestimated; and even as the field becomes more neurologically sophisticated, research is pointing us back to the limbic system and the right brain and the neuronal basis of emotional attachment that ensures our survival as human beings. Underlying therapeutic change and healing are the caring, empathy, and "affective synchrony" (Schore, 1994) that allow us to bear the weight of another's sorrow.

It is my hope that those who need this knowledge, those who generate this knowledge, and those who regulate the professions that use this knowledge will continue to inform each other in ways that improve our efficacy as clinicians. It is not enough for us to attempt to repair traumatic interpersonal damage. We need to support a communal understanding of the interaction between large-scale adverse factors such as racism and mental illness and the severe early abuse and neglect suffered by survivors like Mira. Over the years that I have practiced across outpatient, inpatient, day-treatment, and homeless shelter settings, I have heard many similar stories of intergenerational maltreatment that result from and result in extreme medical and social conditions. Psychotherapy can hope to have only a modest influence on bettering the lives of a relatively small number of people. In addition, even our best clinical work is limited by our personal, professional, and cultural experience. The power of the field of psychotherapy, however, goes beyond the numbers of people we directly engage with to the possibility of our widening influence on social constructions of suffering. Intergenerational, institutional, and social justice perspectives on psychosocial trauma have modified, if not completely changed, a public discourse that is liable to ignore, isolate, and blame victims. Engagement with communal understandings of the pervasiveness and long-term sequelae of psychosocial trauma is a continual challenge for a field that operates in a relatively private arena. Our privileged knowledge can, and should, however, find a larger place in constituting collective responses.

References

American Psychiatric Association. (1994). *Diagnostic and statistical manual of mental disorders* (4th ed.). Washington, DC: Author.

Antonovsky, A. (1987). *Unraveling the mystery of health: How people manage stress and stay well.* San Francisco: Jossey-Bass.

Bhui, K., & Bhugra, D. (1997). Cross-cultural competencies in the psychiatric assessment. *British Journal of Hospital Medicine, 57*(10), 492–496.

Blume, E. S. (1990). *Secret survivors.* New York: John Wiley.

Brown, L. S. (1994). *Subversive dialogues: Theory in feminist therapy.* New York: Basic Books.

Cambridge Documentary Films (Producer). (1998). *Strong at the broken places.* [Motion picture]. (Available from Cambridge Documentary Films, Inc., P.O. Box 390385, Cambridge, MA 02139–3993)

Caplan, G. (1970). *The theory and practice of mental health consultation.* New York: Basic Books.

Chu, J. A. (1998). *Rebuilding shattered lives.* New York: John Wiley.

Esper, J. (1986). Reactions to violence: Normal adjustment is not psychopathology. *Issues in Radical Therapy, 12*(1), 25–54.

Fairbairn, W. R. D. (1952). *An object-relations theory of the personality.* New York: Basic Books.

Felitti, V. J., Anda, R. F., Nordernberg, D., Williamson, D. F., Spitz, A. M., Edwards, V., et al. (1998). Relationship of childhood abuse to many of the leading causes of death in adults: The adverse childhood experiences (ACE) study. *American Journal of Preventative Medicine, 14*(4), 245–258.

Figley, C. (1985). *Trauma and its wake: The study and treatment of post-traumatic stress disorder.* New York: Brunner/Mazel.

Finkelhor, D. (1984). *Child sexual abuse: New theory and research.* New York: Free Press.

Gartrell, N., Herman, J., Olarte, S., Feldstein, M., & Localio, R. (1986). Psychiatrist-patient sexual contact: Results of a national survey: I. Prevalence. *American Journal of Psychiatry, 143,* 1126.

Gere, S. H. (1999). Integrating clinical, personal and academic knowledge: Faculty reflections on training trauma survivors in social work and psychology. Unpublished doctoral dissertation, Simmons School of Social Work.

Gilfus, M. (1999). The price of the ticket: A survivor centered appraisal of trauma theory. *Violence Against Women, 5*(11), 1238–1257.

Harvey, J. H., Barnett, K., & Overstreet, A. (2004). Trauma growth and other outcomes attendant to loss. *Psychological Inquiry, 15*(1), 26–29.

Herman, J. (1981). *Father-daughter incest.* Cambridge, MA: Harvard University Press.

Herman, J. (1997). *Trauma and recovery.* New York: Basic Books.

Hoffman, L. (1990). Constructing realities: An art of lenses. *Family Process, 29*(1), 1–12.

Janoff-Bulman, R. (1992). *Shattered assumptions.* New York: Free Press.

Keane, T. M., Fairbank, J. A., Caddell, J. M., & Zimering, R. T. (1989). Implosive (flooding) therapy reduces symptoms of PTSD in Vietnam combat veterans. *Behavior Therapy, 20,* 245–260.

Kessler, R. C., Sonnega, A., Bromet, E., Hughes, M., & Nelson, C. B. (1995). Posttraumatic stress disorder in the National Comorbidity Study. *Archives of General Psychiatry, 52,* 1048–1060.

Kleinman, A. (1987). Anthropology and psychiatry: The role of culture in cross-cultural research on illness. *British Journal of Psychiatry, 151,* 447–454.

Kobasa, S. C., Maddi, S. R., Puccetti, M. C., & Zola, M. A. (1985). Effectiveness of hardiness, exercise, and social support as resources against illness. *Journal of Psychosomatic Research, 29,* 525–533.

Lugones, M. (1990). Playfulness, "world"-traveling, and loving perception. In G. Anzalhun (Ed.), *Making face, making soul: Haciendo caras* (pp. 390–402). San Francisco: Aunt Lute Press.

MacDonald, M. P. (1999). *All souls.* Boston: Beacon.

Marin, P. (1981, November). Living with moral pain. *Psychology Today, 15*(11), 68.

Marsella, A. J., Friedman, M. J., Gerrity, E. T., & Scurfield, R. M. (Eds.). (1996). *Ethnocultural aspects of posttraumatic stress disorder.* Washington, DC: American Psychological Association.

Masson, J. M. (1983). *The assault on truth: Freud's suppression of the seduction theory.* New York: Farrar, Straus & Giroux.

Neimeyer, R. A. (2004). Fostering posttraumatic growth: A narrative elaboration. *Psychological Inquiry, 15*(1), 53–59.

Noddings, N. (1984). *Caring: A feminist approach to ethics and moral education.* Berkeley: University of California Press.

Poussaint, A., & Alexander, A. (2001). *Lay my burden down.* Boston: Beacon.

Prior, S. (2004). *Object relations in severe trauma.* New York: Rowman & Littlefield.

Rowling, J. K. (1999). *Harry Potter and the chamber of secrets.* New York: Scholastic.

Ruddick, S. (1980). Maternal thinking. *Feminist Studies, 6,* 70–96.

Russell, D. (1984). *Sexual exploitation: Rape, child sexual abuse, and sexual exploitation.* Beverly Hills, CA: Sage.

Rutter, M. (1987). Psychosocial resilience and protective mechanisms. *American Journal of Orthopsychiatry, 57,* 316–331.

Scheier, M. F., Weintraub, J. K., & Carver, C. S. (1986). Coping with stress: Divergent strategies of optimists and pessimists. *Journal of Personality and Social Psychology, 51,* 1257–1264.

Schore, A. N. (1994). *Affect regulation and the origins of the self.* Hillsdale, NJ: Lawrence Erlbaum.

Seligman, M. E. P., & Csikszentmihalyi, M. (2000). Positive psychology: An introduction. *American Psychologist, 55,* 5–14.

Shalev, A. Y., Yehuda, R., & McFarlane, A. C. (Eds.). (2000). *International handbook of human response to trauma.* New York: Kluwer Academic/Plenum.

Tedeschi, R. G., & Calhoun, L. G. (1995). *Trauma and transformation: Growing in the aftermath of suffering.* Thousand Oaks, CA: Sage.

van der Kolk, B., McFarlane, A. C., & Weisaeth, L. (Eds.). (1996). *Traumatic stress: The effects of overwhelming experience on mind, body and society.* New York: Guilford.

Walker, L. E. A. (1984). *The battered woman syndrome.* New York: Springer.

Werner, J. L., & Tyler, J. M. (1993). Community-based interventions: A return to community mental health centers' origins. *Journal of Counseling and Development, 71,* 689–691.

Wilcoxon, S. A., Walter, M. R., & Hovestadt, A. J. (1989). Counselor effectiveness and family-of-origin experiences: A significant relationship? *Counseling and Values, 33,* 225–229.

Winnicott, D. W. (1965). Maturational processes and the facilitating environment. London: Hogarth Press.

9

Hermeneutics and the Moral Dimension of Psychotherapy

John Chambers Christopher

I grew up in the 1970s, a time when many of America's long-cherished images of itself were put to the test. My self-awareness was colored by an awareness of Watergate, a slew of social problems, the energy crisis, pollution and environmental degradation, and our involvement in Vietnam. America's grandiose, narcissistic delusions about its unquestioned role as world leader were in the process of being burst. Like many in my generation, I was confused about my place in the world, and wondered how to best make use of my life. But my questioning soon took a darker turn; I spent much of my adolescence feeling suicidal.

Later in my life, my interest in cultures and in culture theory arose out of these feelings and my ongoing struggle with what Victor Frankl (1963) termed the *existential vacuum,* a condition he considered "the collective neurosis of our age" in which people experience "the total and ultimate meaninglessness of their lives. They lack the awareness of meaning worth living for. They are haunted by the experience of their inner emptiness, a void within themselves" (Frankl, 1963, p. 167). In retrospect, part of my own struggle was due to growing up in those tumultuous times. At a more personal level, as the child of an alcoholic father in an upper-middle-class Anglo-American family, I fought to find meaning in what I experienced as a climate of gloom. Making matters worse was the sense that our society was not facing up to the social and environmental problems we had created. The despair I felt about the world compounded my self-hatred. Inwardly, I was fragmented, torn by conflicting thoughts about how I should live, respond, interact—aware of multiple ways of living but without the means of sorting through and evaluating them. I experienced firsthand Nietzsche's "death of god," the condition in which we recognize that there is no longer a widely accepted authority that can tell us what we are living for, and how we should best spend our lives. To stave off the feelings of emptiness and meaninglessness, I, like many in my generation, embraced the panacea of sex, drugs, and rock 'n' roll.

My first glimmer of hope came in learning about ancient Greek philosophy in a high school history class. It was through exposure to the Otherness of the ancient Greeks that I first became aware that there were other ways of living and of making sense of the human condition. This insight was deepened further in a high school class in East Asian history. These two classes left me with the conviction that it was through a study of history and of other cultures that we could better understand ourselves and the crisis we were in, and perhaps find resources to address our most intractable problems.

I wanted to use my undergraduate education to explore and resolve my need for meaning and my commitment to social change, but I found that I did not fit easily into any of the pre-established majors. Fortunately, the University of Michigan allowed me to design my own major, which I entitled the Psychological and Philosophical Foundations of Culture. I aspired to understand Western and non-Western cultures, their worldviews and views of the individual, and what it meant about human beings that we could exist in such divergent cultural worlds. This was a passion for me; it was literally life-sustaining work, an attempt in using my intellect to create a worldview and philosophy of life that could allow me to endure.

My previous attempts at self-care and self-transformation consisted of trying to think things through rationally, forming endless resolutions that would soon be broken, trying to keep a stiff upper lip, and eventually undergoing some ineffectual psychotherapy. Because my earliest experiences of psychotherapy were not helpful, and because psychology undergraduate classes did not address the crisis of meaning, it was a number of years before I considered a career as a psychotherapist. But in my sophomore year, a friend mentioned seeing a yoga center near the food co-op and this rekindled an interest in the notions of self-cultivation that I first discovered in high school Asian history. In my first yoga class, I had a peak experience in the midst of a guided relaxation. I left the class knowing, "Well, I'm supposed to be doing this!" Both the practice and the philosophy of this ancient Indian tradition gave me, for the first time in my life, the hope that there was something I might do that would truly help me to be a different and better person than I was. Moreover, the practice of yoga and meditation helped to create the kind of peak and mystical experiences that helped me, at least temporarily, feel a profound sense of connection that offset my feelings of alienation. Thus, I found two resources to help me deal with my depression and what I saw as the crisis of late 20th century America—using my mind to analyze what was wrong, and using spiritual disciplines as tools to help bring about personal change, and, ultimately, social change. Both provided my life with purpose, meaning, and sustenance.

Over time, my exposure to and immersion in other cultures and parts of the world, such as Bali, Micronesia, Mexico, East Asia, and several Native American tribes, have reinforced my interest in other cultural traditions. In the remainder of my chapter, I will present the evolution of my ideas about culture and psychotherapy in a semi-autobiographical manner. Included in this process has been my questioning of the predominant Western worldview and values. I will stress how hermeneutic thought provides a powerful framework for understanding the nature of culture and the self, and how culture and the self are interrelated. The hermeneutic framework reminds us that cultures are moral frameworks that orient us in life and help us to establish our identity. I will also address the challenge of attempting to integrate the wisdom of other cultural traditions into our personal and professional lives. Case illustrations will provide examples of the practical significance of this hermeneutic view.

Western Worldview: Dualism, Individualism, Materialism, Mechanism

Through my studies at Michigan, I came to focus on a particular mode of thought that seemed to underlie Western culture. This cognitive style of the West dichotomized life into pairs of opposites: self versus others, subjective versus objective, fact versus values, mind versus body, and so on. For instance, in high school English we were taught to identify the plot of a novel according to which of several themes was being addressed: man versus man, man versus society, man versus nature, or man versus God. As I became more familiar with other cultural traditions, it became evident that this pervasive cognitive style was not universal. I began to gain some perspective on these matters through the philosophy of science and the sociology of knowledge. Thomas Kuhn's (1970) *The Structures of Scientific Revolutions* and Peter Berger and Thomas Luckmann's (1966) *The Social Construction of Reality* were seminal books that provided me with conceptual tools to question the foundations of scientific knowledge and our society's view of reality.

In this quest, I was initially drawn to hermeneutic thought as a method for getting at meaning. Hermeneutics, or interpretation theory, so-named after the Greek god of communication, Hermes, is a way of thinking about how central the process of interpretation is to the human condition; how we are, to use Charles Taylor's (1985) phrase, *self-interpreting animals.*

My search for meaning also led me to existential philosophy. Armed with Victor Frankl, Rollo May, Søren Kierkegaard, and other existential theorists, I came to look at the crisis of meaning as a crisis of worldview. Western worldview has become contrary to most world cultures, and even to Western culture until the 17th century in which human beings were thought to exist within a natural or cosmic order that was imbued with meanings that structured existence. In China, for instance, the natural order was understood in terms of relationships that existed between different elements (earth, air, fire, water, metal/wood). Knowledge of these relationships not only undergirded medical theory and practice, but it also informed ethical and social theory. Similarly, in Hinduism the belief in a metaphysical monism, that all of life was a different manifestation of the Godhead acting out a cosmic drama, shaped philosophy, spiritual practices, and even the caste system. For Plato, the good life required ordering society and the individual psyche to mirror the order of the cosmos. And in the Middle Ages "the world was a great allegory, whose essential secret was its meaning, not its operation or its causes" (Randall, 1940). In light of other historical and cultural traditions, arguably the most radical change in human history has been the European Enlightenment's denunciation of a meaning-infused cosmos and the insistence that the universe (and its inhabitants) could be understood as matter operating in a mechanistic fashion. Nature, rather than expressing a natural order or the purpose of a God, became seen as a neutral arena for human affairs that could be mapped through natural laws. The sociologist Max Weber (1946) described this transition as a movement out of an "enchanted garden" and into a "disenchanted universe" where there was no room for divine intervention, deeper mysteries, or symbolic meanings.

Concomitant with the emergence of this materialistic worldview that operated through mechanistic principles was a different way of thinking about the person—namely, an individualistic outlook that assumed the person could be understood in a decontextualized, atomistic manner. Descartes's *cogito,* the "I" that thinks, epitomizes this move. The birth of individualism during the Enlightenment coincides with and is an expression of an emancipatory thrust to overturn what were perceived as excesses of authority and power by church and state. According to MacPherson's (1962) analysis, individualism arose as a kind of political and social tool, a way of giving the individual person possession over him- or herself, in contrast to institutions like the *munt* in the Middle Ages, which essentially granted the feudal lord guardianship over his subjects (Ullmann, 1966). The means of accomplishing this liberation was to conceive of the person as discrete and autonomous, so important to Locke and Hobbes, as the "man-in-the-state-of-nature" who existed prior to the formation of society. Emerging as a solution to a number of social, economic, political, and religious problems, individualism now lies at the very core of American culture (Bellah, Madsen, Sullivan, Swidler, & Tipton, 1985).

These revolutions in worldview and self-representation ushered in tremendous scientific discoveries, technological innovations, and undreamed of personal freedoms and liberties. We are quite familiar with these great advancements as they were drummed into us from school age on. But it did not take much imagination to see that they also seemed linked to some of the problems in our country and in our world. In Lasch's (1979) view we are becoming a culture of narcissism. Lasch and a number of other social critics have pointed out how our cultural outlook may encourage a destructive emotional isolation and erode the social ties and commitments that alone make freedom or autonomy meaningful. Cushman (1990) developed a trenchant critique of how the "bounded and masterful self" in American society is "empty." Our collective response of "lifestyle solutions," such as rampant consumerism, addictions, compulsive behavior, and even therapy, fail to get to the root of the problem—the empty self. Moreover, there are ways individualism may distort our self-understanding. The myth of rugged individualism, for example, obscures the fact that for our forebears borrowing and lending among neighbors was not only a part of life, but also, as Coontz (1992) writes, "being under obligation to others and having favors owed was the mark of a successful person" (p. 71). Modern individualism, as Selznick (1992) aptly summarized, does indeed bring greater individual freedom; increased equality of opportunity, efficiency, and accountability; and the rule of law; but it does so at the price of what he calls "cultural attenuation," the diminishing of "symbolic experiences that create and sustain the organic unities of social life." Over time, "selfhood itself becomes problematic" (p. 8).

My main concern was, and is, that if we have become "bounded and masterful selves" that are narcissistic, empty, and not fundamentally connected in any deeper or meaningful way, then why should we treat others ethically? It is but a small step for such a decontextualized, bounded, and masterful self to become at best indifferent to disturbing social and environmental conditions and at worst exploitative. Unfortunately, with few exceptions, this concern does not seem to be reflected in psychology.

Problems and Domains Unaddressed by Psychology

In response to my growing clarity about the social construction of reality and the more specific metaphysical and moral commitments of Western culture, I began to wonder in graduate school at Harvard and then the University of Texas why psychology was not dealing with these issues of meaning and worldview more centrally. Individualistic assumptions have been shaping psychological theory, research, and practice. By not being more critical in reflecting on the underlying assumptions and values of Western psychology, are we not complicit in supporting a way of life that was ultimately unsustainable? And why have psychologists not taken more seriously the indigenous knowledge of other cultural traditions—traditions that often were millennia in the making, in contrast to American psychology's brief 100-year history?

Over time, I began to discern that the reasons behind these concerns shared a common origin, a dualistic way of thinking that treats culture and the person as separate entities, thereby minimizing the way we are culturally constituted. Addressing the philosophical questions raised here entails developing alternative ways of thinking and alternative metatheories. Given the interdisciplinary nature of the issues involved, I concluded that what is needed is a metatheory for psychology that sees matters of ontology, epistemology, ethics, and aesthetics as intertwined, separable only for the sake of analysis and at the cost of misrepresenting the underlying subject matter. As Henryk Skolimowski (1981) noted, metaphysics and ethics codefine each other. Psychology as a discipline, however, avoids the metaphysical, and by implication, the moral.

As an academic and professional discipline, American psychology has modeled itself after the natural and medical sciences. The attendant emphasis upon objectivity, quantification, neutrality, and being culture- and value-free has made it more than difficult to take into account the centrality of meaning, values, and culture in our lives. I have found that powerful resources for developing an alternative account of where culture, values, and meaning constitute the self can be found in the theories of such hermeneutic thinkers as Clifford Geertz, Martin Heidegger, Hans-Georg Gadamer, and Charles Taylor.

Coming from an interpretivist, or hermeneutic perspective, Clifford Geertz (1973) characterized culture as "webs of significance" or "webs of meaning." These webs of significance underlie society, human interactions, artifacts, and even our thought and emotions. They provide a background set of assumptions and values that set constraints on human functioning and orient us to what is meaningful. These webs of meaning, in his view, consist partially of worldviews. A worldview (or *weltanschauung*) provides a cognitive map of reality. It makes metaphysical claims that describe and proscribe what reality is, what it is composed of, and how it operates. Multicultural counselors have made good use of this aspect of culture. For Geertz (1973), culture also consists of ethos—a dimension largely ignored within the multicultural counseling literature. Ethos is the affective, aesthetic, and moral dimension of human life that characterizes a culture and its members. It is "the tone, character and quality of their life, its moral and aesthetic style and mood; it is the underlying attitude towards themselves and their world that life reflects" (Geertz, 1973, p. 127).

Over time, I increasingly saw the power and subtlety of Geertz's model. Geertz taught me how to think culturally, how to move beyond definitions of culture and the general claim that it influences psychological theory, research, and practice to achieve the ability to think interpretively and discern specific cultural influences. Every aspect of human behavior, thought, emotion, and social life can be shown to rely on certain metaphysical assumptions that are related to a particular culture's worldview as well as moral commitments and values that are connected to that culture's ethos. I began to take in the notion that culture is in a sense so pervasive that there is no way to neatly separate the individual from culture. I realized that the seemingly most banal parts of our day, such as the first 15 minutes of each morning, are infused with cultural assumptions and values. An "ethnography of everyday life" can reveal how such taken-for-granted social practices as hitting a snooze button on an alarm clock rely on a whole host of cultural values and assumptions.

Another step in my thinking was to realize that an important aspect of culture has to do with making sense of the person and human interactions, a domain that might be called, following Bruner (1990), folk psychology. Extrapolating from Geertz's model, folk psychologies necessarily have two dimensions corresponding to worldview and ethos. The worldview aspect of a folk psychology defines what a person *is*. Research from comparative philosophy, psychological anthropology, and more recently cross-cultural psychology confirm that in different cultures the individual can be understood in dramatically different ways. Geertz (1983) himself challenges our common sense, taken-for-granted view of the person in Western culture by writing,

> The Western conception of the person as a bounded, unique, more or less integrated motivational and cognitive universe, a dynamic center of awareness, emotion, judgment, and action organized into a distinctive whole and set contrastively both against other such wholes and against a social and natural background is, however incorrigible it may seem to us, a rather peculiar idea within the context of the world's culture. (Geertz, 1983, p. 59)

Although there are concerns that Geertz may have overstated the case (Lindholm, 1997; Spiro, 1993), nevertheless it is clear that different cultures regard the capabilities, resources, constituent elements, and even boundaries of the person differently. For instance, the *balians* or traditional Balinese healers with whom I have worked maintain that each person has "four siblings" or parts of themselves that exist on other planes of existence, and that health is based in part on maintaining harmonious relationships among ourselves and our ethereal siblings. In very general terms, people from collectivist cultures typically identify with their extended family; who they are in the deepest way incorporates others. This contrasts, often sharply, with our Western psychological view that people consist of behavior, emotions, and cognitions and that the boundaries of the person coincide with the surface of the skin.

Even less recognized by psychology is how the other dimension of culture, ethos, influences folk psychologies. Folk psychologies define what is normal, what is abnormal, and what is exemplary, influencing our folk theories of development, maturity, and even wisdom (Christopher, 2004). Essentially, this means folk psychologies encapsulate our understanding of what the good person and the good life is. Noticeably, this dimension of folk psychologies also varies across cultures and across time. For contemporary Anglo-American culture, the person should be responsible, independent, self-reliant, authentic, self-directed, and so on. These virtues differ markedly from the emphasis upon faith, hope, and charity prevalent during the Middle Ages. And different still is the mature or good person among the Ifaluk of Micronesia who cultivates *fago,* a sort of bittersweet indigenous emotion that is a combination of love, sadness, and compassion (Lutz, 1988).

Addressing the Moral Nature of Cultural Living

Most helpful to me in thinking more penetratingly about these matters is the hermeneutic contention that the moral or ethical dimension of life is essential to and infused throughout all of human existence. One way of thinking about this is to return to Geertz's notion that we are suspended in webs of meaning or significance. My understanding of the significance of what Geertz meant by significance was substantially deepened by reading (or more accurately struggling to read) the hermeneutic philosophy of Martin Heidegger. Heidegger (1962) maintained concern, care, and signification are central to human existence. We are, as Heidegger put it, beings for whom our being is an issue. Our lives, as a result, are "structures of care." What we do, how we have established our lives, the decisions we make, the way we spend our time all reveal what it is that we care about, either individually or collectively.

From this perspective our behavior and even our thoughts and emotions presuppose care. Heidegger concluded, "the Being of Dasein itself is to be made visible as *care*" (pp. 83–84) and "Dasein, when understood *ontologically,* is care" (p. 84). Building on this, Charles Taylor (1989) evocatively stated that "Selfhood and the good, or in another way selfhood and morality, turn out to be inextricably intertwined themes" (p. 3).

Taylor makes the claim that part of what it means to be a human being is that we are situated within "inescapable frameworks." In his article "The Moral Topography of the Self," Taylor (1988) alleged that we are all situated within a moral topography or moral space that orients us to life by demarcating the good (what we consider valuable, meaningful, desirable, etc.). To illustrate how these moral frameworks underlie our sense of identity and our evaluations of our lives, Taylor observed that we all have a sense of what it means to feel "out-of-joint" through such experiences as being "lost, or condemned, or exiled, or unintegrated, or without meaning, or insubstantial, or empty" (p. 300). But in addition, according to Taylor, we have some sense of what it would mean to be back on track, in alignment, healed, saved, and so forth. And we also have a visceral feel for the internal resources, strengths, or virtues we need to draw upon or cultivate in the process. Taylor's moral space then governs our gut-level sense of how we are doing, how we measure up, and what it is that we need to be doing or not doing. Typically, it is this sense of being out of joint that brings clients into therapy. Sometimes this moral space is explicitly known by us; but whether or not it is consciously articulated, it is still always present in an implicit form that hits us in a kind of visceral way. As Taylor (1985) writes, "these deepest evaluations are the ones which are least clear, least articulated, most easily subject to illusion and distortion. It is those which are closest to what I am as a subject, . . . that shorn of them I would break down as a person, which are among the hardest for me to be clear about" (p. 40). Quite often in therapy we witness our clients profoundly struggle with "these deepest evaluations." Taylor's framework encourages us to see this struggle as a moral struggle, as entailing our deepest senses of what life is about and where we and our clients stand within it.

Worldview and ethos blend to form a *moral vision* that lays out for us what a person *is* ontologically and how a person *should be* morally or ethically. Moral visions are constellations of cultural values and assumptions that provide a framework within which we develop a sense of identity and direction. Implicitly or explicitly, moral visions provide an understanding of the self, the good life, and the good or ideal person. They tell us where to go or how to find those things that we deem higher, deeper, or more meaningful—those things that give us our strength, integration, wholeness, vitality, dignity, and goodness. They simultaneously define for us what we should avoid, resist, oppose, or even combat, both internally and in the outer world. Moral visions recognize that not only is the self or person understood differently in different cultures, thus informing different types of identity, but also that coordinates of the moral space within which the self is located vary across cultures and across time.

To understand other people, other cultures, and other historical periods, it is essential to recognize that there are a "diversity of goods" that underlie notions of the good life and the good person. Gadamer (1975) refers to successful cross-cultural interactions as involving dialogue. This dialogue requires a *fusion of horizons.* A fusion of horizons is a meeting or encounter between ourselves and another in which we allow our deepest convictions and assumptions to be called into question by taking seriously the convictions and assumptions that inform the other's way of life. Doing this requires a stance of profound *openness* on our part. Openness means giving the Other the kind of respect necessary for us to want to understand their perspective from the inside. It also means suspending our beliefs to explore whether the Other's perspective may actually represent an improvement over our own.

Recognizing people's moral visions moves us away from the dualistic tendency to bifurcate facts and values or to conceive of persons as potentially separable from values and from culture. The term moral visions instead suggests that the ontological and moral dimensions of human life interpenetrate to such a degree that it distorts our experience to try to separate them. Indeed, considerable scholarship by theoretical and critical psychologists reveals the extent to which psychology, when it attempts to be objective, neutral, and value-free, ends up nonetheless being shaped by unrecognized cultural values and assumptions or what Bernstein (1978) termed disguised ideology.

Case Examples

A brief example, early on in my clinical training, illustrated to me how differences in moral visions can play out. "Laverne," a Hispanic woman, came in for counseling because she was depressed and anxious. Laverne grew up in an extended Hispanic family in a small southern Texas town. As part of her moral vision, Laverne viewed her primary identity as derived most fundamentally from being a member of a large extended family. Her first priority in life was expected to be her duty to her family and role as one of the first to go to college, thereby helping her family prosper. Laverne's outlook on life is consistent with what cross-cultural psychologists call *collectivism* (Kim, Triandis, Kagitcibasi, Choi, & Yoon, 1994). In collectivism, an individual's worth comes from his or her ability to excel at specific roles and functions within the social order (Moore, 1968). Commonly, within collectivism it is a virtue to harmonize one's relationships with one's ingroup. Accordingly, sensitivity in understanding and anticipating others' feelings and reactions is often cultivated and viewed as an indicator of maturity (Markus & Kitayama, 1991).

Laverne had begun to date "Richard," an Anglo-American from the suburbs of Dallas, shortly after arriving at the university. Laverne reported that Richard was frustrated with her. As Laverne proceeded to describe Richard and their relationship, it became clear to me that Richard had a more stereotypically individualistic moral vision. Richard was apparently quite happy to be away from what he experienced as the stultifying presence of his own family. The true business of life as he saw it was the pursuit of happiness and self-fulfillment; family ties and obligations were little more than a waste of time. Consequently, Richard saw Laverne's family as interfering in her life (and his) and he encouraged Laverne to see herself as a unique, autonomous person capable of forming her own values. Laverne described feeling pressured by Richard to seize control of her life by making her own decisions about how to spend her time (to her credit she suspected that Richard's motives were not entirely altruistic). The result was that each weekend Laverne faced a dilemma—should she go home and help her family or stay on campus with Richard and their friends? Laverne described being frozen with anxiety in deciding what stance to take toward her boyfriend and her family.

Given the 400 or 500 different existent schools of psychotherapy, we have, as counselors, a number of different theoretical lenses to conceptualize Laverne's situation, including models of assertiveness, separation-individuation, empowerment, codependency, acculturation, and so on. Almost all of these theoretical lenses, however, tend to side with Richard's outlook on life—all presuppose an individualistic moral vision. For example, if we draw on the notion of codependency, Laverne is obviously in need of counseling interventions. Yet as Greenberg (1994) detailed, the notion of codependency clearly relies on individualistic preconceptions of what the person is and what maturity and mental health are. Codependency assumes the skin-encapsulated self should be autonomous and bounded. But for most non–Euro-American people and, as feminist writers have pointed out, for many women, the self-other boundary cannot be so sharply defined. Selves are often interdependent, extending to include family and even nation. No doubt there are many cases where dependency issues are too out of balance and people have overly subsumed their own sense of self. Notwithstanding the helpful insights that can come from a notion like codependency, the danger is not placing the concept into cross-cultural and historical context.

Now suppose that as Laverne's therapist, I took it for granted that we first needed to help her to separate and individuate from her family and become less codependent so she could get clear about what she wanted out of life. A second step in her treatment might then be deciding that assertiveness training would be helpful. Assertiveness functions as both a partial criterion of mental health and a social skill that offers us the best chance of "getting our needs met." In the United States, those who are unassertive are subject to criticism and judgment as having "no backbone" and sometimes "no balls." But these judgments presuppose individualistic character ideals such as self-promotion, self-expression, and the ability to negotiate, and ignore or downplay such collectivistic virtues as respect and harmony. Self-discovery, self-awareness, and self-expression are generally unchallenged psychological virtues for Americans who are taught to emphasize their uniqueness and engage in self-promotion and self-assertion (Goffman, 1959; Kitayama, Markus, & Lieberman, 1995). In collectivist cultures, however, the predominant virtues are often diametrically opposed: One should be modest and avoid drawing attention to oneself. In Japan, this is captured by the aphorism, "The nail that sticks out gets pounded down" (Markus & Kitayama, 1991). Assertiveness, it turns out, is not culturally neutral, and this index of mental health for Americans is a true sign of immaturity in many collectivist cultures. It is not simply a question of Laverne deciding between asserting an individualistic or collectivistic identity.

Moreover, thinking of Laverne's situation as a "choice" between individualistic and collectivistic moral visions is itself culturally loaded. The idea of choosing fits in nicely with an individualistic outlook in which one is encouraged to be self-defining. Traditionally, people have not been encouraged to "find themselves." They are expected to adapt to and excel within preordained roles, social offices, and marriages. Commenting on this, Peter Berger (1979) observed that most of humanity has always lived in worlds of "fate." Consequently, presenting Laverne with a choice may be a form of violence to her cultural outlook in which it is not the individual's prerogative to step back from life and decide what she wants out of it.

There is another way in which the idea of a choice introduces an individualistic bias. The idea of being free to choose is central to the individualistic moral vision and to much of social constructionist thought (Richardson & Christopher, 1993; Richardson, Fowers, & Guignon, 1999). But culture and society provide both freedoms and constraints; even if we believe we can choose, we cannot really or at least not to the degree that we think we can. Nonetheless, these cultural outlooks are infused deep in our marrow, residing for the most part far below the levels of conscious awareness. While we can be aware of some of our values and assumptions, we can never be fully aware. Thus, we may always be living out minor variations of the moral visions we were raised with in the kinds of social interactions and practices we take for granted.

I have come to the conclusion that virtually all of our theoretical formulations are similarly problematic, especially when uncritically applied to those not raised with an individualistic outlook (Christopher, 1996, 2001). Triandis (1989) estimated that individualism is most likely the cultural outlook for only 30 percent of the world's population. The implication is that if we fail to address how individualistic values and assumptions influence counseling, then we run the risk that counseling theories and concepts are at best suitable for 30 percent of humanity. Perhaps even worse, these values and assumptions are being extended in potentially harmful ways to the other 70 percent. A strong probability exists that we will distort and misinterpret the experiences of ethnic minorities, women, and those from non-Western cultures if we fail to realize that all of our counseling theories and concepts presuppose moral visions. Given these risks and the reality that most of us have not been trained to think culturally, is it such a surprise that ethnic minorities in the United States have such low utilization rates for mental health services and such high drop-out rates?

As another example of how culture shapes the counseling endeavor, let us consider the theory of acculturative stress and its implications for practice. Berry and Sam (1997) described three levels or "points of view" for considering the level of difficulty individuals have in psychologically acculturating: behavioral shifts, acculturative stress, and psychopathology. The level of "behavioral shifts" addresses those individuals who can relatively easily adapt by changing their "repertoire." At the other end of the three levels, "When major difficulties are experienced, the 'psychopathology' or 'mental disease' perspective is most appropriate" (p. 298). While these levels can certainly capture important behavioral symptoms, it also potentially obscures the concrete fact that we are pathologizing those who struggle the most with such changes. This pathologizing rests on the presupposition that cultural transitions should be relatively facile—those who struggle most are most ill. If we step back and ask why should cultural transitions be easy, we run into our own cultural meanings. For instance, might we by pathologizing these individuals be reinforcing the Western notion that the self should be flexible, adaptable, and highly mobile (Bauman, 2000)? If we consider that what is at stake for such individuals is ultimately their worldview and ethos, their understanding of what it means to be a person, and how life should be lived, then it is highly questionable that cultural transitions should really be so easy or straightforward. The transition to a modern way of life that is urban, pluralistic, and mobile involves a wrenching experience of the breakdown of supporting institutions and the dissolution of human ties of shared purpose and obligation. Are not the symptoms of "psychopathology" an eminently comprehensible reaction given the task involved?

Moreover, might seeing such struggling individuals solely in terms of psychopathology lull us into missing possible strengths and virtues? For instance, might not resistance to shedding identities and indigenous social practices in some cases indicate a form of psychological strength or integrity? Should we instead question the health of those who too easily adjust and adapt, or even that of the society to which we are expecting people to acculturate? The potential risk is that by drawing on or resorting to Western understandings of mental illness and their associated diagnostic classifications, we may forget to situate such struggling individuals within their own frameworks of meaning. We may, as a result, fail to grasp the underlying views of human potential and the good life that are being expressed even in the midst of the most severe expressions of psychopathology. Applying hermeneutic understanding to such situations is a way of attempting to discern what is at stake from the "native's point of view" (Geertz, 1983) and exemplifies that it is interpretation all the way down (Hiley, Bohman, & Shusterman, 1991).

Academic and professional psychology have to build upon the more basic folk psychology that precedes us. This is true both historically in terms of the development of the field out of Euro-American culture, and ontogenetically, as psychotherapists are first and foremost members of their culture who learn a folk psychology before being trained to be theorists, researchers, or practitioners. In other words, all psychologists have already incorporated the moral visions of their cultures before learning the moral visions of psychology.

Recognizing our cultural and historical embeddedness in these inescapable moral visions can remind us that our assumptions about what a person is and what a person should be or become are "contestable and that the choice of assumptions involve controversies that lie deep in the history of Western thought" (Bellah et al., 1985, p. 301).

Much of my scholarship has been directed toward demonstrating in specific ways how individualistic moral visions underlie and shape the domains of psychology that have to do with what we *should be,* such as psychological well-being, moral development, positive psychology, and character education (Campbell & Christopher, 1996; Christopher, 1999, 2003, 2004; Christopher, Christopher, & Dunnagan, 2000). For me, this work is a preliminary step. By helping psychology to recognize how individualistic values and assumptions are pervasive within the field, despite our best attempts to be objective, neutral, and culture-free, we may hope to more openly debate the merits of these contestable assumptions (Richardson & Christopher,

1993). In addition, it may pave the way for psychology to take more seriously the indigenous psychologies of other cultural traditions, psychologies that I have found personally so enriching.

Toward a Hermeneutic Ontology

Lurking around the corners of the hermeneutic view of culture that I have been discussing is a well-developed ontological position about the nature of the self. Much of Western culture buys into a view of the person that is set "over and against," to use Heidegger's phrase, virtually everything, including culture. Such a viewpoint lingers in contemporary society as we tend to assume that to be a mature, individuated person, we need to gain some separation from family and society and turn within to discover who we are and what we want out of life. Ironically, many of the models of racial identity development seem to uncritically presuppose this very trajectory in their developmental stages.

Geertz maintained that it is this atomistic view of the self that complicates our efforts to more clearly perceive how deeply culture shapes us. As an example, he points to "stratigraphic models of the self." These models, like Bronfenbrenner's (1977) ecological model of human development, or more recently that of Gardiner, Mutter, and Kosmitzki (1998), use concentric circles around a biological core to depict the self. While such stratigraphic accounts are a clear improvement in that they do take seriously the influence of culture, culture is potentially reduced to a mere extraneous context. Models and theories that take this approach potentially adopt and reinforce the supposition that the individual is ontologically prior to the social—that it somehow makes sense to think of the individual as a biological entity existing independently of society and culture.

We tend to think of cultural values and assumptions as appendages to our true self. This notion is a distortion of the human condition, according to philosophical hermeneutics, as supported also by an interactivist view of moral development (Campbell, Christopher, & Bickhard, 2002). Hermeneutics addresses the phenomenology of human existence, and concludes that at our most fundamental level we are seamlessly engaged in and situated in a social world. Importantly, such a vision of a situated, engaged, and embodied view of the self gets to a level of agency and experience that precedes dualistic divisions of the world into subjective/objective, self/other, mind/body, and fact/value. Heidegger (1962) suggested that most of the time we are in interaction with the world in such a way that there is no sharp divide. It is this immersion in the activities and social practices of cultural living that most defines us, according to Heidegger, and why he considers us most fundamentally to be *being-in-the-world.* Our normal understanding of ourselves is too cognitive, too intellectual, too individualistic. It mistakes a derivative form of being with our most essential nature. What this means is that our most primordial way of being is actually shaped much more extensively by our culture, by our moral visions than we can comprehend. We are shaped by our social practices that we are *thrown* into at birth and these social practices presuppose notions of what the human being is and what the human being should be or become. Because these social practices, and the meanings implicit in them, are socially constructed and shared, Heidegger (1962) believed we can best understand ourselves in our "average *everydayness*" (p. 38). This holds because "Proximally Dasein [or human being] is 'they,' and for the most part it remains so" (p. 167).

Cultural values and morals are not, in this view, subjective colorings over a more basic world of facts. Values are intersubjective, unavoidable, and inextricably intertwined with facts. "We do not," Heidegger (1962) declared, "throw a 'signification' over some naked thing which is present-at-hand; we do not stick a value on it" (p. 190). Nor is there a self that can completely stand back from, clarify, and manage his or her values. Rather, the self is already and always committed to some set of moral and ontological commitments, which is true for ourselves and clients who come for counseling and psychotherapy. While we can gain some distance from our values, it is never done by a self that is a "dimensionless point of subjectivity." It is done by a person who may be bracketing some of his or her moral underpinnings but always from another position that relies on its own set of values and assumptions, for "every dissolution of one prejudice depends upon a conscious or unconscious reliance on a myriad of other prejudices, and . . . every process of illumination or self-enlightenment rests on a complementary darkening or obscuring of other possible modes of self-understanding" (Warnke, 1987, p. 123).

Thus, Gadamer (1975) claimed that prejudgments or prejudice are the preconditions for us to know anything at all. We are always situated in a horizon of understanding. As a result, psychotherapists can never be strictly neutral or objective. In helping clients understand the meaning of their experience and bring about positive changes, therapeutic conversations always entail the hashing out of two or more moral visions. These moral visions frame both our own and also our clients' notions of what is problematic and what is likely to be therapeutic.

To conclude, hermeneutics begins with ontology, a developed theory that looks in-depth at the concept of the person, the idea of culture, and the relationship between the two. Western psychology, in contrast, has largely attempted to avoid theory not based on empirical research findings. A considerable amount of scholarship suggests that by not taking ontology seriously, Western psychology has simply taken over the categories of our individualistic folk psychology. This is not only not neutral, but it also often precludes an awareness of and sensitivity to the indigenous psychologies of other cultures.

Personal Integration

Moving to Montana 9 years ago posed a bit of a problem for a self-proclaimed cultural psychologist. On the surface, Bozeman lacks the kind of cultural diversity that I had previously been fortunate to take for granted. It has provided, however, an opportunity to look at culture in more subtle ways. For instance, at the counseling center I encourage interns to find out in their intakes exactly where in Montana their clients come from. There is considerable difference between the more liberal and urbane university town of Missoula, the ex-mining town of Butte, and small ranching towns like Two Dot and Ringling. It requires interpretive thinking to then consider how these various social worlds influence clients. Another way of searching for culture in smaller ways is to inquire into the specific ethnic histories of clients even when they appear "White." These ethnic histories can be related to important variations in a more general individualistic moral vision. For instance, a person growing up with one parent who is Irish American and another who is Norwegian American can learn two quite disparate ways of relating to life that can be a source of internal conflict. Moral visions, for example, prescribe the stance we should adopt toward specific emotions. It can be clinically fruitful and interpretively challenging to explore cultural and moral dimensions of the learning histories of different emotions and different interpersonal stances.

For many years, I felt that my spiritual life, my scholarship, and my practice of psychotherapy were not as integrated as I wanted—each essential to me, but not much overlap when viewed externally. Although I knew from personal experience that spiritual practices could lead to the kinds of nondualistic experiences that are meaningful and ethically sustaining, I did not have a sense of how I could introduce these to clients without stepping into the role of a teacher that I felt would compromise a therapeutic relationship informed by humanistic and psychodynamic principles. A partial answer came through learning about Jon Kabat-Zinn's (1990) mindfulness-based stress reduction (MBSR). Kabat-Zinn's well-researched program for teaching mindfulness through meditation, yoga, and a body scan awareness technique to a variety of medical patients provided just the bridge I had been looking for. This led me to develop a MBSR program for the local hospital community and then to integrate MBSR into a graduate counseling class entitled "Mind-Body Medicine and the Art of Self-Care." And because of the growing body of empirical research on mindfulness practices like yoga, meditation, tai chi, chi gong, and even prayer, I have felt much more comfortable recommending these practices to my clients who are so inclined. This integration has been deeply fulfilling personally and the impact of MBSR on patients and students has been far greater than I had imagined. Most striking is the way mindfulness practices help people to accept or tolerate those aspects of their life (like chronic pain) that cannot be altered (Schure, Christopher, & Christopher, 2004).

At this point, what I find most compelling and therapeutic about these practices is not the fostering of transcendent experiences, but how they encourage us to step out of the "bounded masterful self." For example, I believe most of us in American culture have never been taught how to tolerate difficult experiences. We have learned to respond to adversity, stress, pain, discomfort, and the "dark emotions" with attempts to distance and wall off these aspects of life through denial, suppression, and avoidance, sometimes with the help of various strategic, therapeutic interventions. Mindfulness practices instead teach us how to accept our experience whether good or bad, stressful or pleasant. In yoga, for instance, we can learn that even in the midst of a difficult asana (pose) we can learn to eliminate unnecessary tension, relax into the discomfort, and come to explore the sensations and our psychological responses to them.

There is something terribly important about learning how to tolerate life when it is not what we want it to be. I think that with our emphasis on control and mastery, we have lost touch with the art of what has been called *spiritual surrender* (Cole & Pargament, 1999) or what Epstein (1998) poignantly refers to as "going to pieces without falling apart." The emancipatory thrust of the American ethos emphasizes the elimination of suffering and even freedom from unhappiness, as is promised in much of the popular psychology literature. As Barbara Held (2002) observed, this cultural outlook has resulted in a kind of tyranny of happiness. Such a one-sided emphasis on emotional satisfaction and happiness, even found within much of the new positive psychology literature, tends to neglect other more traditional, worthwhile values or virtues such as "the redemptive power of suffering, acceptance of one's lot in life, adherence to tradition, self-restraint and moderation" (Frank, 1973, p. 7; see also Guignon, 2002; Woolfolk, 2002). For instance, "Yoko," a graduate student from Japan in our counseling program, described being socialized as a child to tolerate difficult situations.

Instead of emphasizing freedom from pain and suffering, Japanese culture traditionally regards the ability to endure or "hold the struggle" as a sign of maturity. In this sense, "bad" feelings are not bad—they are a part of life. It is learning to live with bad feelings, unmet needs, and unwanted constraints, and doing so with poise and dignity, that sets off the virtuous or mature person.

A second type of integration that is less developed for me is between the theoretical framework I have discussed and spiritual practice. Hermeneutics is a philosophy of social science, a mode of inquiry, and an ontological-moral framework that helps to situate Western psychology and invites us to take seriously the indigenous psychologies, spiritual practices, and wisdom of other cultures. But increasingly, I see hermeneutic dialogue as a form of spiritual practice, a type of mindfulness. This seems especially true in the context of psychotherapy where the experience of being understood is so central to the healing process. We can only achieve in Gadamer's (1975) sense a fusion of horizons between ourselves and our clients if we treat the Other as a "Thou" and not as an "it," to use Buber's (1970) terminology. In my view, such a stance of nondefensive openness calls for a kind of moral strength and courage that is greatly facilitated by contemplative and spiritual practices. Moreover, I believe that this kind of openness that is both psychological and physical (as it requires learning to relax defensively induced tension in the body/mind) is partial explication of well-being.

At this point, let me mention a case example to ground this notion of openness. While I was in Guam, "Joe," a young Chamorro man who fit the diagnosis of antisocial personality disorder, was referred to me by the judicial system. Joe relayed to me a remarkable history of fighting and assault from an early age and indicated that he came from a family with a reputation for being courageous and fierce fighters. Joe swelled with pride as he conveyed that he had never lost a fight. Although relatively small and slender, Joe claimed he fought with anyone, provided they were bigger. He stressed that he had never walked away from a fight even when he was "looking down the barrel of a gun." Because he was such a good fighter and would not back down, Joe reported that he, along with several other of the "boys" who had demonstrated their fighting abilities, became "protectors" of his village. Joe evidently had developed an infamous reputation and was something of a hero to certain people in his village.

Somewhat tense at the outset because of the way Joe had been objectified by his police records, I found I was able to relax as the session proceeded. What helped me to relax was the realization that Joe was aspiring to live the good life, just as I was. I began to recognize that Joe had constructed his life around the assumption that honor or dignity come from being unafraid, and it is better to be physically injured than to acknowledge fear. Moreover, it is by putting oneself on the line and being a good fighter that one obtains respect and admiration. Although there are clear problems with this outlook, as his police record testifies, Joe's life does not reveal the total absence of moral and ethical consideration that we associate with antisocial personalities. As I opened up to Joe, I saw that he had a compelling moral vision of his identity, the good life, and the good man. One consequence, then, of openness to the Other is that we do not discredit or discount the whole person. Initially, I had been concerned Joe might be very pathological and unlikely to benefit from counseling. If I had clung to such a mindset or initial horizon of understanding, I would have failed to learn that part of him does indeed strive to obtain the good life, no matter how distorted the attempt. I would have failed to see that part of him does strive to be a good person, no matter how distorted the definition, as discussed in Schmitz and Christopher (1997).

I have come to believe that it is not the moral vision that is generally problematic: it is how these moral visions are interpreted and applied. For instance, with Joe, there is much to respect about his commitment to the moral sources of honor and dignity. Indeed, in the midst of current corporate and political scandals it would appear that we could do with a large dose of these virtues. Joe's problem, from the vantage point of the courts and society, is how he defines and tries to obtain honor and dignity—the particular implementation of these moral sources. Counseling, in this case, entailed helping him to realize that the specific ways he did implement them was actually a problem for him (i.e., in terms of court costs, having to attend counseling, jail time) and that there might be other ways he could find honor and dignity that did not rely on violence.

Using dialogue to work with a client's moral vision has a number of potential therapeutic benefits. Recognizing clients' moral visions means acknowledging their deepest vision of life and deepest motivations and this can give them a deep sense of being understood. Such an experience of being understood can only help strengthen the therapeutic alliance. Working with clients' moral vision by redefining but not eliminating it is a way of building upon their strengths. It can also help reduce resistance as clients do not experience us as challenging or rejecting their whole way of being. Indeed, I believe that clients are more likely to become more allied with the change process as they sense there may be better ways of getting what they most want out of life (see also Christopher, 1996).

One implication of this is that we cannot be neutral as psychotherapists. I originally found cultural relativism to be a powerful tool to break the hegemony of the Western scientific worldview. Working across cultures, I discovered relativism was disempowering. It left me no grounds from which to question behaviors like Joe's that are dangerous. We are left trying to navigate between the Scylla of wanting to be culturally respectful of our clients and the Charybdis of needing to make evaluations and intervene in what seems to be psychologically unhealthy. I think this is where Gadamer's (1975) notion of hermeneutic dialogue and the struggle to achieve a fusion of horizons proves helpful. The counseling process can thus be viewed as a form of hermeneutic dialogue in which meaning is collaboratively discerned and both parties are potentially changed in the process.

As I finished this chapter, I stumbled across a portion of Heidegger's thought that I was not familiar with. The later Heidegger (1966) was concerned with the impact of technology upon human life and the increasingly exclusive reliance on a type of thinking he calls "calculative." He worried that "the approaching tide of technological revolution in the atomic age could so captivate, bewitch, dazzle, and beguile man that calculative thinking may someday come to be accepted and practiced as the *only* way of thinking" (p. 56). And for him calculative thinking, while useful, is ultimately a type of "thoughtlessness" as it remains within the "conditions that are given" and fails to contemplate "the meaning which reigns in everything that is" (p. 46). Fortunately, Heidegger believed we also have the capacity for "meditative thinking" and that "the proper exercise of this capacity, difficult though it is in terms of releasement toward things and openness to mystery, can lead to a new ground of meaning" (p. 21). So, from an unexpected quarter, I found more support for the idea that social change is linked with different kinds of thinking and different states of awareness and modes of consciousness.

All of this for me is part of an ongoing search. As I see it now, much of life boils down to not what I believe but the ethical quality of my day-to-day life—how much responsibility I take for my life, the quality of my relationship with other people and the rest of nature, and living as fully and consciously as I can with the limited amount of time I have on earth. The intellectual issues continue to be important to me as a way of trying to bring about social change. But I confess that the focus of my scholarship is narrower than I had originally hoped, and I worry whether critiquing and working toward alternative theories of well-being, psychotherapy, and the self will really bring about the kinds of collective changes that seem so necessary. But in my own personal life, the intellectual questions and issues do not burn in the same ways, perhaps in part because I feel a greater sense of peace about meaning in life. It is here where contemplative and spiritual practices have been so vital for me. They provide the means to put life in perspective and to see the richness in each moment—richness that is often found in the Other.

References

Bauman, Z. (2000, July). *Identification in the times of globalization.* Paper presented at the Congress of the International Association for Cross-Cultural Psychology, Pultusk, Poland.

Bellah, R. N., Madsen, R., Sullivan, W. M., Swidler, A., & Tipton, S. M. (1985). *Habits of the heart: Individualism and commitment in American life.* New York: Harper & Row.

Berger, P. L. (1979). *The heretical imperative: Contemporary possibilities of religious affirmation.* Garden City, NY: Anchor.

Berger, P. L., & Luckmann, T. (1966). *The social construction of reality.* Garden City, New York: Anchor.

Bernstein, R. J. (1978). *The reconstructing of social and political theory.* Philadelphia: University of Pennsylvania Press.

Berry, J. W., & Sam, D. L. (1997). Acculturation and adaptation. In J. W. Berry, M. H. Segall, & C. Kagitcibasi (Eds.), *Handbook of cross-cultural psychology: Vol. 3. Social behavior and applications* (pp. 291–326). Boston: Allyn & Bacon.

Bronfenbrenner, U. (1977). Toward an experimental ecology of human development. *American Psychologist, 32,* 513–531.

Bruner, J. (1990). *Acts of meaning.* Cambridge, MA: Harvard University Press.

Buber, M. (1970). *I and Thou.* New York: Scribner.

Campbell, R. L., & Christopher, J. C. (1996). Moral development theory: A critique of its Kantian presuppositions. *Developmental Review, 16,* 1–47.

Campbell, R. L., Christopher, J. C., & Bickhard, M. H. (2002). Self and values: An interactivist foundation for moral development. *Theory and Psychology, 12,* 795–822.

Christopher, J. C. (1996). Counseling's inescapable moral visions. *Journal of Counseling and Development, 75,* 17–25.

Christopher, J. C. (1999). Situating psychological well-being: Exploring the cultural roots of its theory and research. *Journal of Counseling and Development, 77,* 141–152.

Christopher, J. C. (2001). Culture and psychotherapy: Toward a hermeneutic approach. *Psychotherapy: Theory, Research, Practice, and Training, 38,* 115–128.

Christopher, J. C. (2003, October). *The good in positive psychology.* Paper presented at the International Positive Psychology Summit, Washington, DC.

Christopher, J. C. (2004). Culture and character education: Problems of interpretation in a multicultural society. *Journal of Theoretical and Philosophical Psychology, 23,* 81–101.

Christopher, J. C. (2004). Moral visions of developmental psychology. In B. Slife, J. Reber, & F. C. Richardson (Eds.), *Critical thinking about psychology: Hidden assumptions and plausible alternatives.* Washington, DC: American Psychological Association.

Christopher, S., Christopher, J. C., & Dunnagan, T. (2000). Culture's impact on health risk appraisal psychological well-being questions. *American Journal of Health Behavior, 24,* 338–348.

Cole, B. S., & Pargament, K. I. (1999). Spiritual surrender: A paradoxical path to control. In W. R. Miller (Ed.), *Integrating spirituality into treatment: Resources for practitioners* (pp. 179–198). Washington, DC: American Psychological Association.

Coontz, S. (1992). *The way we never were: American families and the nostalgia trap.* New York: Basic Books.

Cushman, P. (1990). Why the self is empty: Toward a historically situated psychology. *American Psychologist, 45,* 599–611.

Epstein, M. (1998). *Going to pieces without falling apart.* New York: Broadway Books.

Frank, J. D. (1973). *Persuasion and healing: A comparative study of psychotherapy.* New York: Schocken.

Frankl, V. E. (1963). *Man's search for meaning.* New York: Pocket Books.

Gadamer, H.-G. (1975). *Truth and method.* New York: Crossroad.

Gardiner, H. W., Mutter, J. D., & Kosmitzki, C. (1998). *Lives across cultures: Cross-cultural human development.* Boston: Allyn & Bacon.

Geertz, C. (1973). *The interpretation of cultures.* New York: Basic Books.

Geertz, C. (1983). *Local knowledge: Further essays in interpretive anthropology.* New York: Basic Books.

Goffman, E. (1959). *The presentation of self in everyday life.* Garden City, NY: Doubleday Anchor.

Greenberg, G. (1994). *The self on the shelf: Recovery books and the good life.* Albany: State University of New York Press.

Guignon, C. (2002). Hermeneutics, authenticity and the aims of psychology. *Journal of Theoretical and Philosophical Psychology, 22,* 83–102.

Heidegger, M. (1962). *Being and time* (J. Macquarrie & E. Robinson, Trans.). New York: Harper & Row.

Heidegger, M. (1966). *Discourse on thinking.* New York: Harper & Row.

Held, B. S. (2002). The tyranny of the positive attitude in America: Observation and speculation. *Journal of Clinical Psychology, 58,* 965–992.

Hiley, D. R., Bohman, J. F., & Shusterman, R. (Eds.). (1991). *The interpretive turn: Philosophy, science, culture.* Ithaca, NY: Cornell University Press.

Kabat-Zinn, J. (1990). *Full catastrophe living.* New York: Delta.

Kim, U., Triandis, H. C., Kagitcibasi, C., Choi, S. C., & Yoon, G. (Eds.). (1994). *Individualism and collectivism: Theory, method, and applications.* Thousand Oaks, CA: Sage.

Kitayama, S., Markus, H. R., & Lieberman, C. (1995). The collective construction of self esteem: Implications for culture, self, and emotion. In J. A. Russell & J.-M. Fernâandez-Dols (Eds.), *Everyday conceptions of emotion: An introduction to the psychology, anthropology and linguistics of emotion* (pp. 523–550). Dordrecht, The Netherlands: Kluwer Academic.

Kuhn, T. S. (1970). *The structure of scientific revolutions.* Chicago: University of Chicago Press.

Lasch, C. (1979). *The culture of narcissism: American life in an age of diminishing expectations.* New York: Warner Books.

Lindholm, C. (1997). Does the sociocentric self exist? Reflections on Markus and Kitayama's "Culture and the self." *Journal of Anthropological Research, 53,* 405–422.

Lutz, C. A. (1988). *Unnatural emotions: Everyday sentiments on a Micronesian atoll and their challenge to Western theory.* Chicago: University of Chicago Press.

MacPherson, C. B. (1962). *The political theory of possessive individualism.* Oxford, UK: Oxford University Press.

Markus, H. R., & Kitayama, S. (1991). Culture and the self: Implications for cognition, emotion, and motivation. *Psychological Review, 98,* 224–253.

Moore, C. A. (1968). *The status of the individual in East and West.* Honolulu: University of Hawai'i Press.

Randall, J. H., Jr. (1940). *The making of the modern mind.* New York: Columbia University Press.

Richardson, F. C., & Christopher, J. C. (1993). Social theory as practice: Metatheoretical options for social inquiry. *Theoretical and Philosophical Psychology, 13,* 137–153.

Richardson, F. C., Fowers, B. J., & Guignon, C. B. (1999). *Re-envisioning psychology: Moral dimensions of theory and practice.* San Francisco: Jossey-Bass.

Schmitz, S., & Christopher, J. C. (1997). Troubles in Smurftown: Youth gangs and moral visions on Guam. *Child Welfare, 76,* 411–428.

Schure, M., Christopher, J. C., Christopher, S. E. (2004). Mind/body medicine and the art of self-care: Teaching mindfulness to counseling students through yoga, meditation and qigong. Unpublished manuscript.

Selznick, P. (1992). *The moral commonwealth: Social theory and the promise of community.* Berkeley: University of California Press.

Skolimowski, H. (1981). *Eco-philosophy.* Boston: Marion Boyars.

Spiro, M. E. (1993). Is the Western conception of the self "peculiar" within the context of the world cultures? *Ethos, 21,* 107–153.

Taylor, C. (1985). *Philosophical papers: Vol. 1. Human agency and language.* New York: Cambridge University Press.

Taylor, C. (1988). The moral topography of the self. In S. B. Messer, L. A. Sass, & R. L. Woolfolk. (Eds.), *Hermeneutics and psychological theory: Interpretive perspectives on personality, psychotherapy, and psychopathology* (pp. 298–320). New Brunswick, NJ: Rutgers University Press.

Taylor, C. (1989). *Sources of the self: The making of the modern identity.* Cambridge, MA: Harvard University Press.

Triandis, H. C. (1989). The self and social behavior in differing cultural contexts. *Psychological Review, 96,* 506–520.

Ullmann, W. (1966). *The individual and society in the Middle Ages.* Baltimore: Johns Hopkins University Press.

Warnke, G. (1987). *Gadamer: Hermeneutics, tradition and reason.* Stanford, CA: Stanford University Press.

Weber, M. (1946). Religious rejections of the world and their directions. In H. H. Gerth & C. W. Mills (Eds.), *Max Weber: Essays in sociology* (pp. 223–259). New York: Oxford University Press.

Woolfolk, R. L. (2002). The power of negative thinking: Truth, melancholia, and the tragic sense of life. *Journal of Theoretical and Philosophical Psychology, 22,* 19–27.

10

Cultural Conflict, Values, and Relational Learning in Psychotherapy

Del Loewenthal

This chapter attempts to open up some implications of considering cultural conflict and values from a relational perspective, with particular reference to Emmanuel Levinas, the French philosopher. Levinas speaks of the importance of accepting, without attempting to know, the Other's otherness. Using his ideas, I examine the implications for psychotherapy and counselling of a more macro view of cultures in conflict, including the potential of some implicit values of the therapeutic relationship for exacerbating, rather than mitigating, cultural conflict. The context for the discussion is the exploration of meaning in a world where such developments as the decentering of the subject has implications for how potential transformation takes place through counselling and psychotherapy, enabling clients to return to learning from experience. I will comment on the implications of Phenomenology in the post-modern era and the contemporary world. While the term "postmodernism" is problematic for some (for example, Eagleton, 1996) it is nevertheless regarded as being very important for exploring how relationships are examined.

My intention overall is to pose questions for those involved in clinical practice and psychology/counselling/psychotherapy education. The chapter is in three sections; the first explores the personal, the second the political, and the third values, leading to the call for a radicalised modernism in the training of psychologists, counsellors, and psychotherapists.

The Personal

As with other authors, I have been asked to be transparent about my beliefs and values and to show how I integrate my personal with my professional worldviews in working "within the cultural realm." In responding to how I integrate the personal with the professional in thought and action, there are several problems for me. The first is the issue that one can never speak fully of the culture that one is in. The second is that much of this apparent transparency can be seen as attempting to present current culturally acceptable cover stories for unconscious processes (which may be similar to the previous point). The third is the contradiction between acknowledging beliefs and values and Bion's (1970, p. 35) suggestion that we should take a therapeutic stance where we have "no desire and no memory," which is further enforced for me by phenomenological notions of the importance of laying one's own self temporarily aside. The fourth is that in taking up the request to talk about the personal, I am faced with many interwoven concerns: the inappropriateness of being self referential, the taboo of revealing myself, which I have acquired through my scientific and subsequent humanistic, analytic training; and my own vulnerability that I might enjoy doing this and then others eventually will come to see how limited I am. Finally, there is the concern that it is all about a return to me as more egocentrism when I am apparently writing here about the value of putting the other first.

Yet I have also become increasingly convinced that what makes us speak or not speak has to do with current cultural values. So, when a patient, *in my opinion,* used her daughter to punish her estranged husband and I felt that the child was not considered as a person, I commented on this. What helps me to express this is the relational ethics of Emmanuel Levinas and consideration of my responsibility for her (the patient's) responsibility.

Levinas was born in Lithuania in 1905 of Jewish parents. He moved to the Ukraine, where he was during the Revolution of 1917, then went as a young man to France. He was to live most of the rest of his life in France, surviving a prisoner of war camp, and dying in France in 1995. From 1928 to 1929, however, he had gone to Freiburg, Germany where he attended Husserl's lectures. This was the decisive encounter with Phenomenology and, through this, Martin Heidegger. Levinas is now credited with bringing Phenomenology to France and greatly influencing Jean-Paul Sartre, Simone de Beauvoir, and Maurice Merleau-Ponty and such postmodern thinkers as

Jacques Derrida and Jean-François Lyotard (Loewenthal & Snell, 2001). There, again, the focus of these influential thinkers is more about a larger picture of the hoped-for politics of a better way of being in the world with others (Deleuze & Guatarri, 1977; Heidegger, 1963).

Yet how do I come to be making such references for my assumptions? In writing this, I wonder more in terms of *nachträglichkeit* (afterwardsness) that I have for a long time been particularly interested in conflict. Perhaps this is because I was born into a family in which my father was Czech/German/Jewish and my mother was Welsh/English/Church of England. Both had lost their families in very different ways with various resulting insecurities, yet, with the exception of this topic, I was at home with conflict being expressed. I later found more difficult the religious, class, and sexual conflicts that initially appeared as if they were outside my immediate family.

Politically, my father took a right-wing newspaper but had no problem with a left-wing shop steward and a conservative tax collector being long-term lodgers in the house. My father voted Labour and my mother, Liberal. Aneurin Bevan, the postwar minister of health for the Labour party, who is identified with the inauguration of the National Health Service, had used my mother's parents' house as a local party office but she never voted Labour. In terms of conversation and action, it was a relatively liberal upbringing when it came to aspects such as politics and race. Though there were many contradictions, I can remember my mother telling a visitor that she would move if "Black people" came to live next door; but not only did we have "Black people" living next door, I also often came home to find these Black children and their friends happily playing in our house. When I attempted to point out this contradiction to my mother, she replied, "They're not Black." One aspect this raises is that apparent words and actions need not be at one. Indeed, those who speak of the good may not be good (though they could still do some good). From a psychoanalytic perspective this could be seen as a reaction formation; others might see it as a power base derived from doing the opposite of what is being "preached" by those who wish to set the standards by which to judge others. Am I any different when suggesting one should consider putting the other first?

One of my degrees was in management science, in which one might see the main component, operational research, as being about dealing with conflicting resource demands through finding methods of optimisation. It was the module on industrial relations, however, that really captured my interest, and I later got a master's degree in this followed by a doctorate. Here, I became more interested in the conflicts and (productivity) of individuals within themselves. I subsequently worked as a lecturer and management consultant and became particularly interested in the conflict within organisations where social objectives were greater or equal to their economic ones. For my psychological practice, I trained initially in more humanistically orientated counselling and later in individual and group analytic psychotherapy, and was particularly influenced by the social phenomenology of R. D. Laing's Philadelphia Association. Laing set up his first treatment centre in the 1960s (he was particularly able to communicate to a wide public his horror of the harshness of routine treatment in mainstream mental hospitals at the time), providing a place of safety in which patients could rediscover themselves. For him, the treatment is about how we treat people (Laing, 1967). When I joined the training programme he devised, the aims were to provide a place of safety, where people in torment could live through what they must, without jeopardy. It was a network of households staffed with people who were concerned about building means of helping people whose relations with themselves and others had become abject. Through this therapy, a better understanding was hoped for of how the highs and lows of life were experienced, as well as of how we might lose and find ourselves, and each other, again.

Cultural change in exploring conflict, in and between individuals, is evidenced by the change in use of language during this period. For example, when I started my training as a counsellor, the humanism of Abraham Maslow and Carl Rogers would mean I would listen to clients in terms of their *need,* though behavioural influences regarding assertiveness together with certain readings of person-centred approaches could sometimes hear this as *demand.* I was particularly influenced by my psychotherapeutic/psychoanalytic and postmodern training, and subsequently heard what the patient was saying in terms of *wishes* and various notions of *desire.* What was also becoming clear was the effect such cultural changes on language have in terms of the nature of relationships (therapeutic and others). If the dominant discourse is primarily about demand and assertiveness, the other is more there to service this demand; if the language is about "need," then there is a place for both user and professional to determine it. If the language is about "desire," then the therapist cannot say what another's desire can be, yet such desire can emerge in the relationship with another. Culture, therefore, has a fundamental effect on how we hear and what we might say as psychologists and practitioners.

There are changing cultural assumptions about what it means for the world to be an alive and meaningful place for us. I therefore found myself changing responses to my clients' or patients' demands. I think I am currently giving a primacy to the person's ability to move toward realizing his or her desires, and also developing the sense when an individual can consider, and not attempt to know, another's "otherness." I am interested in Continental Philosophy where the question of what we are "subject to"—for example, language—is addressed. For some this can be seen as enabling a return to Freud's idea of being "subject to the unconscious," which modernism seems to ever water down. Postmodern writing attacks the egocentrism of modernism (Loewenthal & Snell, 2003) by attempting to show that we are really subject to the unconscious (Freud, 1915), language (Lacan, 1977), writing (Derrida, 1996), and ethics (Levinas, 1969). I am particularly interested in the notion of being subject to ethics, and hence putting the other first, a body of thought developed by Emmanuel Levinas.

Before going into more details about Levinas's ideas on privileging heteronomy over autonomy, I wish briefly to note with my own history the importance of the changing use of language in both previous fashions of therapeutic theories and research approaches. In the 1970s, conceptually my research had been about "physical," "intellectual," "social," and "emotional" development. These have changed to "embodiment," "thoughtfulness," "responsibility," "emotional learning," and "the unknown." Research methods have also moved from questionnaire design to interviews to relational research (Loewenthal, in press), and existential phenomenological interest in meaning has moved through Postmodernism to a state where various approaches of Continental Psychology have led to decentering of the subject, raising questions of agency. Thus, for example, for Lacan, "I think therefore I am" becomes "I am where I do not think," and for Levinas, "We are subject to putting the other first" (Loewenthal & Snell, 2003).

How does one then explore meaning in the contemporary world, and how can psychotherapy help people? I would suggest that one important aspect of psychotherapy, as a means of learning from experience, involves understanding how to deal with common sense.

Valuing Common Sense

To what extent does the therapist represent current notions of commonsense, and where is the concept of common sense helpful and where is it unhelpful? For example, at the time of writing, a major European political party was stating that it would be unnatural to allow a Muslim country into the European Community. Is this an example of bigoted racism, or is it pragmatic politics? Whose common sense do we psychologists value? Yet culturally, we are all inevitably coming from somewhere. I find Heaton (1999) useful here. He suggests that

> Common sense here does not mean the same as common opinion. . . . Without common sense we merely have a dyadic relation to other people. We

> understand them as orientated by their horizon or ours alone. So experience is seen as theory laden and context dependent. Theories are not grounded in any way and relativism prevails. Hence the huge numbers of theories in psychotherapy and the impossibility of reconciling them. (Heaton, 1999, p. 77)

Heaton argues that our relationship with others is triadic in that we are oriented by both the person and our feeling of orientation toward him or her, which is formed from immediate discriminatory judgments and ordinary judgments of experience. Immediate discriminatory judgments orient us to our theoretical framework, and ordinary judgments are oriented by our theoretical framework. A practitioner's presence in the relationship therefore is infused with instinct and preference, which mediate with what is possible from our time.

One way of exploring European notions of common sense is to examine the values of the Judeo-Christian and Greek cultural values that have been important parts of their foundations. An area that they may have particularly in common is on notions of justice. Some of the Greek ideas of democracy that have led to our jury system are about what appears right from a particular situation. If, however, one takes the Levinasian view, truth and justice are what emerge in the moment with another. Both can be seen to not start with rules and regulations, but out of the *relationship*. One's reaction to "the other" in a therapeutic relationship also involves such discernment. Thus, truth, justice, and ethics in the therapeutic encounter emerge out of this relationship. The therapist would not therefore start with external rules from so-called ethical codes or psychotherapeutic theories, though both may have implications for what emerges as common sense.

I find that aspects of phenomenology enable one to explore "what is," and that regardless of the extent to which we may wish to try to bracket our own predilections, what we perceive is inevitably through language, and with it, the values of our culture including current notions of common sense. What, for example, is a client telling you when he answers the phone shouting aggressively, "Yeah! What do you want?" after he has told you that he has installed a telephone with an answering machine as he wants to make new friends? For at least those therapists whose work is based on the relational, this might be commented on in the session, and the therapist would probably be comparing what the client said on the phone with the client's hope of making friends and current cultural norms in answering the telephone.

This example, it is hoped, is obvious, but I cannot think of anything I have said or not said as a psychotherapist that is not bound by cultural notions. When somebody is of a different culture, religion, sexual identity, and so on, then some argue that culture is particularly important. I think if anything it is even more important to examine issues of difference and culture for somebody who appears to be of the same culture, religion, sexual identity, and so forth; it may just be more difficult to initially see the difference, but this difference may be no less important. I like the idea that everyone's text has its own specific context and that the association of words, as in chain of signifiers, inevitably leads to important different meanings. And yet one can never really think outside and be critical of the culture one is in: It defines us inextricably through the language we use.

The Ethics of Putting the Other First

I am interested in relational learning. At the Centre for Therapeutic Education at Roehampton University, London, we are particularly interested in relational learning through counselling and psychotherapy. I would wish to argue, however, that the relational is also fundamental to much of teaching and learning in general. I have three children and I do not think I am alone in seeing their interests in their school subjects changing dramatically as their teachers change. One question is whether the *face-to-face,* rather than just the interface, provides a basis for ethics as transformative practice. If so, this has implications for many professional practices, including counselling and psychotherapy.

It could be that there is an implied transformation in psychology where being for others comes before being for myself. I have attempted to develop a framework for testing the hypothesis that ethics as practice is not in any way separate from psychological practice. Rather, if ethics is defined as putting the Other first (Levinas, 1969), then should we not all be striving toward this? The argument here is that ethics is not extraneous to transformative practice or theory. To separate ethics from practice is untenable and fundamentally unethical. This has profound implications for psychological practice, and learning and teaching in psychotherapy as the practice of ethics (Loewenthal & Snell, 2001).

An essential question should be: "What does it mean for the practitioner to put the client first?" A corresponding question could be: "What does it mean for the client to put the practitioner first?" I think it is useful to explore what it means "to put the Other first." It seems very different to be giving one's life for others, and helpful in clarifying consumerist confusion about the term "client-centred," which is currently being bandied about in the UK and other European public services. But let me explain what Levinas may be offering in this regard.

It has been suggested that "In the twentieth century, continental philosophers developed a new type of foundation for ethics. . . . A relatively new line of thought made a distinctive relation to other people the central feature of ethics. . . . Martin Buber . . . and Emmanuel Levinas are the most prominent members of this tradition" (Becker & Becker, 1992, pp. 528–529). In examining the ethics of any relationship, subjectivity, as defined by Kierkegaard (1944) for example, is an important starting point. Another important related concept is that of phenomenology, starting with Husserl's (1960) "to the things themselves." Next comes Heidegger's (1963) notion that any inquiry into being must make transparent the being of the inquirer. However, as the interest here is the *relationship*, the question of intersubjectivity, rather than subjectivity, becomes important. Thus, the intersubjective theories of ethics of Buber and Levinas are the main focus here, as opposed to other notions of ethics that do not make a distinctive relation to other people the central feature. But why Levinas rather than Buber?

Buber's (1958) two fundamental relations of "I–It" and "I–Thou" can be seen to exist between psychotherapist and client. In the "I–It" relation, the psychotherapist offers him- or herself only partially, using the client as a means to some predefined end, grasping the client as a type and experiencing him- or herself as a detached, isolated, separate subject. In an "I–Thou" relation, the psychotherapist offers him- or herself wholly, participates with the other in an event that takes its own course, grasps the concrete particularity of the client, and emerges as a person in terms of reciprocity. For Buber, only in the "I–Thou" relation does the psychotherapist achieve genuine presence. The "I" of the "I–Thou" is not the same as the "I" of the "I–It." Buber would, however, have acknowledged that in practice, psychotherapist and client live in continuous dialectics between these two poles. Furthermore, the "I–Thou" relation does not really unite them; instead, they achieve a reciprocity that acknowledges their distinctness. For Buber, the "I–Thou" relationship cannot become a goal in itself. The psychotherapist should risk and offer him- or herself fully and be genuinely addressed by the other, and therefore become a genuine person.

A practitioner who did not experience the "I–Thou" would be greatly impoverished, and so hence would psychology, as in the Henry James story, "The Real Thing." This is where a commercially successful photographer earns his money selling photographs of what appear to be royalty, but are in fact photographs of actors. One day, however, some actual royalty, down on their luck, offer to pose for him. What happens is that soon there is a tension brought about by a photographer telling "real" royalty how to look, and the photographer reengages the actors; the "royalty," after further unsuccessful employment as domestics, are fired. Now, it can be argued that perhaps there would have been better photographs and potentially more transformation if the photographer had photographed and shown that tension ("I-Thou" rather than "I-It").

Nonetheless, I will argue that Buber is modern, with the "I" in the centre, such that the "Thou" is seen in relation to the "I," so that even a claim for distinctness is a difference in relation to the "I." Thus, the "Thou" or client, is only seen as being different in comparison to something of the psychotherapist. There is always a return to the practitioner—the client cannot be "other" when that is the case. This centering of the individual self or "I" reflected the modernist assumption of mainstream Western cultures, which did not fully appreciate the postmodern implications of the "face-to-face."

Levinas, on the other hand, is postmodern in that he believed we are subject to putting the other first. For Levinas, "my duty to respond to the other suspends my natural right to self-survival" (Levinas, 1995, p. 189). This "right to exist" is in the face of the Other which asks us both, "Do not do violence to me" and "Do not let me die alone" (as to do so would be to become an accomplice in his death). "In the relation to the face, I am exposed as an [sic] usurper of the place of the Other" (Levinas, 1995, p. 189). The relation of the psychotherapist to the client would define the ethical, but the Other would remain wholly alien and not to be assimilated. The client's proximity is prior to the psychotherapist's "presence." So no totality can integrate psychotherapist and client. The relation to the client is like a relation to infinity—perpetually beyond experience, making the organising structures of experience possible. In other words, *sociality,* through the *ethical relation,* precedes and conditions individual experience.

Unlike Buber, for Levinas the client's absolute transcendence prevents symmetry and reciprocity. From a Levinasian reading, the client becomes manifest through "the face". "The face is exposed, menaced as if inviting us to an act of violence. At the same time, the face is what forbids us to kill" (Levinas, 1985, p. 86). It is the face of the client that both commands the psychotherapist not to harm and solicits the psychotherapist's aid. For a practitioner to acknowledge the client's face is to have responsibility to the client and for the client. Thus, the ethics of psychological practice would concern primarily the relation to the Other. I believe it is this notion of *heteronomy* from the Hebraic element of European culture, rather than the Greek notion of *autonomy,* that can have more important implications for psychology and psychological practice.

As psychologists and practitioners, we will always be subjective, our values determining how we hear and what we say. That is insofar as we are able to say what our values are—for we are suffused with the values of our culture, which we can only partly step outside, and are subject to unconsciously. So it is vital for our practice that we attempt to consider what we regard as essentially human. That is, under what circumstances is the world an alive and meaningful place? Rather than assertively go after that which appears important to us (autonomy), we begin with putting the other first (heteronomy) in a way that recognises the "otherness of the other." In this way, our values and ethics are linked. (When speaking of ethics, this is not meant as being synonymous with codes of conduct. Codes can, in fact, be seen as unethical, because however well intended in their systematisation, as in professional codes, the code may be put first rather than the Other being first.) Levinasian ethics is not therefore about my right to exist; it is not even just about the Other's right to exist, but can be seen as my responsibility for the "other's responsibility to others."

As suggested in Loewenthal and Snell (2001), if we start with questions of being, what seems to happen is that we slip into questions where transformations have to revolve around *my* being, such that should we then ever look at another's being, we do so only by taking ourselves as the measure. Levinas argues that ethics—putting the other first—must always precede ontology (the study of being). Yet, for Hamlet, as for Heidegger and most of Western thought, the question has been "To be, or not to be"? Primacy is thereby given to the ontological, in the mainstream Western cultural sense of individual being, with perhaps devastating consequences. This philosophical orientation has formed the unquestioned basis of most Western psychology and psychotherapy, with its emphasis on autonomy, egocentricity, or notions of a bounded, unitary self, and so on (Loewenthal, 1996).

Levinas was very interested in Hamlet. Levinas challenged the ontological by suggesting that ethical questions must always come before those of being, a phenomenological rather than a moral necessity. For Levinas, as perhaps for Shakespeare, Hamlet is asking the wrong question, the result of which is that those he is closest to are killed off. This is because he puts himself first rather than the other first. By asking the question, "To be, or not to be?" Hamlet shows himself to be concerned with himself before he is concerned with anyone else. There was also a related important reading in that by asking this question, it was as if Hamlet could be in charge of his own death. "Hamlet is precisely a lengthy testimony to this impossibility of assuming death" (Levinas, 1989, p. 42). The tragedy of Hamlet, existentially, is that he tries to stay on top of that which he cannot. It may be the case that most psychologists encourage a similar fate for themselves and their clients.

A Psychologist's Ethical Window

I have devised a framework summarizing the previous discussion on the implications of Levinasian ethics for psychology and psychotherapy. This can be used to discuss specific psychological theories and psychotherapeutic stances. The psychologist's ethical window typically is a two-dimensional model; the main axis concerns whether the psychologist puts the psychologist first or the client. The other axis is whether the client puts the client or the psychologist first. In bringing this second dimension, reciprocity is not intended; "I'll put you first if you put me first." Both dimensions, however, seem needed for responsible relatedness to exist. Again, for the psychologist or any psychotherapist to put the client first is a complex notion. It does not necessarily mean doing what the client wants, or denying the psychologist's desire, as both would not necessarily be putting the other first. Moreover, if speaking of the Other as other is yet another way to seduce others in the name of putting the Other first, then is it really me first, yet again? I worry that such notions as Levinas's ethical practice might be used as the new ever-more-subtle seduction. Perhaps Hegel's (1979) fable of master/slave, where we have no choice but to be either master or slave, is always inevitable—both in the macro sense with regard to the position between countries and in the micro sense within the consulting room. If this is the case, then the seducer must always only appear to be open and never really reveal the thinking behind what is happening.

One obvious difficulty that may emerge from this framework is that what the psychologist or practitioner puts first may not match at all with what the client puts first and vice versa. Another serious limitation is that other people are left out. An implication of Levinas's writing is that if we put our individualistic theories first, rather than the Other, we are at best privileging a position that gives primacy to autonomy at the expense of others and our society in general.

But what of the politics of society and my place in it as a psychological practitioner? What exploration is allowed of cultural values that I may "teach" my clients and the values regarding cultures in conflict?

Culture, Conflict, and Globalisation: Psychology and Ideology

I examine next, drawing on Loewenthal (2003), some implications for psychotherapy and counselling of a more macro view of cultures in conflict. Second, with the help of a case example, I consider the potential of the therapeutic relationship for exacerbating, rather than mitigating, cultural conflict. Finally, I end with the call for a radicalised modernism in the training of counsellors, psychotherapists, and psychologists.

Should psychologists and other professionals question their ideological stances underpinning their therapeutic practices as a result of current culture wars? At the time of the initial shock of the September 11 terrorist attack in New York, there was some questioning. I was at a conference at the Management Centre of a British university where many people seemed to ask "Why do they hate us so much?" This also happened in mainstream political debate, as reflected for example in the following quote from *The Financial Times* (Barber, 2001) which, given the lack of attention to such wider culture issues when considering psychotherapy, I wish to quote at length.

> If democracy is to be the instrument by which the world avoids the stark choice between a sterile cultural monism (McWorld) and a raging cultural fundamentalism (Jihad), neither of which services diversity of civic liberty, then the US, Britain and their allies will have to open a second civic and democratic front aimed, not against terrorism *per se,* but against the anarchism and social chaos—the economic reductionism and its commercialising homogeneity—that have created the climate of despair and hopelessness that terrorism has so effectively exploited. (p. 1)

Is therapeutic theory helpful or unhelpful here? How often do we acknowledge and question these cultural forces when working with others in psychotherapy?

Although Barber was not entirely correct in equating Jihad with fundamentalism, he suggests that a second democratic front will be advanced not only in the name of retributive justice and secularist interests, but also in the name of distributive justice and religious pluralism. He questions how many of what he called "enemies of McWorld," given the chance, would prefer to enjoy modernity (he does not use the term "postmodernity") and its blessings if they were not so often the victims of modernity's unevenly distributed costs. For some in the second and third worlds, globalisation appears not as opportunities for liberty and prosperity, but as (primarily U.S.) economic imperialism as rationalisation for exploitation and oppression. He suggests that it is hypocrisy rather than democracy that is the target of their rage.

"McWorld" celebrates market ideology with its commitment to the privatisation of all things public and the commercialisation of all things private. Consequently, it insists on total freedom from government interference in the global economic sector (laissez-faire). Yet freedom from interference—the rule of private power over public goods—is another name for anarchy. And terror is merely one of the contagious diseases that anarchy spawns. Ironically, even as the United States fosters an anarchic absence of sovereignty at the global level, it has resisted the slightest prospect of surrendering its own national sovereignty—whether to NATO commanders, to supranational institutions such as the international criminal tribunal, or to international treaties such as those banning land mines or regulating fossil fuels. As if still in the 19th century, the United States has persuaded itself that its options are to preserve an ancient and blissfully secure independence, or to yield to a perverted and compulsory interdependence that puts foreigners and alien international bodies such as the United Nations or the World Court in charge of U.S. destiny (Barber, 2001).

To what extent is the position taken up by psychologists essentially similar to the American position of cultural dominance? If psychological theories only promote autonomy then where is the Other? For if the Other is only there to shore up an attempt at autonomy, does this not lead to greater impoverishment in the quality of relational life for all?

Another article in the same issue of *The Financial Times* (Prowse, 2001) questioned the myth of value-free economics and suggested that "The view that liberal capitalist values are superior encapsulates the aggression of the US and its Western allies," and that "A theocratic Muslim state has every reason to fear a US-led globalisation because market institutions are unlikely to be compatible with the communal life it favours." We should question where counselling and psychotherapeutic theories stand in relation to all of this, and where psychotherapists position themselves. As we can be considered one of the most independent of professions, such capitalist ideologies and arrangements have favoured our way of being and shaped the way we practice.

To explore how our ideology as therapists may reinforce through our practices the conflicts outlined above, I wish to describe what might be taken as a spoof, a story amongst stories. In Bram Stoker's *Dracula*, the victims are identified by a mark caused by Dracula's embrace (Stoker, 1994). Dracula was someone else who came from Central Europe (besides others already mentioned, including Freud and Husserl). In the countries of Europe and elsewhere, one can imagine a consistent mark left on trainees, and through them, their clients or patients.

I once saw a sign on a French provincial town wall; it read "G8 ASSASSINS." This reflects concern that the rich countries of the world meet in order to sustain and enhance their position in relation to the Third World, which we are being asked to refer to as "less economically developed countries." Within these eight rich countries there is also a relational economic pecking order that used to be called a class system. All these countries also have counsellors, psychotherapists, and psychologists examining their relationships with their clients to help these clients with their relationships with others. What connection, if any, is there between these macro and micro situations? If one accepts that the privileged few, in terms of world economies, are living from the added value generated through the manipulation of third world economies, then is this mirrored in the consulting room? Europe, as with the

United States, through its colonial and postcolonial policies has managed to create and maintain an economic ascendancy for its people over some others. It seems that such policies have attempted to put their populations' minds at rest through developing an ideology or norm where ideology is a dirty word. Now, too many Europeans would reach into their pockets if they were to meet for more than a fleeting moment a young child making, for example, sports shoes for us Europeans, but then there would be concern that our economy as we know it may collapse. The markup from such products is such that we, the purchasers, gain both the shoes and a well-heeled system.

What then of the relationship between therapist and client or patient—is it not a microcosm of the global economy? Is it in any way possible that therapy has to do with maintaining and enhancing privilege and advantage through a form of Dracula-like bloodsucking where, for example, the patient is instructed in the ever-changing cultural forms of seduction within our own social order and encouraged to collude with that culture's bid for dominance? For the behaviourist, conceptually, "demand" was the buzzword that one would be assertive enough to take one's shoes back to the shop and get them changed, without really much notion of the shop assistant as "other." The humanists seemed more interested in "need," where the individual primarily puts him- or herself first as the subject, with the associated danger of putting the other second as object. And I am not sure that the analyst's interest in, for example, "wishes or desire" is any less selfish.

Deleuze and Guattari (1977) described various ways in which the seductions of power, status, and money encourage the repression of nonconforming revolutionary desire. They oppose themselves to Freudian and Lacanian emphasis on Oedipus and Signifier, and with this the psychoanalytic priesthood. Yet such texts rarely appear in psychotherapeutic and counselling training. So therapists can continue to make political choices without having to realise this, even though as therapists we are all the time translating or mediating something between the client and the culture we are in (Loewenthal & Snell, 2003). This is what would appear to be a vital ingredient in the case example presented later where the apparent cultural conflict might be seen as less about the implications of national identity and more about consumerist rather than ethical relations and their resulting values.

Perhaps the only prospect of influencing the fashions of schools of counselling and psychotherapy in psychology is that change is required when the manipulative elements of the current dominant schools become overt. As with any management ideology, a manipulative seduction may be essential to all these systems of thought. People are taught to show that they appear to listen, but were they really to listen they would be brought face-to-face with the potential exploitation of their relationships, their societies, and that third world child making those shoes. What is fostered instead is a way of thinking in which an examination of the way we think politically throughout our society, including in our consulting rooms, is taboo. Thus, uncovering our covert agenda is essential.

There are a few examinations of politics and social responsibility in psychotherapy, for example, Samuels (2001). It can be argued that these attempts are continually necessary for, as with the drops of blood at the end of those Dracula films, everyone knows that this means that the monster within has not been eradicated but only suppressed and needs always to be fought again. Indeed, it may be considered too grandiose a thought for what we as therapists can do, if it did not have the further backing of Deleuze and Guattari (1977), for it was a mission launched from a "lunatic asylum" (a place familiar to many of us) that "destroyed" Count Dracula. Deleuze and Guattari stress the collective nature of desire with "no separation between the personal and the social, the individual and the collective" (Sarup, 1993, p. 93). Following Reich's interest in the mass psychology of fascism, they believe that "the unconscious is a political force and that fascism dwells in it as much as on the historical stage or in political parties" (Sarup, 1993, p. 93). Deleuze and Guattari argue that there are two types of desire: the paranoid (a reactionary desire—based on the authoritative structure of the hierarchical state) and schizophrenic (a real desire—centred on flight). These respectively correspond, in social terms, to the authoritarian (insistence on centralised power) and the libertarian (loose organisations without territorial limits or a system of hierarchy). For Deleuze and Guattari, Freudian psychoanalysis is an example of interpretation as impoverishment—where a patient's life is rewritten in terms of Freud's family romance. What has just been presented is not typical of therapeutic training, and in this way the mainstream bands of psychoanalysis, counselling, psychotherapy, psychology, and psychiatry are similar in lacking an ideological thoughtfulness. Our students seem rarely allowed to consider such radical alternatives. There is thus less chance that we can fight and leave a different mark, if only at best for a while. Or is such talk just a minor safety valve in the process of globalisation so that we can have the delusion of free speech? But let us look at a case example.

A Case Example

This case example is provided as initially this might be seen as a suitable case for cultural treatment in terms of the client's concerns around national identity. What appeared to emerge, however, was a more important underlying question of culture in terms of consumerist versus ethical relations. Mimi is in her late 30s. At first it appeared that her main issue was a cultural conflict in terms of her father being French and her mother Algerian. This problem was exacerbated by her attending a French school in Algeria where those of mixed race were treated very much as second-class citizens, as was her experience of visiting France. She seemed to want to look up to her father and yet when she described his cold pragmatism when an early hospitalisation might have ordinarily called for a caring relationship in either culture, she spoke of this in her International English in a cut off jovial way. She did wonder whether she looked to others more Algerian or French.

When Mimi arrived she hardly spoke, looking at me both childishly and erotically from one eye, the rest of her face being deliberately covered with her hair. Her reason for seeing me was to receive a therapy required for her to train as a counselling psychologist. Over time, she revealed her face more and one aspect that emerged was that she had had a late abortion, and that a reason for her slight figure was that she wanted to starve herself to death in order to meet "it." Eventually, "it" became her son, and was named, and the eating disorder crisis passed. Seeing others as commodities may have in some ways helped her anaesthetise herself to earlier trauma, but this commodification was not sustainable for her; she could only overcome her abortion when she saw her unborn son as a human being. After this, more ways emerged in which she had commodified the relational to the current detriment of her own being.

Her twice-weekly visits to me, though very important to her, appeared as if she was paying for a service industry. I was an "it"—not a "thou" in Buber's terms and certainly not "an other" in terms of Levinas. Inasmuch as she started to see both her brother and her friend treating others as objects, she could not for what was to be a considerable time, treat me as an "other."

It emerged that her parents had split up when she was 15 and she had had to live with her father whom she relied on for her foundations (perhaps particularly so as her parenting was not good enough). Her father's "efficient parenting" included ensuring that she got an electric shock when she wanted to help him with some wiring, and then shouting at her afterwards as a way of teaching her about electricity.

Similarly, early in her life she had been held responsible for her brother constantly wetting his bed. Her apparent feelings toward authority, and her resentment, particularly toward men, seemed to have resulted in her hatred of male doctors, her husband, and who I represented.

Mimi and her husband's difficulty with her appearance, which seemed more his problem than hers, resulted in potential medical interventions, which she described in such resentful terms. She had a very idealised notion of true love and felt unable to help her husband in any way with his problem as this would not be what she dreamt of. She complained of her husband paying for a service—so she could look how he wanted her to rather than working through this with her. It is this paying for a service, the McWorld values of which Mimi and her husband partook in an international lifestyle, that might be seen as a defence for her being with me as an "other". To let me in would be to start to let in that which she previously could not cope with. Perhaps in this way, consumerist relations, reinforcing the consumerist world, can be seen to be developed and reinforced through unresolved constrictions from emotional distress. These produce a consumerist lifestyle that is a compensation, rather than a movement arising from and toward a human potential for relating with others. It was only when Mimi, eventually, after learning how she defended against it, could start to relate to me as an "other" that she could be open to the difference in me that she could never know, rather than see me simply as a service to be bought. Given what she had had to survive in responding to others, in terms of her parents and schooling, it was difficult for her to be open to learning from experience and her own humanness. To have only gone down the pathway of cultural conflict in terms of questions of nationality might have missed this, though they were an important part in the weave of the tapestry of her story. I do find it easier, however, to link the ethics of the cultural values of the relational than the political with my practice, but this may be more to do with how we are trained.

Concluding Thoughts: Call for the Radical in the Therapeutic Enterprise

In my knowledge, British students of counselling, psychotherapy, and psychology learn little formally about politics and ideology. While it is widely acknowledged that the lack of radicalised modernism is apparent in all forms of cultural practice (Lyotard, 1984; Parker, 1997), it is particularly pronounced in psychotherapy and counselling. I wish to pose the following questions in examining the contest of meaning within and between countries, based on a popular book (Bolton, 1989) written not for students of psychotherapy and counselling, but of photography. *What are the social consequences of psychological and psychotherapeutic and counselling practices?* An important and complex question for psychologists and others engaged in counselling practice concerns the encouragement of "tradition and continuity rather than rupture and change" (Bolton, 1989). Related questions include: *How do we individually and, particularly, collectively orchestrate meaning? What other ways of understanding have been dismantled and destroyed?* With the success of late modernism, the political basis of modernism has been pushed aside so that we think of our practice as apolitical. Modernism therefore has restructured knowledge, and one should consider what effects our classification systems and professionalisation processes had on meaning. Mainstream psychology and the psychotherapy and counselling literature appear to be largely apolitical. Where change for the individual is examined, the social consequences in terms of notions of how we view "the good," "health," or "madness," let alone war and terror, are not left open to close scrutiny for long.

How is psychology used to promote class and national interests? As with the individual and client or with war (as in Iraq), do claims of lifting repression lift off the chains of oppression or do they become part of a more sophisticated oppression? Mainstream psychology and counselling and psychotherapeutic practices offer little by way of analysis of the effects of power in representation, generally encouraging the reverse and implying that what is discussed in the consulting room is neutral and above ideology. This tendency is expressed in the frequent refusal of the profession to consider anything other than to incorporate all that is said into an uncritical history of psychotherapy that is self-contained, self-referential, and self-justifying. This potentially strengthens the role of psychology and the psychotherapy and counselling enterprise as the voice for the status quo. We need more critical histories of the field of counselling and psychotherapy.

What are the politics of psychology and counselling and psychotherapeutic truth(s)? Danto (1998) uses archival and oral history in attempting to show that Freud proposed the creation of clinics providing free treatment. We could for example ask: What is the importance of this article appearing, opening up what is claimed to be a "little known aspect of the history of psychoanalysis" in terms of changes in the economics of private practice? An analysis of any counselling or psychotherapeutic truth requires in turn an analysis of power, which in turn depends upon our understanding of the social and political aims of psychology, counselling, and psychotherapy. Thus, the expectation of the enterprise in itself confines psychotherapy into a particular discursive space. There again, what are the effects of notions of liberalism and objectivity on psychotherapeutic practice? Can they actually supplement social activism and, if so, is this a legitimate aim? To raise such questions is to call into question the ideological closure that would appear to generally characterise counselling and psychotherapy training.

To borrow a final example from Bolton (1989), psychotherapy "can be used to honour or repress its subjects," to either compliment the "ceremonial presentation of the bourgeois self" or "establish and delimit the terrain of the other." In this way, psychology and psychotherapy and counselling are seen to aid in "the construction of social and moral hierarchies." Derrida (1996) has shown us how the concept of the archive is fundamental to our understanding of meaning. Yet I am not sure if such developments will find their way into our Psychology programmes. As Bolton would say, the questions raised here are intended to be productive rather than exhaustive.

Behind the above questions is perhaps a whole further set of assumptions, arguments for change in psychology and for change in the history of history and interpretation of interpretations, and arguments for acknowledging the changing relationships within society. Is it too grandiose to consider how counselling and psychotherapy can best change society? Is it something that just happens? In other words, do we simply accept the attempted separation of culture and society promoted by late modernism? In England, the development of, for example, a Society for Socially Responsible Psychotherapy may be the start of a more socially motivated critical practice. There is also some expressed interest in social justice in psychology and counselling in the United States (e.g. Goodman et al., 2004).

Perhaps the most important question is why are such questions (including that of sexual differences) so seldom explicitly discussed? Could it be a combination of current stakeholders and vested interests successfully allowing those counselling and psychotherapy approaches that appear "natural," such that seriously questioning the current status quo is marginalised, if not considered "wrong"? The 11th of September in all its contextual horror may yet provide the opportunity for us to reconsider our values and relationships between countries and between ourselves, and to consider anew how our theory and practice may serve as help or hindrance. Psychotherapy and counseling, I hope, are not still too conservative for such questioning.

References

Barber, B. (2001, October 20). Ballots versus bullets. *Financial Times*, p. 1.

Becker, L., & Becker, C. (1992). (Eds.). *Encyclopedia of ethics*. New York: Garland Publishing.

Bion, W. (1970). *Attention and interpretation*. London: Karnac.

Bolton, R. (1989). *The contest of meaning*. Cambridge, MA: MIT Press.

Buber, M. (1958). *I and thou*. New York: Scribner.

Danto, A. (1998). The Ambulatorium: Freud's free clinic in Vienna. *International Journal of Psychoanalysis*, *79*, 287–300.

Deleuze, G., & Guattari, F. (1977). *Anti-Oedipus: Capitalism and schizophrenia*. Minneapolis: University of Minnesota Press.

Derrida, J. (1996). *Archive fever*. Chicago: University of Chicago Press.

Eagleton, T. (1996). *The illusions of postmodernism.* Oxford, UK: Blackwell.

Freud, S. (1915). The unconscious. In J. Strachey (Ed., Trans.), *Standard edition of the complete psychological works of Sigmund Freud, 1953–1964: Vol. 14* (pp. 161-215). London: Hogarth Press.

Goodman, L. A., Liang, B., Helms, J. E., Latta, R. E., Sparks, E., & Weintraub, S. R. (2004). Training counselling psychologists as social justice agents: Feminist and multicultural principles in action. *The Counseling Psychologist, 32*(6), 793–837.

Heaton, J. (1999). The ordinary. In L. King (Ed.), *Committed uncertainty in psychotherapy: Essays in honour of Peter Lomas* (pp. 62–81). London: Whurr.

Hegel, G. (1979). *Phenomenology of spirit.* Oxford, UK: Oxford University Press.

Heidegger, M. (1963). *Being and time* (J. MacQuarrie & E. Robinson, Trans.). New York: Harper & Row. (Original work published 1927)

Husserl, E. (1960). *Cartesian meditations: An introduction to phenomenology* (D. Cairns, Trans.). The Hague, The Netherlands: Martinus Nijhoff.

Kierkegaard, S. (1944). *The concept of dread* (W. Lowry, Trans.). Princeton, NJ: Princeton University Press.

Lacan, J. (1977). *Ecrits: Selected writings* (A. Sheridan, Trans.). London: Routledge.

Laing, R. D. (1967). *The politics of experience and the bird of paradise.* London: Penguin; New York: Pantheon.

Levinas, E. (1969). *Totality and infinity: An essay on exteriority* (A. Lingis, Trans.). Pittsburgh, PA: Duquesne University Press.

Levinas, E. (1985). *Ethics and infinity: Conversations with Philippe Nemo* (R. Cohen, Trans.). Pittsburgh, PA: Duquesne University Press.

Levinas, E. (1989). Time and the other. In S. Hand (Ed.), *The Levinas reader.* Oxford, UK: Blackwell.

Levinas, E. (1995). Ethics of the infinite. In R. Kearney (Ed.), *States of mind: Dialogues with contemporary thinkers on the European mind.* Manchester, UK: Manchester University Press.

Loewenthal, D. (1996). The post-modern counsellor: Some implications for practice, theory, research and professionalism. *Counselling Psychology Quarterly,* 9(4), 373–381.

Loewenthal, D. (2003). War and terror: Conflict, ideology and the therapeutic relationship. *Psychodynamic Practice,* 9(3), 384–392.

Loewenthal, D. (Ed.). (in press). *Case studies in relational research.* London: Palgrave Macmillan.

Loewenthal, D., & Snell, R. (2001). Psychotherapy as the practice of ethics. In F. Palmer-Barnes & L. Murdin (Eds.), *Values and ethics in the practice of psychotherapy and counselling* (pp. 23–31). Buckingham, UK: Open University Press.

Loewenthal, D., & Snell, R. (2003). *Post-modernism for psychotherapists.* Hove, UK: Brunner Routledge.

Lyotard, J. F. (1984). *The postmodern condition: A report on knowledge.* Manchester, UK: Manchester University Press.

Parker, I. (1997). *Psychoanalytic culture: Psychoanalytic discourse in Western society.* London: Sage.

Prowse, M. (2001, October 20). Why a peace loving nation is seen as a threat. *Financial Times,* back page.

Samuels, A. (2001). *Politics on the couch.* London: Profile Books.

Sarup, M. (1993). *An introductory guide to post-structuralism and postmodernism.* Hemel Hempstead, UK: Harvester Wheatsheaf.

Stoker, B. (1994). *Dracula.* Harmondsworth, UK: Penguin. (Original work published in 1897)

11

Summary and Conclusion

Lisa Tsoi Hoshmand

What can we learn from the perspectives and practice experiences of our group of authors and therapists? Their case examples illustrate cultural considerations that clearly have social and moral dimensions as well as implications for theory and practice. While the readers can derive their own thematic understanding from the various chapters, I would like to provide a summary in the light of the broad implications of culture and the issues in the field of psychotherapy and counseling identified earlier. The collective input of the authors can be organized in terms of both critique and integration of the field. The reflective integration of the personal and the professional at the individual level is further discussed as a continuous developmental process for students and practitioners. Finally, I examine the ideas on psychological and social well-being put forth directly or indirectly by the authors, in the hope that they will suggest additional criteria for evaluating the social value and cultural validity of the practice of psychotherapy and counseling. I close with a call to the profession to more fully accept the cultural nature of the therapeutic and counseling enterprise, and to more openly engage in critical, moral dialogue as part of our academic and professional discourse. Implications for teaching and professional training are also discussed.

Voices of Critique and Questioning of the Enterprise

One of the criticisms made by the authors is the inadequate questioning of cultural assumptions in American psychology. This shortcoming is reflected in a relative lack of interest in learning about non-Western traditions and other psychologies, a point made most forcefully by William Mikulas. In addition to echoing Mikulas in making this observation, William Rezentes and John Christopher further commented on the importance of understanding the cosmology and ethos of other cultures. It is a broader emphasis than the focus on psychotherapeutic techniques or counseling interaction styles that are congruent with a given cultural and ethnic group. In terms of cultural worldviews, John McLeod considered psychotherapy to be perpetuating an individualism that erodes community. Furthermore, American psychology reflects the dualistic and mechanistic biases of Western science. For Doralee Grindler Katonah, such biases have resulted in a circumscribed understanding of the person, and a less than holistic approach to the human capacity for healing and growth. She suggested that in privileging cognitive forms of knowing, we deprive ourselves and our clients of attention to embodied, integral emotional processes in making meaning of experience. For Christopher, the assumptions associated with objectivist science and its avoidance of the metaphysical have limited moral discourse in psychology, and excluded moral considerations from our theory and practice. This limitation parallels the exclusion of the religious and spiritual realm that is constitutive of the moral, and defining of identity for many individuals and groups here and in other parts of the world. The holistic approach to healing in the Hawaiian culture, described by Rezentes, is an example of the significance of a spiritual orientation.

McLeod and Loewenthal commented on the commodification of all aspects of cultural life, including human services and counseling. It is perhaps not surprising that with the materialistic and consumerist tendencies of modern society, the therapeutic culture seems no more prepared than the popular culture in offering insights into human struggles and suffering as part of life and one's character development. The pursuit of happiness and success, driven by materialistic values and individualism, has resulted in disappointments and psychological distress. According to Loewenthal, this consumption-driven attitude can undermine the relational and one's ability to engage authentically with the other. McLeod sees modern life as destructive of social capital, historical consciousness, and what it means to be in human community. It takes thoughtful comparison with other cultural ways of being for us to know that there are other kinds of existential meanings and forms of fulfillment. Mikulas referred to the tantric way of life in the Buddhist tradition as an example of what seems to be lacking for many young people. At the same time, he reported an increasing number of Americans seeking the Buddhist way, which suggests that there is some movement toward finding alternative forms of cultural existence.

Some of the existential anguish witnessed by psychotherapists and counseling practitioners is created by unjust conditions and people's mistreatment of others that can be found in all cultures. As Christopher, Gere, Loewenthal, and others implied, however, to the extent that we are reluctant to engage with the moral or to view the human condition from a value stance, it is not likely that we can help our clients respond to their difficulties in living. Dana Becker was critical of the insufficient attention to gender and social class issues. She and Susan Gere both regarded the profession's tendency to overemphasize the psychological over the social, and the individual over the systemic, as unhelpful. Again, it appears that the individualistic assumptions of American culture and psychology have reinforced the tendency to treat the individual person as a locus of control and responsibility for problems. This has been at the expense of understanding systemic factors and finding collective or systemic solutions.

Although psychologists have become more aware of the differences between individualistic American culture and the more collectivist cultures of many non–Euro-American groups and traditional societies, our authors are concerned that this does not always translate into reflexivity in our practice with cultural minorities and immigrant or international clients. As Christopher noted, it is too easy to expect the other to adapt to one's own cultural environment. Cultural domination through assimilation is the domestic equivalent of cultural imperialism abroad. Rezentes has tried to give voice to this fact, carrying the history of Native Hawaiians and knowing their continuing struggles. The simultaneous presence of ethnocentrism and unwitting cultural imperialism, further supported by political and economic structures, should be of concern from a social justice standpoint. Susan Gere commented on the positionality demanded of practitioners in relation to the lived realities of clients for whom justice and well-being are out of reach. It would not be possible to negotiate such positionality from a detached, neutral stance. Loewenthal pointed to the lack of attention to macro-level social inequities, and emphasized from a relational perspective the need for cultivating social responsibility in professional training. He expressed the concern that psychology might otherwise be used to promote class and national interests. Both acknowledged the existential alliance-building necessary for moral solidarity with the other, or one's clients in this case.

To varying degrees, our authors seem to acknowledge the possibility of changes in the culture of psychotherapy over time. Biases in the clinical treatment of women, and social and professional perceptions of problems such as trauma, sexual abuse, and violence have undergone some changes as the field evolves. Susan Gere cited the naming of racially based psychological trauma only within the last decade. Dana Becker noted, however, that the social construction of differences continues to reflect insensitivity to systemic realities and social class issues. Furthermore, there continues to be a medicalization of problems experienced by women as a result of political, economic, and social arrangements. Loewenthal illustrated this with the case example he provided, expressing concerns about the effects of capitalism and consumerism. He cautioned against ideological closure in perpetuating the cultural status quo if we do not take a critical approach to the history and current ideology of psychological practice. Mikulas commented on the complacency that has taken away the momentum of the feminist movement. Dana Becker seems to think that we have a long way to go in raising consciousness about these issues. While acknowledging ecological and narrative therapies that are more oriented to social action, McLeod seemed doubtful that psychotherapy and counseling will be explicitly a form of cultural work without more critical reflexivity on the part of practitioners. He recommended that critical attention be directed at the discourse technologies of psychotherapeutic practice in particular.

Mikulas, Rezentes, and others suggested that we could learn from the wisdom of other cultural traditions by expanding our academic studies and professional training. McLeod conceptualized this not only in terms of additional cultural resources, but also as opportunities to enter and participate in cultural worlds with different moral outlooks and practices. Susan Gere cited the value of a global perspective in recognizing the ecological factors that contribute to problems of inequity. Small gains in altering the prevailing understanding or the actual social realities do not come easily. To assume the cultural validity of our theories and models of practice when faced with increasing diversity, or when addressing the realities of the less privileged, is simply not justifiable. This is likely to continue if we do not learn to modify our assumptions in the light of practice knowledge that can be derived from working with culturally different clients and clients with different sexual orientation, religious identity, and socioeconomic background. McLeod observed that the discourses and practices of psychology have not been consistent with cultural curiosity and the cultivation of cultural resources. He attributed this partly to the over-reliance on paradigmatic research in academic psychology that takes a detached stance toward the culture of the other.

The context of practice, on the other hand, offers valuable opportunities for culture learning in which the practitioner has to consider how his or her own cultural identity enters into the encounter with the client's cultural world and identity. It appears that our authors have benefited in various ways from working with clients from other backgrounds. Some of the case examples illustrate the critical questioning that comes with learning from one's clients and the therapeutic encounter. Susan Gere wrote about practitioners growing with their clients, and learning to honor the strengths of trauma survivors for instance. Yet, the attitude of humility necessary for culture learning and critical reflection is not often found in settings that have ingrained power differentials. Becker, Gere, and Rezentes commented on the realities of power dynamics in mental health and other professional settings. Rezentes reminds us that sensitivity to such dynamics needs to be extended to students as well, who may have to negotiate their cultural identities and worldviews as they are being socialized into the academic and professional cultures of American psychology. This also happened in the experience of McLeod, who commented on the monoculture of psychotherapy and how professional training can alienate individuals from their own cultural roots in favor of the culture of psychotherapy. Genuine self-critique of our academic culture and the induction process for students and trainees may pave the way for reflective evaluation of the culture of psychotherapy and counseling and what Loewenthal refers to as the macrocultures.

Our authors seem to feel that they are representing minority points of view and that their stances on issues are not characteristic of the mainstream. McLeod suggested that having been a cultural outsider could serve practitioners in their cultural positioning while standing with different cultures. Mikulas was sensitive to the fact that he is being critical of North American mainstream psychology in which he has membership and acceptance. Rezentes expressed concerns about how his views would be received by those from whom he is asking for more self-reflection and critical examination. Loewenthal expressed a sense of vulnerability in self-disclosure, concerned about appearing to be focused on himself when advocating putting the other first. Grindler Katonah recognized that practicing from a holistic perspective is a rare opportunity in the prevailing medical and therapeutic culture. Becker acknowledged her frustration with women's place and choices in society, but was careful not to be apologetic about how she feels. There is obviously a risk in speaking out and being critical of the enterprise and one's community. This unfortunately reflects the state of our discourse. As culture wars intensify in societal discourse, and there is decreasing tolerance for disagreement and dissent, academic and professional discourses are similarly constrained. That is why in proposing integrative perspectives, one has to be careful so as not to suppress divergent points of view under a grand narrative. With this in mind, I would like to revisit the question of what a cultural meta-perspective can bring to the field of psychotherapy and counseling.

Integrative Perspectives on Psychotherapy and Counseling

Rather than considering the prospect of unifying the field, I would reframe the question in terms of how a culture-centered view and cultural metatheory can improve psychological practice. My goal here is to minimize the polarization between scientific and humanistic views of psychological theory and practice by acknowledging the dual nature of psychotherapy as both science-based and fundamentally a cultural enterprise. I believe this will allow different systems of rationality, ideologies, and practices to be understood in cultural terms. Under the current polarization, there is a cultural and sociological divide within the profession (Hoshmand, 2003). Issues concerning the moral and the political are seldom included in the prevailing academic discourse that is based on scientific ideology and norms of objective detachment. Understanding psychotherapy and counseling as a fundamentally cultural enterprise enables us to broaden our inquiry and discourse. We can, as Grindler Katonah, Loewenthal, and others suggested, entertain questions such as what constitutes and sustains aliveness in human experience. Acknowledging the dual nature of the enterprise allows us to overcome the difficulties that result from trying to fashion our professional identities and position ourselves in a field that is defined by this unresolved schism. For the profession, the cultural meta-perspective can provide a common language for describing the ideas and practices in the field of psychotherapy and counseling.

One of the clearest conclusions from the therapist accounts presented in this book is the importance of culture learning and cultural reflection in the context of practice. Our authors, like other reflective practitioners, find themselves revising their background understanding in the light of practice experience. They also draw on their clients' meanings and lived realities in broadening their own cultural horizons. To the extent that they allow the larger social backdrop and cultural realities to be considered, it helps to illuminate the client's experience that is in the foreground. In the discussion about clinical trauma theory and related diagnostic and therapeutic practice, for instance, it is evident that the emergent knowledge of practice can inform current theoretical understanding and how the profession should approach women who are victims of perpetration. This reciprocal relationship between theory and practice will be more likely if the experienced knowledge of reflective practice is regarded as being as valuable as academic theories and formal research knowledge.

I have in the first chapter discussed the multiple dimensions of culture, emphasizing that the cultural is more than scientifically described differences. Our authors have in different ways addressed the implications of culture as diverse worldviews and traditions of healing, culture as human practices, culture as moral ontology, and culture and identity as politics of difference. This multifaceted approach to culture is more comprehensive than the historical focus on cross-cultural differences. It changes the way we define our professional role and position ourselves in relation to the clients we work with. It also places us, as world citizens, closer to the global dynamics of cultural conflict and the moral responsibility for ensuring social justice. Grindler Katonah argued that people are oppressed when they are only viewed as instances of cultural categories, whereas understanding the complexities of how personal meanings interact with an individual's cultural environment and experience can help to preserve human dignity.

In a cultural view, the psychotherapist or counseling practitioner is a cultural worker, as explained by McLeod, and not infrequently, an agent of social control. At the same time, we all have membership in particular subcultures and communities, and bear particular social, political, and cultural histories. It is therefore essential that we acknowledge our identity experience and how we are positioned in relation to others when engaged in the work of psychotherapy and counseling. This acknowledgement has to be part of our developing professional identity. The preceding chapters have provided some glimpses into how our group of therapists sees the integration of their personal and professional worldviews.

Pathways to Integrating the Personal and the Professional

The therapist accounts shared here will, I hope, model for students the type of authenticity needed to achieve an integration of the personal and the professional. Our authors were generous with their transparency, and courageous in communicating their convictions. Each demonstrates a different path, but each shows a sense of integrity. It would appear that professional convictions evolve over time with reflection on one's personal beliefs and values and how they interact with one's environment and enter into one's work. It is a developmental process that demands narrative coherence when communicated. From a narrative, cultural point of view, the accounts are engendering of identity and future development (Hoshmand, 1998). That is why I recommend that students and practitioners in training engage in this effort of self-reflection and integration, a process that continues throughout one's development as a professional.

We can expect students to begin this developmental integration if we model a similar willingness to account for the personal in the professional, and provide learning environments that are supportive of such integration. As in psychotherapy and counseling, safety and acceptance are necessary for self-inquiry and growth. For students to explore their culture and identity in the midst of otherness, there has to be a discourse environment that would permit the kind of self-narrative and dialogue involved in sharing one's worldview and encountering one's own encapsulation. This cannot happen when there is fear of judgment or risk of being marginalized.

Although not all of our authors spoke directly about the moral nature of their therapeutic and professional stances, they all acknowledge the beliefs and values that inform them. Christopher contrasted different interpretations of his clinical case under individualistic and collectivist worldviews. Loewenthal wrote about putting the other first as an existential obligation, acknowledging also his interest in conflict related to class and other political differences. Rezentes told us about the Hawaiian culture, describing his experience in the native language that is imbued with indigenous meanings and values. Each account conveys the importance of formative experiences, including the culture learning from one's clients mentioned earlier. Gere, Becker, and Christopher described the surprising elements of their clients' worldview that reminded them of other cultural and social realities.

In various ways, our authors live in more than one cultural world. Mikulas and Christopher seem to have internalized a significant Buddhist orientation in their way of being that is evident also in their counseling practice and professional work. Grindler Katonah described herself as living and practicing a holistic philosophy in the midst of dualistic Western culture and science that inform medical and psychological practice. Rezentes tries to navigate between Euro-American and Hawaiian understandings of psychological healing, and hopes to educate others about his native culture. Dana Becker is keenly aware of her identity as a middle-class White woman when she works with poor, ethnic minority women. One can imagine the identity choices and moral conflicts that can emerge when these therapists are confronted with the differentness represented by the other, or when their own different cultural inclinations demand resolution.

We have in this collection of narratives a sampling of different cultural horizons, some yet to be negotiated to satisfaction. But one may ask, what is the end goal in each case, whether it is mainstream versus feminist, Euro-American versus Hawaiian, or Western versus Eastern in discourse? Mutual education, increased understanding, and some degree of merging of horizons may be helpful. The ultimate test for those of us involved in psychotherapy and counseling practice is whether the expanded cultural horizons will better serve the public and our clients. This leads to the question of how we should evaluate the good that comes from psychotherapeutic and counseling practice. One source of potential answers may be the therapists' ideas of psychological and social well-being.

Collective Visions of Well-being as Criteria of Practice

What are the visions of individual well-being held by our authors? Several of them alluded to a holistic integration of one's being in the spheres of action, experience, and spiritual or moral outlook as essential to psychological well-being. The need for meaning and a philosophy of life seems to be borne out by the authors' personal experience or the case examples given. McLeod emphasized the ability to live creatively with what is culturally given, and with the multiplicity of cultural choices. The model depicted by Grindler Katonah offers a process definition of health involving the capacity to not be rigid with meanings, and to welcome change without deferring to repressive forces. Finding socially acceptable ways of expressing one's cultural being and community values is another component. If the therapeutic encounter or counseling relationship is reflective of what ideally could be the case in one's ecological context, then the opportunity to work on identity projects and to evaluate one's life choices in a supportive environment seems crucial to a person's development. There is also a recognition that health and well-being are relative to the person's existential context. Only when we can fully empathize with the existential struggles of the other would we be able to see that there is dignity and courage in suffering. It will be appropriate for professionals to exercise more caution in bringing judgment to what appears to be less than optimal functioning by individuals, families, and groups.

As far as ideas about social well-being, concern about issues of social equity and justice is a theme for many of the authors. All of us are aware of global disparities in well-being. Our assumption is that one's appreciation for otherness may translate into ways of being that lead to social well-being. I tend to agree with the Native Hawaiian belief articulated by Rezentes that individual well-being and social well-being are intertwined and co-defining. At the same time, I share our authors' weariness about the status quo and unquestioning attitudes of complacency. McLeod and Loewenthal were openly critical of economic and military forces that have been presumed to bring solutions to human problems. Whereas critical voices and perspectives potentially can be instrumental in social change, politics of power and cultures of discourse that discourage critical questioning could be barriers to social improvements.

No one seems to doubt that diversity could be a strength, and that learning from other cultural traditions and ways of being may improve one's own society. On the issue of the latitude of cultural choice, our authors appear to fall on a continuum, from believing in human agency and a relative freedom from cultural constraints to recognizing the power of social and economic circumstances in limiting the possibilities for individuals and groups. Both McLeod and Grindler Katonah emphasized culture learning that goes beyond the apparent content and known cultural patterns to understanding and working with the creative processes of meaning-making and cultural transformation. McLeod seems to think that improving clients' access to, and creative uses of, cultural resources is the essence of the cultural work of psychotherapy and counseling. Grindler Katonah presented a holistic, interactional understanding of the symbolization process in furthering new meanings that entail new patterns of cultural living in an ever-evolving relationship between the person and his or her cultural environment. She expounded on the idea that only when a behavioral pattern is halted could new understanding emerge for the person. The parallel for large-scale cultural change would be that communities need to pause in their routine cultural patterns (including cultural stories, as McLeod explained) to potentiate the capacity for a responsive order that is conducive to change.

How would we incorporate these ideas related to psychological and social well-being in evidence-based practice and the outcome evaluation of psychotherapy and counseling? In terms of psychotherapy and counseling process, it would be appropriate to look at the extent to which clients are encouraged to explore all spheres of being and especially what holds meaning for them. If we grant the moral as a dimension of the therapeutic encounter, it should not be far-fetched to examine whether the practitioner is being facilitative of the client's moral reflections and deliberations. The ability to provide a supportive environment and to instill hope, as acknowledged in the research on common factors, continues to be important. Given the differences in what may be culturally relevant and existentially pertinent among clients, outcome measures of the benefits of psychotherapy and counseling should have local and cultural validity. Consulting clients and indigenous practitioners about the choice of indicators and evidence of benefits will be more than necessary. Including social functioning and community-level indicators will ensure that we do not overemphasize the individual psychology of the client to the neglect of the social environment or group to which the client has to successfully belong. In other words, we should consider the ecological validity of our interventions and their evaluation. Furthermore, the chosen indicators should reflect not just symptom relief or only what is readily measurable, but holistic and qualitative changes that can be evaluated in case study and multimethod research.

It is difficult to move from traditional psychotherapy research to the evaluation of its contribution to social well-being on a large scale. As Rezentes commented, communal well-being is a process and a valuing of certain ways of life, not just an outcome measure. Minimally, we should look at the extent to which psychotherapy and counseling facilitates clients' culture learning and behavioral and attitudinal flexibility in interacting with others who are different. Furthermore, McLeod suggested that it is not sufficient to focus on niche-building to improve the relationship between a person and his or her cultural environment, but that social organization and the formation of other forms of collectivity are essential to cultural existence. Affirming clients' efforts in engendering their identity in a culturally complex world, and empowering those who need to exercise their critical voices are some aspects of the psychotherapeutic experience relevant to social well-being. We may have to develop new inquiry approaches and to use interviews, other narrative methods, and community-oriented research to capture those experiences and changes believed to be relevant to social well-being in the long run. This is one of several needed changes and hopes for the future.

Hopes for the Profession

My first hope is for changes in our discourse so that there can be more dialogue about critical and moral issues such as social equity and justice, as urged by so many of our authors. In both academic discourse and our discourse in the professional context of practice, there needs to be a greater willingness to engage in moral dialogue and to acknowledge our role in a moral enterprise. This should include the unapologetic use of the language of moral compassion for human suffering, such as demonstrated by Susan Gere. It is encouraging that principles of social justice and social action are being considered in counseling curriculum and training (Goodman et al., 2004; Lee & Walz, 1998).

Given the latent ethnocentrism in the underlying assumptions of psychological theory and practice, culture learning has to become a priority for psychology and related professions. McLeod and Mikulas suggested, respectively, the use of cultural objects, including art and other media, and learning other cultural practices such as meditation in professional training. By valuing the reflective knowledge of practice and local indigenous knowledge, professionals would be more inclined to engage in, and therefore benefit from, culture learning in the context of practice. Such immersion can be combined with participatory modes of inquiry and action research in ethnically and culturally diverse communities. In other words, it calls for methodological pluralism in our approaches to inquiry. Psychotherapy research can involve qualitative case studies and relational research modalities, as recommended by McLeod, Loewenthal, and myself.

As I have commented earlier, there are polarizing forces that keep us from changing our discourse, professional cultures, and hierarchy of values. Getting to the roots of the cultural divide within the profession between objectivist science and the new philosophy of science, and acknowledging the sociology of separation between academic researchers and practitioners will be essential (Hoshmand, 2003). Any future dialogue on such differences can be in the communitarian spirit of following hermeneutic ideas for an expansion of one's cultural understanding in the hope of a fusion of horizons. Faculty development in relation to the above may be helpful. This can include learning how to bring social and cultural realities (domestic and global) into classroom discussions, how to facilitate hard conversations about differences, and how to optimize both convergence and divergence while containing conflict as opportunities for transformative learning and personal growth (Hoshmand, 2004). Curriculum development can involve more inclusion of multidisciplinary perspectives (including discourse analysis and cultural studies) and greater openness to methodological pluralism. Questions on the relationship between person and society in choosing personal and social ways of being require responses from across the disciplines. Psychology can collaborate with other fields in evolving global theories of human development and personhood, and in shaping cultural realities.

To the extent that we can engage in constructive dialogue of differences among ourselves, more teaching and learning can take place about the moral implications of therapeutic conversations and the negotiation of cultural horizons in the broader societal context. It is clear also that training in cultural competence has to go beyond skills of intervention to encompass more ethnographic culture learning, cultural immersion, and exposure to alternative worldviews. The moral dimension of psychotherapy and counseling suggests that the teaching of ethics has to be expanded beyond compliance with professional codes to wide-ranging moral conversations and in-depth exploration of how to achieve professional and personal integrity. As Rezentes suggested, an investment in the person of the healer points to a more holistic professional education. I have seen how academic programs can have an emphasis on issues of culture and identity in the development of students and trainees (Hoshmand, 2004). This is critically related to the continuous developmental process of integrating the personal with the professional. I have also seen cases where there is a lack of such emphasis, and where there are barriers to reflective integration. Owning the power dynamics in academic settings, and being sensitive to how the culture of Western psychology impacts the international and minority students or the less privileged, are some of the challenges that we face.

In conclusion, a broadly conceived cultural perspective and cultural psychology can be used to guide theory, research, practice, and training. The issues and lessons learned in psychological practice will continue to provide us with both possibility and challenge.

References

Goodman, L. A., Liang, B., Helms, J. E., Latta, R. E., Sparks, E., & Weintraub, S. R. (2004). Training counseling psychologists as social justice agents: Feminist and multicultural principles in action. *The Counseling Psychologist, 32*(6), 793–837.

Hoshmand, L. T. (Ed.). (1998). *Creativity and moral vision in psychology: Narratives of identity and commitment in a postmodern age*. Thousand Oaks, CA: Sage.

Hoshmand, L. T. (2003). Can lessons in history and logical analysis ensure progress in psychological science? *Theory and Psychology, 13*(1), 39–44.

Hoshmand, L. T. (2004). The transformative potential of counseling education. *Journal of Humanistic Counseling and Development, 43*(1), 82–90.

Lee, C. C., & Walz, G. R. (1998). (Eds.). *Social action: A mandate for counselors*. Alexandria, VA: American Counseling Association; Greensboro, NC: ERIC Counseling and Student Services Clearinghouse.

Author Index

Subject Index

About the Editor

Lisa Tsoi Hoshmand is Professor of Counseling and Psychology at Lesley University, Cambridge, Massachusetts. She is the author/editor of 3 books and over 40 other publications. Her recent work includes an edited book, *Creativity and Moral Vision in Psychology: Narratives of Identity and Commitment in a Postmodern Age* (Sage, 1998); an article "Narrative Psychology" in the *Encyclopedia of Psychology* (American Psychological Association and Oxford University Press, 2000); the book chapter "Psychotherapy as an Instrument of Culture" in *Critical Issues in Psychotherapy* (Sage, 2001); and an article "Narratology, Cultural Psychology, and Counseling Research" (*Journal of Counseling Psychology*, 2005, volume 52, issue 2). She has published and presented on cultural psychology, qualitative research methodology, clinical teaching, reflective practice, and transformative education. A Fellow of the American Psychological Association and a licensed psychologist, she has served on the editorial boards of a number of journals in counseling psychology, theoretical and philosophical psychology, and community psychology.

About the Contributors

Dana Becker, PhD, is Associate Professor of Social Work at the Bryn Mawr College Graduate School of Social Work and Social Research, Bryn Mawr, Pennsylvania. She has degrees in both social work and developmental psychology and has practiced as a feminist psychotherapist for over 20 years, specializing in both individual and family therapy. She has also served as clinical training director on a number of federally funded grants aimed at refining family therapy treatments for drug-abusing, inner-city youth and their families. She is the author of the books *Through the Looking Glass: Women and Borderline Personality Disorder* (Westview, 1997) and *The Myth of Empowerment: Women and the Therapeutic Culture in America* (New York University Press, 2005) as well as articles and book chapters focusing on family therapy, gender, and psychiatric diagnosis.

John Chambers Christopher, PhD, is Professor of Counseling Psychology in the Department of Health and Human Development at Montana State University, Bozeman, Montana, and a senior staff psychologist at the MSU Counseling Center. He is the recipient of the 2003 Sigmund Koch Early Career Award by the Division of Theoretical and Philosophical Psychology of the American Psychological Association. He specializes in cultural psychology and theoretical and philosophical psychology. He has written on the cultural, moral, and ontological underpinnings of theories of psychological well-being, moral development, and psychotherapy. His primary interests are in using interactivism and philosophical hermeneutics to develop alternative conceptions of the self and of well-being and metatheories for psychological inquiry. His recent publications include *Counseling's Inescapable Moral Visions, Situating Psychological Well-Being: Exploring the Cultural Roots of its Theory and Research,* "Culture and Psychotherapy: Toward a Hermeneutic Approach," "Moral Visions of Developmental Psychology, Culture and Character Education: Problems of Interpretation in a Multicultural Society," and "Values and the Self: An Interactivist Foundation for Moral Development."

Susan H. Gere, PhD, is Associate Professor of Counseling and Psychology and Director of the Division of Counseling and Psychology at Lesley University, Cambridge, Massachusetts. Over the past 35 years, she has practiced, taught, consulted, and administered programs in the community and in graduate education. While continuously working with teaching and clinical practice, her most recent areas of interest are in psychological trauma and post trauma therapy and community consultation. Her scholarship includes work on understanding the role of clinical trainers with student trauma survivors, the aesthetics of clinical teaching, cultural identity issues of refugees and homeless women, and feminist pedagogy. She is the first author (with Hoshmand and Reinkraut) of the book chapter "Constructing the Sacred: Empathic Engagement, Aesthetic Regard and Discernment in Clinical Teaching" in *Passion and Pedagogy* (Peter Lang, 2002).

Doralee Grindler Katonah, PsyD, MDiv, is a clinical psychologist with special interests in spirituality and health psychology. She is currently Associate Core Faculty at the Illinois School of Professional Psychology, and staff psychologist and faculty at Advocate Medical Group Center for Complementary Medicine, Park Ridge, Illinois. Dr. Grindler Katonah is also faculty and a certifying coordinator for The Focusing Institute in New York. She has taught Focusing for over 20 years, presented nationally and internationally, and conducted research on Focusing with people who have cancer. She was the first director of The Focusing Institute and has published in the area of Focusing and medicine. She especially enjoys bringing a Focusing-oriented approach to deeper issues of personal and spiritual growth.

Del Loewenthal, DPhil, is Chair of the Centre for Therapeutic Education in the School of Psychology and Therapeutic Studies at Roehampton University, London. A chartered psychologist in the United Kingdom, he originally trained as a psychotherapist with the Philadelphia Association founded by R. D. Laing. He is the editor of the *European Journal of Psychotherapy, Counselling and Health* (Routledge). He is the coauthor (with R. Snell) of the books *Postmodernism for Psychotherapists* (Brunner Routledge, 2003), and (with D. Winter) *What Is Psychotherapeutic Research?* (UKCP/Karnac, in press). The author of *Case Studies in Relational Research* (Palgrave Macmillan, in press), he has various publications on emotional learning and psychotherapeutic training.

John McLeod, PhD, is Professor of Counselling at the University of Abertay Dundee, Scotland. His publications include *Narrative and Psychotherapy* (Sage, 1997), *Qualitative Research in Counselling and Psychotherapy* (Sage, 2001), *An Introduction to Counselling* (3rd ed., Open University Press,

2003), and *The Handbook of Narrative and Psychotherapy* (coedited with Lynne Angus, Sage, 2004). He is interested in the potential of qualitative inquiry as a means of generating knowledge that can inform the practice of psychotherapy, and in the role of counselling in relation to social inclusion, participation, and generativity.

William L. Mikulas, PhD, is Professor of Psychology at the University of West Florida, where he has received many awards for research and teaching. He is also a permanent Visiting Professor at Chulalongkorn University in Thailand and an Honorary Professor at the University of Flores in Argentina. A leader in the integration of Eastern and Western psychologies, he belongs to several international organizations that are involved in such integrative efforts. He is the author of the book *The Integrative Helper* (Brooks/Cole, 2002), and has published numerous books and articles on psychotherapy and the integration of different healing traditions.

William C. Rezentes III, PhD, is a practicing psychologist on O‘ahu, Hawai‘i. He specializes in transcultural therapy and research with Hawaiians. His work includes individual and family therapy, organizational consultation, research, writing, student mentoring, and community forums and workshops on Hawaiian psychology. He is also a Hawaiian musician, recording artist, and song and chant composer. He is the author of the book *Ka Lama Kukui* [Hawaiian Psychology]: *An Introduction* (‘A‘ali‘i Books, 1996), and several other publications on Native Hawaiian acculturation.

Made in the USA
Lexington, KY
06 January 2015